IN THE
Camera's Eye

Other Volumes in Brassey's Terrorism Library

Alexander & Latter TERRORISM & THE MEDIA: DILEMMAS FOR
GOVERNMENT, JOURNALISM & THE PUBLIC

Hanle TERRORISM: THE NEWEST FACE OF WARFARE

Other Titles of Related Interest

Charters & Tugwell ARMIES IN LOW-INTENSITY CONFLICT

Leventhal & Alexander NUCLEAR TERRORISM: DEFINING THE THREAT

O'Neill INSURGENCY & TERRORISM: INSIDE MODERN REVOLUTIONARY
WARFARE

Paschall LIC 2010: SPECIAL OPERATIONS & UNCONVENTIONAL WARFARE
IN THE NEXT CENTURY

Taylor THE TERRORIST

Related Journals*

Armed Forces Journal International

Defense Analysis

Survival

*Sample copies available upon request

IN THE
Camera's Eye

NEWS COVERAGE OF TERRORIST EVENTS

EDITED BY Yonah Alexander

AND Robert G. Picard

BRASSEY'S (US), INC.

MAXWELL MACMILLAN PERGAMON PUBLISHING CORP

Washington . New York . London . Oxford . Beijing
Frankfurt . São Paulo . Sydney . Tokyo . Toronto

U.S.A. (Editorial)	Brassey's (US), Inc. 8000 Westpark Drive, 1st Floor, McLean, Virginia 22102, U.S.A.
(Orders)	Attn: Order Dept., Macmillan Publishing Co., Front & Brown Streets, Riverside, N.J. 08075
U.K. (Editorial)	Brassey's (UK) Ltd. 50 Fetter Lane, London EC4A 1AA, England
(Orders)	Brassey's (UK) Ltd. Headington Hill Hall, Oxford OX3 0BW, England
PEOPLE'S REPUBLIC OF CHINA	Pergamon Press, Room 4037, Qianmen Hotel, Beijing, People's Republic of China
FEDERAL REPUBLIC OF GERMANY	Pergamon Press GmbH, Hammerweg 6, D-6242 Kronberg, Federal Republic of Germany
BRAZIL	Pergamon Editora Ltda, Rua Eça de Queiros, 346, CEP 04011, Paraiso, São Paulo, Brazil
AUSTRALIA	Brassey's Australia, P.O. Box 544, Potts Point, N.S.W. 2011, Australia
JAPAN	Pergamon Press, 5th Floor, Matsuoka Central Building, 1-7-1 Nishishinjuku, Shinjuku-ku, Tokyo 160, Japan
CANADA	Pergamon Press Canada, Suite No. 271, 253 College Street, Toronto, Ontario, Canada M5T 1R5

Brassey's (US), Inc., books are available at special discounts for bulk
purchases for sales promotions, premiums, fund-raising, or educational use
through the Special Sales Director, Macmillan Publishing Company,
866 Third Avenue, New York, NY 10022.

Library of Congress Cataloging-in-Publication Data
In the camera's eye : news coverage of terrorist events / edited by
  Yonah Alexander and Robert G. Picard.
    p.   cm. — (Brassey's terrorism library)
  Includes bibliographical references.
  ISBN 0-08-037452-2
  1. Terrorism in the press. 2. Terrorism in mass media.
3. Terrorism and mass media. 4. Press and politics—History—20th
century. I. Alexander, Yonah. II. Picard, Robert G. III. Series.
PN4784.T45I5 1990
303.6'25—dc20   90-33326
                                        CIP

British Library Cataloguing in Publication Data
In the camera's eye : news coverage of terrorist events.
  (TLBS Brassey's terrorism library).
  1. Terrorism. Reporting by news media
  I. Yonah, Alexander II. Picard, Robert G.
  070.44932242
  ISBN 0-08-037452-2

PUBLISHER'S NOTE

Brassey's Terrorism Library

THE MONOGRAPH SERIES

As terrorism continues as one of the most serious and lasting threats to the security of nations and to the safety of innocent citizens everywhere, the systematic and rational analysis of terrorism becomes even more important. Brassey's is thus publishing the Terrorism Library, a series of books designed to educate a concerned worldwide public. In order to provide the widest possible dissemination of information about terrorism, Brassey's will also publish monographs such as this one as part of the Terrorism Library. By disseminating these valuable monographs of terrorism-related collections, documents, papers, and studies, we hope to play some small part in the understanding of and response to terrorism.

CONTENTS

Contents

PART III   Evaluating Media Performance

PART IV   Covering Terrorism

FOREWORD

Brassey's (US)

TERRORISM

Library

Terrorism, as a process of deliberate employment of psychological intimidation and physical violence by sovereign states and subnational groups to attain strategic and political objectives in violation of law, is not new in history. In modern times, along with the nuclear age, we are in the midst of the new "age of terrorism" with all its frightening consequences for the continuity of civilized order.

Indeed, terrorism has become a permanent fixture of contemporary life. It poses a variety of threats, including those related to the safety and welfare of ordinary people, the stability of the state system, the health and pace of economic development, and the expansion and even the survival of democracy. Today's terrorists are better organized, more professional, and better equipped than their historical counterparts. Technological developments offer new targets and new capabilities. Tomorrow's terrorists might resort to chemical, biological, or nuclear violence to achieve mass disruption or political turmoil.

In light of this likelihood, Brassey's (US), Inc., has developed its Terrorism Library. The purpose of this series is to offer books, written or edited by recognized experts, on a variety of subjects including the causation and control of terrorism; national, regional, and global perspectives on terrorism; and specific case studies. Although each volume will stand on its own merit, the Terrorism Library will provide a comprehensive intellectual and professional framework for better understanding the nature, scope, intensity, and consequences of the threat of modern terrorism and what society can do to cope with this phenomenon in the 1990s.

PROFESSOR YONAH ALEXANDER
Series Editor

PREFACE

It has been generally suggested that "terrorism is the deliberate employment of violence or the threat of use of violence by sovereign states or subnational groups encouraged or assisted by sovereign states to attain strategic
and political objectives by acts in violation of law. These criminal acts are
intended to create overwhelming fear in a target population larger than the
civilian and military victims attacked or threatened."[1] Whether this definition is accepted or not, the fact remains that ideological and political violence as forms of criminality as well as low-intensity conflict have become
a permanent fixture of our "Age of Terrorism."

Acts of terrorism make daily headlines around the world. It is for this
reason that in 1984 the Mass Communication and Society Division of the
Association for Education in Journalism and Mass Communication established the Terrorism and the News Media Research Project. Its purpose was
to promote and facilitate research intended to produce substantive evidence
about the roles of media in the planning, implementation, and conclusions
of acts of terrorism. In addition, the research focuses on methods employed
in covering such acts, the content of coverage, and the effects of coverage
on official responses to terrorism, public perceptions of organizations engaged in political violence, and terrorist groups. Researchers selected to participate in the project have backgrounds in mass communication, criminal
justice, political science, and sociology, and were drawn from both within
and outside the association.

This book contains ten selected and edited papers that were among three
dozen presented at the "Communication in Terrorist Events" conference
held by the project in Boston from March 3 through 5, 1988. The conference
specifically focused on the intended and unintended meanings conveyed in
news coverage of terrorism, the ways in which media covered different terrorist acts and perpetrators, and how the media performed during coverage
of terrorism.

The volume is divided into four sections focusing on how news coverage
is construction of reality, on relations between media and terrorists, how
media perform during events, and what is conveyed.

George Gerbner, the leading authority on the effects of media-portrayed
violence, explores the symbolic communication of terrorist acts and the
struggle for control of the meaning placed on those acts by news reports.
His study is followed by an examination of the differences in meaning

attached to the same events by individuals and nations with adversarial relations. This exploration by Thomas W. Cooper discusses how these perspectives affect the import and meaning attached to acts of political violence. Jack Lule provides another view by looking at the dramatic meaning of news reports about terrorist acts. He explores how the killing of Robert Dean Stethem during the hijacking of TWA Flight 847 was reported and the implications of the symbolic meaning attached to the event.

Richard M. Pearlstein focuses on the psychological rewards of media coverage provided members of groups who commit acts of terrorism and how it is used to help provide identities to individuals and groups. The ways in which victims of terrorism interact with media are investigated by Louise F. Montgomery, whose chapter explores the impact of extensive media coverage on victims and their families. Why and how journalists become targets of terrorism is explored by Robert G. Picard, who notes that media tend to support dominant social values and established political structures and thus are considered opponents of some of those who engage in terroristic acts.

Robert Terrell and Kristina Ross consider efforts to construct voluntary guidelines for news coverage of terrorism and argue that the narrowness and single-purposeness of the guidelines can conflict with democratic ideals and harm the perspectives on terrorist acts that are conveyed. Timothy Gallimore reviews available media coverage guidelines and considers the extent to which media have complied in their coverage of political violence.

L. John Martin and Joseph Draznin explore the pressures on broadcasters during coverage of terrorism and the views of news executives about the need and extent to which terrorism should be covered and what should be conveyed. Judith M. Buddenbaum looks at coverage of the conflict in Namibia to determine what differences exist when news is constructed by journalists with different perspectives and finds they are significant.

This volume is intended to provide an overview of the increasing and important avenue of inquiry into the communicative nature of terrorist acts and the role of media during such violence. Many questions remain in search of answers. Research is needed on the content of news coverage of acts of political violence, manipulation of news coverage, the role of staged and unstaged acts of terrorism, the effects of coverage on outcomes of incidents, differences in coverage in various types of media, the legitimacy of coverage, and the role of coverage in inducing subsequent acts of terrorism.

It is hoped that this volume will further stimulate research in the important field of terrorism with a view toward advancing the cause of peace and justice.

YONAH ALEXANDER AND
ROBERT G. PICARD

NOTE

1. See Ray S. Cline and Yonah Alexander, *Terrorism as State-sponsored Covert Warfare* (Fairfax, Va.: HERO Books, 1986), p. 2.

PART I

Coverage as a Construction of Reality

CHAPTER 1

Symbolic Functions of Violence and Terror

by George Gerbner

MOST OF WHAT WE KNOW, or think we know, we do not personally experience. Perhaps the most distinguishing characteristic of our species is that for all practical purposes we live in a world erected through the stories we tell.

Violence and terror have a special role to play in this great story-telling process. They depict social forces in conflict. They dramatize threats to human integrity and the social order. They demonstrate power to lash out, provoke, intimidate, and control. They designate winners and losers in an inescapably political game.

These are symbolic functions. They are not acts or threats of hurting and killing but of representations or symbolic re-creations of such acts or threats. Whether they are presumably factual or apparently fictional, they have similar sociopolitical consequences. In discussing what is known about these consequences, I will draw on research of our own "Terrorism and the Media" project as well as of others I have summarized in a report for the United Nations, Educational, Scientific and Cultural Organization (UNESCO).[1]

My argument is simply that symbolic uses of violence tend to benefit those who control them, usually states and media establishments. Isolated acts of small-scale insurgencies or bold strikes of a few individuals may force media attention and convey a public message of outrage and defiance. But in the last analysis, that challenge is often made to seem even more outrageous and serves to enhance media credibility ("we report facts no matter how bad") and to mobilize support for repression, often on a higher scale than warranted by the threat, as in the form of wholesale state violence and terror or military action, which is presented as justified by the provocation.

The highly selective and politically shaped portrayals of violence and terror conceal rather than reveal the actual incidence and distribution of real violence and terror. These portrayals, including the choice of labels, serve as projective devices that isolate acts and people from meaningful contexts and set them up to be stigmatized and victimized.

Stigma is a mark of disgrace that evokes disgraceful behavior. Calling some people barbarians makes it easier to act barbarically toward them. Presuming some people to be criminals permits dealing with them in ways otherwise considered criminal. Labeling a large group "terrorists" seems to justify terrorizing them. Declaring nations as enemies makes it legitimate to attack and kill them. Calling some people crazy or insane makes it possible to suspend rules of rationality and decency. Stigma brands deviation from the norm as not only unusual and perhaps unjustified but as evil and sinful. It is one way a culture has to enforce its norms.

The persons stigmatized are the obvious targets, but the real victim of the process is the community's ability to think rationally and creatively about injustice.

The context in which this type of demonstration and socialization goes on is the historically unprecedented mass ritual of television violence and its cultivation of an inequitable sense of power and vulnerability. For the first time in human history we have manufactured a compelling symbolic environment not of the family, the neighborhood, the school, the church, and the selectively used print and film media but the mass ritual of television. It presents a world that, especially in prime time, is largely power-oriented. Its action dramas are by far the major sources of vivid images about violence and terror most people absorb daily, beginning in infancy. News by and large has to compete in a marketplace of these dramatic appeals and preconceptions.

Prime time is a world in which men outnumber women three to one. Young and old people and minorities have less representation and fewer opportunities and power, but more than their share of vulnerability and victimization. Violence and terror perform the tasks of the unequal distribution of power. That is their symbolic function.

The typical viewer sees every week an average of 21 criminals (including "terrorists," domestic and foreign). Arrayed against them are 41 public and private law enforcers. (If they "live" so long, there are also an average of 14 doctors, 6 nurses, 6 lawyers, and 2 judges to deal with them.) Violence occurs an average of 6 times per hour in prime time, and over 20 times per hour in weekend daytime children's programming. We absorb an average of 2 entertaining murders a night.

Neither fictional nor factual (news) violence and terror bear much relationship to their actual occurrence in our communities and the world, but they do cultivate an accommodation to the structure of power. Our research on television found that exposure to the pattern of media violence cultivates a differential sense of vulnerability and stigmatization, placing heavier burdens on selected minorities and nationalities. This is the general context of pervasive and inescapable violent representations within which the labeling and depiction of terrorism and terrorists play out their symbolic social functions.

Much of the controversy over press coverage of terrorism revolves around control more than substance. Media systems can tolerate almost any challenge on camera as long as they control the camera and select the shots and the context. That is why live coverage or documentaries that let insurgents explain themselves are risky; they may wrest control and context— even if briefly—from the system.

When that happens, the state threatens to step in and restore control of the system. The friction recalls the symbiotic relationship of cooperation and conflict between the medieval state and church, in which the church usually emerged as the more credible cultural arm of society, while the state ran the army better. The mass media has replaced the church, and modern states tend to come to similar conclusions. The Prevention of Terrorism Act, for example, was enacted in the United Kingdom in the wake of an Irish Republican Army (IRA) bombing in 1974 that killed twenty-one people and injured over 160. The act suspends civil liberties for anyone suspected of supporting the IRA terrorism or withholding information about it. Under its provisions, the police seized a copy of a fifteen-minute untransmitted film shot by a British Broadcasting Corporation (BBC) crew at an incident at Carrickmore. After a long debate in Parliament and in the press, the government decided not to prosecute the BBC, but broadcast rules on reporting terroristic acts were tightened.

Comparative studies of terrorist coverage reveal unreliable statistics and blatantly political uses. As with racist and sexist terms now in disrepute, the word *terrorist* lives on as invective but is useless for analytical purposes.

Although the media in the United States continued to put increasing emphasis on international terrorism throughout the 1970s, Edward Mickolus's authoritative chronology of transnational terrorism has shown that the frequency of incidents peaked in 1972 with 480 that year and subsequently declined to an average of 340 per year.[2] Many of the reports focused, and still focus, on the Middle East. There has been no comparable coverage of prevalent state and antistate terrorism in many countries of Africa, Latin America, and Asia.

While the physical casualties of highly publicized terrorist acts have been relatively few, the political and military consequences have been far-reaching. The fate of governments, relations among states, scientific exchanges, tourism, and trade have been affected. International tensions, domestic repression, and support for counterviolence have increased. For example, although less than 1 percent of all casualties of international terrorism in 1985 were American, they prompted the forcing down of an Egyptian airliner and the bombing of Tripoli (probably based, as it turned out, on faulty intelligence).

Although international terrorism by and against states received most attention, M. Cherif Bassiouni and others have pointed out that terrorist acts in a national context far outnumber international ones.[3] Disappearances, bombings, kidnappings, and state violence in many countries, often unreported, claim thousands of times more victims than do well-publicized acts of international terror.

Sandra Wurth-Hough documented the role of media coverage of terrorism in selecting events and defining issues for the public.[4] David L. Paletz, Peter A. Fozzard, and John Z. Ayanian analyzed the *New York Times's* coverage of the IRA, the Red Brigades, and the Fuerzas Armadas de Liberación Nacional (FALN) of Venezuela from July 1, 1977, to June 30, 1979, and found no basis for the charge that coverage legitimizes the cause of terrorist organizations. On the contrary, 70 percent of the stories mentioned neither the cause nor the objectives of the terrorists; almost 75 percent mentioned neither the organization nor its supporters; and the 7 percent that did mention names surrounded them with statements issues by authorities.[5]

In a follow-up study of U.S. network news, Milburn et al. have also noted the frequent omission of any causal explanation for terrorist acts and the attribution of mental instabilty to terrorists and their leaders. (Similar acts directed against countries other than the United States were more frequently explained.) The implication, the researchers noted, was that "you can't negotiate with crazy people."[6]

Graham Knight and Tony Dean provided a detailed account of how the Canadian press coverage of the siege and recapturing of the Iranian embassy in London from Arab nationalist "gunmen" served to assert the efficiency and legitimacy of violence by the British Special Forces. In the process of transforming crime and punishment into a selectively choreographed newsworthy event, the media "have to some extent assumed the functions of moral and political—in short, ideological—reproduction performed previously (and limitedly) by the visibility of the public event itself."[7] It is not accidental, the authors claimed, that highly publicized and "morally coherent" scenarios of violence and terror have made public punishment unnecessary as demonstrations of state ideology and power.

Typically isolated from their historical and social context, denied description of conditions or cause, and portrayed as unpredictable and irrational, if not insane, those labeled "terrorists" symbolize a menace beyond the reach of rational, humane, and democratic means.[8] Understanding becomes a costly luxury, if not treason. In a domestic context of racial violence, Paletz and Robert Dunn studied the effects of news coverage of urban riots in the United States. They concluded that the attempt to present a view acceptable to most readers failed to illuminate the conditions in the black communities that led to the riots. News of civil disturbance shares with coverage of terrorist activity the tendency to cultivate a pervasive sense of blind fear and danger and of the consequent attraction of harsh measures to combat it.[9]

Connie De Boer summarized survey results in five countries and found that although terrorists claimed relatively few victims, media coverage cultivated a sense of imminent danger that only unusual steps could overcome. Terrorism was considered a "very serious" problem by nine out of ten Americans and nearly as many British respondents. Six out of ten people in the Federal Republic of Germany considered it "the most important public event of the year."

Six or seven out of ten respondents in the United States, the United Kingdom, and the Federal Republic of Germany favored the introduction of the death penalty for terrorists. Similar majorities approved using a "special force" that would hunt down and kill terrorists in any country; placing them "under strict surveillance, even though our country might then somewhat resemble a police state"; using "extra stern and harsh action" unlike against other criminals; and "limitations of personal rights by such measures as surveillance and house searches" in order to "combat terrorism."

Eight out of ten Germans in the Federal Republic approved a news embargo instituted after a kidnapping, and six out of ten thought that conversations between the accused and their lawyers should be monitored to prevent new acts of terrorism.

From one-fifth to over half of the respondents in the Federal Republic of Germany said that "one has to be careful" of what one says to avoid being considered sympathetic to terrorists. Sympathizers were considered to be those who oppose the death penalty, who believe their "lawyers have the right at all times to visit terrorists in prison," who think their "criticisms of our society to be justified in some respects," or who feel pity for them.[10]

Psychological research on individual aggression and violence has been the most widely publicized. It has also been relatively easy to refute. Critics of aggression research point to the difficulty of relating experiments to real-life situations, question the validity of relating aggressive tendencies to actual violence, and charge that blaming most individual aggression or violence on the media distracts attention from underlying social influences and the greater threat of collective, official, organized, and legitimated violence. They recall Friedrich Schiller's complaint: "It is criminal to steal a purse, daring to steal a fortune, a mark of greatness to steal a crown. The blame diminishes as the guilt increases."

Indeed, most research on the effects of violence has been generated by fears that violence and terror in the media brutalize children and undermine the social order. While that may be partly true (and a nonsequitur), seldom asked and rarely publicized have been broader questions of policy: Why should media organizations, established institutions of society, undermine their existence by promoting violence? Are incitation and imitation really the principal consequences of exposure to violence? Are there consequences that may benefit media institutions and their sponsors? If so, what are they? Can they help explain the persistence of media policies despite public criticism and international embarrassment over flooding many cultures with images of violence and terror?

The conventional debate between those who fear imitation and those who claim popular demand begs the point. Although conflict is essential and violence is legitimate in news and drama, there is no evidence of popular demand for violence per se. Perhaps one or two out of the ten highest-rated television programs are violent shows. Most television (and news) violence is formula-bound, cheap to produce, "travels" better than other fare, has a minimal attention value, and can thus be profitable commodities despite mediocre ratings.

It is clear that violence-inspired mayhem poses no threat to modern societies. On the contrary, the violence-terror scenario, as circuses of old, may function to isolate and annihilate, or at least combat such threats.

Yet, the research evidence also suggests that prolonged exposure to stories and scenes of violence and terror can mobilize aggressive tendencies, can desensitize some and isolate others, can trigger violence in a few and intimidate the many. But lawlessness and massive disorder relate more to illicit commerce, wars, unemployment, and other social trends than to the violence index we have been compiling since 1967. Small-scale terrorists have toppled no state without a collapse of power from other causes; mostly they have provoked reprisals, repression, and an excuse for invasions.

It may well be that a media system strikes an implicit balance between the costs and benefits of violence scenario. On one hand there is the cost of public anxiety and accommodation to injustice and inhumanity. On the other hand are the less visible but historically and empirically demonstrable gains in power—personal and institutional—derived from the ability to depersonalize enemies, to cultivate vulnerability and dependence in subordinates, and to achieve instant support for swift and tough measures at home and abroad in what is presented as an exceedingly mean and scary world. The scenario provides its producers with the sense and reality of power, and its persistence may be understood, among other things, in terms of its utility for those who define and control its uses.

NOTES

1. George Gerbner, "Violence and Terror in the Mass Media," *Reports and Papers in Mass Communication,* no. 102 (Paris: UNESCO, March 1988).

2. Edward F. Mickolus, *Transnational Terrorism: A Chronology of Events, 1968–1979* (Westport, Conn.: Greenswood Press, 1980).

3. M. Cherif Bassiouni, "Terrorism, Law Enforcement, and the Mass Media: Perspectives, Problems, Proposals," *Journal of Criminal Law and Criminology* 72, no. 1 (1981); and M. Cherif Bassiouni, "Media Coverage of Terrorism: The Law and the Public," *Journal of Communication* 33, no. 2 (1982): 128–43.

4. Sandra Wurth-Hough, "Network News Coverage of Terrorism: The Early Years," *Terrorism* 6, no. 3 (1983): 403–422.

5. David L. Paletz, John Z. Ayanian, and Peter A. Fozzard, "The I.R.A., the Red Brigades and the F.A.L.N. in The *New York Times,*" *Journal of Communication* 32, no. 2 (Spring 1982): 162–71.

6. Michael A. Milburn, Claudia Bowley, Janet Fay-Dumaine, and Debbie Ann Kennedy, "An Attributional Analysis of the Media Coverage of Terrorism," paper presented at the 10th Annual Meeting of the International Society of Political Psychology, San Francisco, California, July 6, 1987.

7. Graham Knight and Tony Dean, "Myth and the Structure of News," *Journal of Communication* 32, no. 2 (1982): 144–61.

8. Michael A. Milburn et al., "An Attributional Analysis."
9. David L. Paletz, and Robert Dunn, "Press Coverage of Civil Disorders: A Case Study of Winston-Salem," *Public Opinion Quarterly* 33, no. 3 (1969): 328–45.
10. Connie DeBoer, "The Polls: Terrorism and Hijacking," *Public Opinion Quarterly* 43, (Fall 1979): 410–18.

REFERENCES

Bassiouni, M. Cherif. "Media Coverage of Terrorism: The Law and the Public." *Journal of Communication* 33, no. 2 (1982): 128–43.

Bassiouni, M. Cherif. "Terrorism, Law Enforcement, and the Mass Media: Perspectives, Problems, Proposals." *Journal of Criminal Law and Criminology* 72, no. 1 (1981).

DeBoer, Connie. "The Polls: Terrorism and Hijacking." *Public Opinion Quarterly* 43 (Fall 1979): 410–18.

Gerbner, George. "Violence and Terror in the Mass Media." *Reports and Papers in Mass Communication,* no. 102. Paris: UNESCO, March 1988.

Knight, Graham, and Tony Dean. "Myth and the Structure of News." *Journal of Communication* 32, no. 2 (1982): 144–61.

Mickolus, Edward F. *Transnational Terrorism: A Chronology of Events, 1968–1979.* Westport, Conn.: Greenswood Press, 1980.

Milburn, Michael A., Claudia Bowley, Janet Fay-Dumaine, and Debbie Ann Kennedy. "An Attributional Analysis of the Media Coverage of Terrorism." Paper presented at the 10th Annual Meeting of the International Society of Political Psychology, San Francisco, California, July 6, 1987.

Paletz, David L., John Z. Ayanian, and Peter A. Fozzard. "The I.R.A., the Red Brigades and the F.A.L.N. in The *New York Times*." *Journal of Communication* 32, no. 2, 162–71.

Paletz, David L., and Robert Dunn. "Press Coverage of Civil Disorders: A Case Study of Winston-Salem." *Public Opinion Quarterly* 33, no. 3 (1969): 328–45.

Wurth-Hough, Sandra. "Network News Coverage of Terrorism: The Early Years." *Terrorism* 6, no. 3 (1983): 403–422.

CHAPTER 2

Terrorism and Perspectivist Philosophy: Understanding Adversarial News Coverage

by Thomas W. Cooper

IN THE MADE-FOR-TELEVISION MOVIE *The U.S. vs. Salin Ajimi,* aired by CBS-TV on January 10, 1988, many U.S. audiences were exposed during prime time to the perspective of a fictional terrorist who articulately accused the United States of state terrorism. Typically, *terrorism* is a term used to describe the action of others—other countries; other political, religious, and ethnic groups; other belief systems than one's own.

Thus the broadcasting of *The U.S. vs. Salin Ajimi* was unique for many Americans: the defense lawyer within the trial of Ajimi noted that "terrorists" frequently assume that they are at war and thus that their actions pale in comparison to the dropping of atom bombs on Japan, the napalm bombings of civilians in Vietnam, and continuing U.S. activities in many foreign countries. Such actions and reported actions of the Central Intelligence Agency (CIA) make the United States appear no better than, or perhaps the same as, seemingly distant and mad terrorists.

Behind the script, and its novelty to many audience members, was the notion that mass media do not usually depict the full perspective of terrorists or, from a larger context, do not typically report threatening foreign perspectives in a serious, accurate, and comprehensive manner. Americans, like most citizens, are not taught to view their own national actions as "terrorism." This implication supports the notion that, while the press of various nations tends toward the posture of neutrality or objectivity, the press usually inclines toward its own government's perspective: when controversial incidents occur involving a country's rival, usually the home country is depicted as heroic, if at all possible, and the rival country depicted as a villian.

While there is insufficient research to date to prove that adversarial coverage follows this pattern as a general rule in all countries, this chapter cites numerous examples of such coverage by the United States and the Soviet Union, and posits the likelihood of such coverage patterns taking place among other adversaries, such as North and South Korea, Israel and the Palestine Liberation Organization (PLO), or the United States and Libya.

Particularly helpful in understanding the motivation of such stigmatizing coverage is the notion of *perspectivism,* as described by Friedrich Nietzsche, which accounts for enormous differences in the viewpoints of rival or competing entities. This chapter explains, applies, and adapts his thought toward a clearer understanding of culturally biased reporting by the press of adversaries in two types of situations: 1) terrorist activities affecting the reputation, citizens, or wealth of one of the rival nations; and 2) incidents involving direct contact or tension between the rival nations.

In the English edition of *Moscow News,* May 13, 1986, a five-paragraph article features the one-inch headline "CIA Engineered Berlin Disco Explosion."[1] Quoting the Anatolia News Agency (ANA) as its source, the article claims that both the CIA and the Israeli special service (or Mossad) sponsored the planting of a bomb in the La Belle Disco Club in West Berlin on April 5, 1986, by a U.S. soldier who was involved in an underground drug syndicate.[2]

Major U.S. newspapers and broadcasts reported the same bombing but attributed the bombing to Libyan or Libyan-sponsored terrorists, or quoted U.S. officials who claimed that Libya was responsible. One example of such coverage appeared, on April 6, 1986, when the *New York Times* ran two adjacent stories that occupied priority positions on the front page, totaled over fifty paragraphs, as continued on later pages, and opened with the headlines, "2 Killed, 155 Hurt in Bomb Explosion at Club in Berlin; Libyan Role Is Suspected" and "U.S. Sees Methods of Libya in Attack."[3] Most such accounts, including the follow-up stories in all major U.S. media throughout the week of April 6–13, stated, indicated, or suggested that Libya was either responsible, or assumed by U.S. (and in many reports by West German) authorities to be responsible, for the Berlin bombing.

Rare exceptions to this coverage pattern, such as the *St. Petersburg Times*'s lead story on April 6, noted early in the article and prior to any mention of Libya, that at least three phone calls had been received—one day by a news agency in London, two others in West Berlin—claiming that the bombing was the work of a West German radical group, an Arabic group, and a West European left-wing group, respectively.[4]

The majority of U.S. reports did not mention that Libya denied any connection with the Berlin incident. The *New York Times*'s front-page story only briefly reported Libya's denial in its thirty-eighth (final) paragraph, which appeared on page eighteen.

In short, a thorough reading of primary news coverage of the April 5, 1986, West Berlin disco explosion leads to two primary views of the bombing's cause. Soviet news sources explained the incident as part of a larger series of CIA-sponsored or *allegedly* CIA-sponsored terrorist activities. U.S. news reported the explosion as related to, or *allegedly* related to, a larger fabric of Libya-trained terrorist crimes, as masterminded or supported by Colonel Muammar al-Qaddafi.[5] Reports that a message of congratulations from Qaddafi to the terrorists had been intercepted by U.S. officials were given an average of two consecutive days of coverage, while the corresponding story of the Soviet press, that the message from Qaddafi was forged and delivered by the CIA, was a "counterpart" report wherever the Soviet press responded in depth to the U.S. version of the Berlin disco explosion.[6]

These *counterpart* stories, when fully researched, suggest that no major press outlet in either the United States or the Soviet Union was committed to emphasizing "both sides," or in fact, several sides (U.S., West German, Soviet, Libyan, Turkish—one of the two fatalities was a Turk; the other, an East German) or other perspectives of the Berlin explosion. Neither gave "equal time" to foreign spokespersons nor revealed their sources. The *New York Times* reporters repeatedly mentioned "a senior American official" as their primary source about the Libyan connection, while *Moscow News* repeatedly credited only one source, the ANA news agency, for all its facts relating to the bombing.

Neither news system contextualized the incident by trying to answer the question, Why Berlin? The various other news stories about Germany within the *New York Times*, for example, which might have been related to Berlin events during April 6–13, included a tug of war between the United States and the Soviet Union over German research that the United States was attempting to include within the Star Wars program. This was only part of a major U.S. policy involving many U.S. attempts (Secretary of Defense Caspar Weinberger was at that time hoping to win the support of Japan, where he was negotiating) to gain foreign support for Star Wars research. This story is not related by journalists to the bombing. The U.S. and Soviet foreign policy struggle had been highly dramatized in the *New York Times* the day before the explosion, and missiles in Germany, as well as Berlin tensions, had been and continued to be a zone of contention. Many lesser-reported incidents had shown hostility by Germans themselves, especially left-wing and pacifist groups, to Americans, particularly to nuclear-related military installations and, to a lesser degree, to all reminders of foreign occupation, to which Berlin is a monument.

Much Western coverage, however, did seek to contextualize the story within the more geographically scattered string of "terrorist" hostilities. Indeed the *New York Times*, among others, sought to point out possible causality by drafting a separate three-column box four-fifths of one page long with the headline "Twelve Months of Terror: The Mideast Connection." A list of isolated violent actions was provided with their possible terrorist instigators so as to suggest relatedness, if not conspiracy.[7]

More politically conservative papers ran more outright conspiratorial columns and stories amplifying the notion, and to some extent the fear, of an invasion by Libyan terrorists. The *St. Petersburg Times*, for example, ran a daily front-page series by Charles Stafford entitled "They Will Come," which was introduced by the ominous logo of an Inquisition-style hooded terrorist, who is presumably en route to invade the United States. Many of these stories also cited the Soviet Union as a major force behind Qaddafi and implied some level of Soviet support for, if not masterminding of, unified terrorist activity.

Similarly, *Pravda, Izvestia, Moscow News,* Gosteleradio, and other prime news outlets for the Soviet Union were not hesitant to link not only the Berlin bombing but also the Korean Airlines Flight KAL 007 airliner tragedy, attempts to photograph Chernobyl by satellite, defections, border incidents, and other controversial international actions with premeditated Western collaboration, whether spying, anti-Soviet propaganda, or Western terrorism, usually crafted by the CIA. Soviet coverage also reported news supporting the premise that fighting in South America, Afghanistan, the Philippines, and many other locations was sponsored or aided by the CIA and other Western forces.

FROM TERRORISM TO PERSPECTIVISM

Close research of such patterns of news coverage between rivals over several years within major news sources demonstrates a larger tendency: the official national attitudes of political adversaries are, by and large, and with few notable exceptions, reflected in the international news coverage of their press. Whether that press emphasizes *ecomomic* press freedom, as in the Soviet Union, or *political* press freedom, as in the United States, neither seems free to give "equal time" to both, or several positions about terrorist bombings, particularly those occurring in aligned or strategic countries. These tendencies raise questions about whether "terrorism" coverage may ever be studied ahistorically or apolitically.

For example, the Berlin disco explosion had little journalistic life of its own. Most journalistic commentary, rather than seeking far greater detail about the German incident, sought to ferret out hidden connections of the story to a political background and, more important, to a *political* foe or political *threat* to the home nation of the reporter. In this light, it is interesting to note that the use of the word *terrorism* in journalism usually appears in commentary about *foreign* events or domestic events with *foreign* sponsors. Imagine a U.S. or Soviet lead story that begins, "Today *our* best terrorists attacked innocent children in France, killing seven out of a possible twelve."

Despite the feigning of objectivity and despite many journalistic crusades against ethnocentrism and racism, mainstream journalists largely partake of a worldview in which terrorism is not associated with one's self but comes from "the other," as an aspect of what Nietzsche called "perspectivism." Perspectivism describes the worldview an individual or group constructs to associate value and dominance with its own strengths. In so doing, "the other" or others are made inferior, less valuable, and relatively weak or wrong. For example, Nietzsche was able to demonstrate how the Roman Empire established strength and power as the ultimate values, thus legitimizing its empire and conquest by brute force. Conversely, Nietzsche notes that the Christians created a counterbalancing vision of self-supremacy by proclaiming meekness and piety as the ultimate values, thus creating a dominant *perspective* that made Roman values look inferior and barbaric.

Perspectivism allows an invisible shield of insulation from domestic problems. For example, when U.S. authorities speak of terrorism as foreign, they ignore acts by the Ku Klux Klan, the U.S. Nazi Party, "Right to Life" bombing groups, and others who participate in similar actions within the United States. By the same token, perspectivism allows Soviet journalists to associate terrorism with U.S.-inspired activities in Nicaragua, El Salvador, and many other countries, most of which are, or or said to be in the Soviet press, inspired by the CIA, while avoiding use of the word *terrorism* in association with Communist-inspired activities or those of aligned countries that are responding "defensively against Western imperialism."

ADVERSARIAL PERSPECTIVISM

The phrase *adversarial perspectivism* has been chosen to indicate a specific and well-known type of reciprocal perspective-building and maintenance between adversaries. In this specific case, counterpart media are (wittingly or unwittingly) used to maintain a superior and self-righteous posture by the perspectivists (those creating and maintaining self-serving perspectives) involved. For example, both the U.S. and Soviet press suspect an incident such as the Berlin bombing as probably being created by "the other."

While Nietzsche's term *perspectivism* has been chosen so as to imply not simply different perspectives (as in *relativism*), but rather deliberately constructed *apex* perspectives (superior to all others), the terminology is also akin to the helpful philosophical term of E.R. McGilvary—*perspective realism.*[8] As with Prichard's (and Chisholm's) "theory of appearing," perspective realism maintains that direct realism can deal with perceptual relativity by claiming that sensible qualities are related to point of view and usually to some standing conditions.[9]

Thus in perspective realism, or the theory of appearing, it becomes important to state in viewing an object that "the table is round *from here*," or, similarly, "the table is elliptical *from here*." But, in perspectivism, the perspectivist (or creator of the perspective) usually neglects the words "from here," whether to obtain or maintain power, or whether because his view is isolated or prejudiced through domestic conditioning.

Nietzche's favorite example of this type of power maintenance, as described in *On the Genealogy of Morals,* suggests that Christianity created and broadcast a particular type of morality for protection against and power over Roman amorality.[10] However, it is within his later work, *The Will to Power,* that Nietzsche outlines the notion of perspectivism as concomitant with the human longing for power over or dominance, and thus equivalent to a ruling perspective.[11] Thus the mind is deliberately and defensively used to selectively interpret sensations from the environment with a protective, dominating, and self-elevating perspective.

Adversarial perspectivism implies not simply two rival perspectives, but a structural relationship between them. For example, if both are competing for world support and attention, as is the case between the Soviet and U.S. superpowers, certain types of coverage will be given to global incidents of mutual self-interest. If terminology from optics is employed, the two types of coverage, or perspectives, might be called concave and convex, that is to say, one superpower distorts the picture of what has happened in one way, while the rival distorts the picture in the opposite direction. Concave and convex mirrors in an amusement park serve as helpful examples of distortion in opposite directions that makes a person look extremely thin or fat. To each other, Americans and Soviets look exceedingly indulgent or restricted.

A transcendent view of adversarial perspectivism differs considerably from the subjective research perspective of taking sides, thus assuming that the rival country alone creates propaganda and that one's own national mirror of the incident remains clear and unbending. However, the notion of adversarial perspectivism does not imply some arbitrary pure truth zone at the exact midpoint between the adversaries' points of view. Coverage of one incident may be slightly convex from side A and slightly more concave from side B. It may be grossly distorted by both in another incident. In a case where there is little political clout at stake or where there were numerous eyewitnesses from the international press, both press groups may overlap considerably in their accounting to appear objective or to increase their credibility, among other reasons.

Finally, adversarial perspectivism is not simply self-promoting or protective. It may also intentionally seek to deflate the image of the rival and undercut a competitive perspective. At the micro level, the verbal tilting between Oscar Wilde and George Bernard Shaw (Wilde [sarcastically]: "Wish I'd said that, Shaw." Shaw [flippantly]: "You will, Oscar, you will.") served this one-upmanship function by undercutting the opposition's uppercut. Adversarial perspectivism may target and diminish the credibility of particular policies or goals of the opponent such as the Star Wars program or occupation of Afghanistan.

CHERNOBYL COVERAGE EXAMPLES

The drastically different types of coverage given the 1986 Chernobyl nuclear explosion by the U.S. and Soviet press are well-known examples of perspectivism. *Pravda* printed a short report about an "industrial accident" among numerous other unrelated articles, some of which were much longer and presumably of more interest to domestic readers. Western news took the opposite approach and serialized the story as its lead, often for many days, both in broadcast and print media.

Well-known incidents of exaggerated stories (two thousand fatalities, a second explosion, *War of the Worlds*–style evacuation pandemonium) dramatized the coverage in Western news outlets and were often more widely circulated by other Western outlets whose editors did not check the accuracy or context of the original sources. In response, the Soviet press made its lead story the "anti-Soviet and inhumane attacks of the West against the unfortunate at Chernobyl" and similar turning of the tables away from Chernobyl and toward Western news coverage.

Spartak Beglov's *Moscow News* editorial "Poisoned Cloud of anti-Sovietism" epitomized this perspective, which was first printed in *Pravda* (April 30) by V. Bolshakov, and one week later in *Pravda* (May 6) by Yurily Zhukov, and by A. Shainev in *Sovetskaya Kul'tura* (May 6). Beglov's editorial stated:

> Yes, what we are witnessing is a premeditated and well-organized hullabaloo aimed at polluting to the maximum the political atmosphere in East-West relations with miasmas of anti-Soviet hysteria and to use this poisoned cloud to hide the chain of crimes committed by the US and NATO militarism against peace and the security of nations: the recent US aggression against Libya, the nuclear blasts in Nevada, and the militaristic Star Wars program.[12]

Beglov, like many others, had used the images of Chernobyl ("poisoned cloud," "polluted atmosphere") to sustain the Soviet perspective that the United States would use any excuse to defame the Soviets and to contextualize Chernobyl *coverage* (the accident itself is not discussed) as part of a long-standing and unfair anti-Soviet attack as well as a smokescreen to cover U.S. international military operations.

The image of Beglov as a conspiring fabricator is broken down during first-hand interviews with him in his Novosti office, just as the image of U.S. journalists as international fabricators of the now absurd figure of two thousand fatalities crumbles during direct dialogue with U.S. correspondents to Moscow such as Nicholas Daniloff.[13] Both Beglov and Daniloff are experienced journalists and talented writers who share the basic assumptions and convictions of their patriotic colleagues. Moveover, both have been trained to mistrust the "journalism" of their rival.

Other aspects of the perspectivism involved in the Chernobyl coverage have been widely researched. Indeed Tom Gervasi's "Charting the Double Standard in the Coverage of Chernobyl" shows the lengthy history of suppressed imformation about radiation exposure in both the United States and the Soviet Union. He includes incidents in both countries that were reported days or weeks later and even some incidents never publicly reported at all, such as the Soviet blackout of possibly the worst nuclear disaster of all—the probable Kyshtym explosion of 1957, eight hundred miles east of Moscow.[14] Thus, adversarial perspectivism leads to Soviet emphasis upon the perils and delayed reporting of Three Mile Island, among others, and the reciprocal approach by U.S. news wires in write-ups on Chernobyl, but both are part of a historical pattern of delayed and concealed information.

Another U.S.-based research point of view is expressed by Ellen Jones and Benjamin Woodbury II in "Chernobyl and Glasnost," in which the highlights of Soviet internal response to and external publicity about Chernobyl are chronologically documented.[15] Unlike Gervasi, Jones and Woodbury are employed by the U.S. Defense Intelligence Agency and emphasize a shift in Soviet media policy away from stonewalling and toward manipulation of more candid coverage.

A third type of U.S. research about Chernobyl coverage is published by V.P.I. (Virginia Polytechnic Institute) professor Timothy Luke under the title "Chernobyl: The Packaging of a Transnational Ecological Disaster." Luke emphasizes overlapping goals shared by the superpowers—the preservation and growth of nuclear energy plants within their countries. Within his own terms, Luke demonstrates that both countries successfully controlled the image that "no price is too high" to pay for energy sources, despite the evidence of Chernobyl.[16]

Whatever their differing emphases, and the internal political loyalties of the U.S.-based authors, all three types of research share within their conclusions the premise that news about Chernobyl was not apolitical. Indeed all three assume national political goals toward nuclear power, in one or both countries, which are to some extent censored with awareness of public relations overtones, both foreign and domestic.

THE GORBACHEV-CHERNOBYL ISSUE

Response to Gorbachev's first post-Chernobyl public address provides another useful case study. On May 14, 1986, eighteen days following the Chernobyl explosion, Soviet leader Mikhail Gorbachev first addressed the Soviet public (and indeed, in abridged format, a much larger international audience) about Chernobyl by means of Soviet national television. Naturally, the emphasis of *Pravda* and other primary Soviet news conduits was upon the speech itself, although it had been fully available by television the evening before. *Pravda,* without introductory commentary, published a transcription of the speech in its actual order of delivery. Flattering photos of Gorbachev, whether posed prior to the speech or taken live during the telecast, were positioned at the top center of most articles, typically in *Pravda,* May 15, 1986.[17] The televised the speech used minimal commentary and camerawork, giving the illusion of a person-to-person talk by Gorbachev with each member of his audience.

In discussing the speech the following day Dean Yassen Zassoursky, dean of the Moscow State University School of Journalism, noted its many positive features, emphasizing Gorbachev's compassion for the victims, use of the incident to take steps toward peace (the proposed meeting with Reagan at Hiroshima), and candor about the incident.[18] Other Soviets and reports from Soviet media were equally positive.

However, a survey of some of the better-known U.S. and English newspapers the following day proves enlightening. The *New York Times, USA Today,* and *The Times* of London used the phrase that Gorbachev had "broken his silence," while *The Financial Times,* the *Boston Globe, The Guard-*

ian, and *The Wall Street Journal* also noted the "first public talk since Chernobyl," or similar commentary, usually with language that implied the important story was not what Gorbachev said, but rather that he had not said anything in the eighteen preceding days. However, in the Soviet Union such public silence of leadership has been customary for centuries. Behind the scenes, Gorbachev and many of his assistants had said and done much.

None of the leading Western papers mentioned above treated the Gorbachev speech as the undisputed lead story by virtue of either space or position, although it was among the lead stories in three. Both the *Boston Globe* and *New York Times* ran smaller one-column photos of Gorbachev, which, by virtue of the cropping and facial expression, more closely resembled mug shots than did the flattering Soviet photos. While important items in the Soviet press were that Gorbachev sought to establish peace, compassionately consoled the families of victims, and so forth, many of the Western articles began with contextualization of his remarks: he "tried to regain some lost credibility" (The Guardian), he withdrew from silence, or he broke his secrecy.

Perhaps the most demeaning coverage given the Soviet leader appeared in papers noted for equally rough treatment of most world leaders. *The Daily Mail,* which led with a gossipy full-page story about a nineteen-year-old black man (with a photo of him that measured six inchs by three inchs) who raped a seventy-nine-year-old white woman twice, devoted one column on page ten with an one-inch-by-one-inch exceptionally unflattering mug shot of Gorbachev to a story that quickly mentioned Western sources calling the speech a "propaganda ploy." Similarly, *The Sun* devoted 650 percent more space to a story entitled "The Racist Banana," about a local racial incident, than to the Kremlin-based story adjacent to it, and devoted 4,000 percent more space to "Andrea, the Jet Set Pet," a "cheesecake" topless pinup photo, than to a micro mug shot of Gorbachev, which appeared above the memorable headline "Kremlin Chief's 'Sorry' to Nuke Victims."

A detailed content analysis reveals that of thirteen leading U.S. and English newspapers studied (which includes national, urban, upper-class, and working-class [tabloid] samples, over 70 percent of the total words of all articles about the Gorbachev speech are not within quotation marks, that is, have been interpreted from translations.[19] Of the 30 percent which appeared within quotations, the majority of quotations are interrupted—that is, incomplete sentences, sentences taken from context, or paragraph fragments out of chronological order. Only the *New York Times* ran unanalyzed excerpts of the speech and these appeared nine pages after the condensed article of interpreted and contextualized highlights.

Soviet media have given similar stigmatized coverage to the speeches by Ronald Reagan. Unlike U.S. television, Soviet television uses very limited dialogue by adversaries, so images of Reagan giving speeches are shown with Soviet narrative voiceover, rather than with Reagan's synchronized voice and simultaneous Russian translation. Thus one startling surprise to Soviet television audiences was the pretaped appearance of Reagan sending

New Year's greetings to the Soviets on January 1, 1987; its broadcast appeared in most Soviet homes without explanation.[20]

REVIEWING KOREAN AIR LINES FLIGHT 007 COVERAGE RESEARCH

Possibly the best-known coverage of a recent U.S.-Soviet controversy occurred when Korean Airlines (KAL) Flight 007 was shot down by the Soviet military August 31, 1983. Research by Manny Paraschos and Jo Ann Stewart (1985) indicated that once again U.S. media (based upon their analysis of three major television networks and three major newspapers) relied heavily "on Western sources, on the executive branches of government in particular."[21]

Douglas McLeod and Bob Craig (1986) inspected more wide-ranging literature—705 news articles, broadcasts, and telecasts from the media of seventy-three nations, including the United States and the Soviet Union. The researchers categorized the other seventy-one countries such that sixteen countries were considered Soviet-aligned; thirty-nine, U.S.-aligned; and sixteen, neutral. McLeod and Craig's conclusions posited that "news coverage of an ambiguous event reflects international political alignments. . . . This study lends further evidence to attest to the power of social controls in the production of news."[22]

From a commonsense standpoint, this and other recent research indicates that, rather than adopting a neutral position, the U.S. press shows overwhelmingly more trust in reports by U.S. and U.S.-aligned news sources than in Soviet and Soviet-aligned news sources and vice versa. The "watchdog," or investigative, role of the U.S. press, which seems adversarial toward the U.S. government—particularly in episodes such as Watergate, the Pentagon papers, and the Iran-Contra affair—creates the false impression that, in general, the U.S. press is particularly skeptical of U.S. sources and equally open to all points of view.

Numerous Soviet documents—such as the rules of duty of journalists, V.M. Tepluk's important guidebook on the reponsibility of Soviet journalists, and other guidelines—also seek to create the impression that the Soviet journalist is entirely fair, accurate, and responsible.[23] Indeed members of the Soviet and U.S. press have met to study how such fairness and accuracy might be best implemented with less bias against rival superpowers.[24]

A TURNING TIDE?

Larger sectors of both the U.S. and Soviet public have been increasingly exposed to selected perspectives from the "adversary." The noted "Spacebridges," hosted by Vladimir Pozner in the Soviet Union and Phil Donahue in the United States, which promised "candid discussion between U.S. and Soviet ordinary citizens," permitted national audiences in the Soviet Union and major urban markets in the United States to be exposed to opposing views on Afghanistan, Soviet Jews, Star Wars, unemployment, and other issues.[25]

Of equal interest are the tendencies in both countries to import previously censored perspectives, if only on an experimental basis. Soviet *glasnost* has included a loosening up of jamming U.S. based radio signals such as the Voice of America, and U.S. news bureaus, particularly ABC-TV, courted Soviet spokespersons such as Vladimir Pozner, Georgiy Arbatov, and others to appear on major television and radio programs and even as counterpoint to an address by President Reagan.[26]

Moreover, some American audiences, particularly late-night television viewers, are occasionally exposed to alternative definitions of terrorism. Of particular relevance was the January 8, 1988, airing of "Nightline" on ABC-TV, in which host Ted Koppel interviewed Yassir Arafat, leader of the PLO.[27] Arafat repeatedly included the notion of *state terrorism* during the broadcast. He was particularly alluding to Israel, but he also implied that the United States was involved in state terrorism, by which he meant terrorism carried out on behalf of an entire nation, often in warlike fashion, against threatening or adversarially aligned targets.

Although Koppel challenged Arafat repeatedly, the PLO leader was given many openings to pose an alternative view of terrorism. This is only one of many examples in which U.S. audiences are hearing, if not precisely equal time for previously veiled or trivialized perspectives, then at least increasingly credible (if only to those predisposed to nonmainstream perspectives) foreign voices that challenge U.S. governmental and media perspectivism. Nevertheless, this exposure should be viewed as the exception, not the rule. The *Moscow News* article about CIA sponsorship of the Berlin disco bombing, like Michael Parenti's radical but nevertheless American accounting of the downing of KAL Flight 007 in *Inventing Reality,* would still seem farfetched to most U.S. audiences and "total propaganda" to others.[28]

Moreover, *glasnost,* despite its tendencies toward more criticism, both of and by the press, is not a policy that welcomes equal time to all foreign viewpoints. Fyodor Burlatsky's now famous article "Two Views on the International Journalist" makes clear three important problems for the Soviet journalist in the age of *glasnost:*

> 1) We have failed to promptly inform our public about the new technological revolution that has gained rapid momentum in Japan, the U.S., and the West European countries since approximately the mid-1970's.
> 2) We still lack . . . extensive information about social and cultural life abroad. Yet the fact is that 90% of the population of Western societies is made up of working people, and they are by no means utterly deceived, manipulated, and illiterate but perfectly normal people. . . .
> 3) A third problem is to shift from the simplistic concept of an enemy to the far more complex concept of partner, rival and competitor in portraying the Western countries' ruling circles.[29]

Burlatsky, like Koppel, seems ahead of his time, by pointing toward a vision of the future, in which unguarded dialogue between U.S. and Soviet "adversaries" (now becoming "partners," as Burlatsky proffers) at all levels is the rule and not the exception. Moreover, as Robert Stevenson et al. conclude in "Soviet Media in the Age of Glasnost," "Some changes seem evident in Soviet media, particularly in television, but criticism of Soviet officials and activities is still limited, and coverage of the United States is uniformly critical."[30] With noted exceptions, such as the positive coverage of the leadership summits, there are still many parallels in American media.

TOWARD RECIPROCAL UNDERSTANDING

The exchange of information between adversarial journalists and similar cultural exchanges within other components of society are only a tiny beginning toward the type of understanding that is required for both to move toward a more complete picture of the other. Despite both countries being a "melting pot" of many cultural and ethnic groups, they contain a national identity different in underlying personality, not just in political beliefs, from the other. Soviet media, as Soviet society, move at a different underlying metabolic rate than U.S. high-intensity culture. Within Soviet culture, it is no more unusual for Gorbachev to gather data and reflect upon Chernobyl before speaking than for a Native American to sit in silence at a tribal council for several days before speaking.

Likewise, the Soviet administrator who cannot understand the U.S. penchant for seemingly nonstop press conferences and coverage must understand American media operations, in part created by competitive pressures and deadlines and in part created by the adventuresome and aggressive spirit of the pioneering personality who "tamed" America. The Soviet must see the U.S. hunger for "tips," "scoops," photos, and seemingly trivial "updates" as domestically perceived as a service to customers, not as a uncontrolled disturbance of the peace.

This type of deeper understanding of internal wavelengths and cultural predispositions permits a gradual shift in the perception of "adversary" as propagandist, a view still widely held in both countries, to "colleague" with a different (not better, worse, or alien) point of view. It is important to understand these various psychosociological national traits. For example, excepting Native Americans, U.S. citizens are "defectors" from other countries, including the descendants of captured, imported slaves, while Soviets are primarily descendants of survivors of (attempted) conquests of their native lands, which they incessantly defended for millennia. Different styles and functions of media make sense within particular historical, social, and linguistic contexts.

In a similar manner, both U.S. and Soviet journalists need a deeper understanding of "terrorists." The sum total of people categorized as terrorists does not fit a pat, unchanging stereotype. In-depth interviews with those depicted as terrorists in many countries do not reveal a uniform pattern of deranged, hostile, illiterate, macho, and psychotic madmen. While such people exist, much, if not all, of the monolithic image of terrorists is presented to Americans not by people who call themselves terrorists, but by the mass media. Therefore, keep in mind that, in many countries, similar images of American "terrorists" are presented to audiences who have not known Americans firsthand. Instead they have seen tourists, often at a psychological distance, and upon foreign turf, and have also viewed selected examples of U.S. media in which gratuitous crime and violence reinforce the notion that the United States is a country ruled by terror.

The global distribution of *The Godfather,* the *Rambo movies,* "Dallas," and numerous other popular exports reinforces the notion that, to Americans, human life and repect for others are secondary to the imposition of power and a rigid, self-serving worldview. To many, these appear to be the native attitudes of the terrorist. A country that appears to assassinate its own leaders, engage in far-reaching drug wars, create racial struggles, catalyze union-management battles, foster urban combat zones, thrive on sex and violence, and deploy napalm, Agent Orange, and even the atomic bomb (no other country has done so) seems absurdly naive or hypocritical when it complains of relatively minuscule forms of "terrorism" to smaller countries.

By the same token, when Arafat speaks of himself as a freedom fighter and compares himself to De Gaulle against the Nazis or Washington against the British, is he able to dispel his own association with cruel atrocities involving babies and third parties, and re-create a perspective by which he is the flawless, compassionate, and innocent patriarch of his people? It is mass media coverage, more than Arafat himself, that determines the view of Arafat that audiences find convincing.

CONCLUSIONS

Both the term and concept of *terrorism* are deeply rooted in media- and superpower-dominated understandings of reality. Incidents such as a reported bomb exploding in a German nightclub are no less likely to be colored by adversarial perspectivism than events that appear to be directly caused by U.S. or Soviet (or other adversary) powers.

Even seemingly trivial (if any destruction of human life may be said to be trivial) and isolated acts of terrorism, if traced deeply, may be psychologically and sociologically related to feelings toward authority, adversaries, or harbingers of social or geographical displacement. Such displacement, authority, or adversarial conditions are frequently the effects of superpower (and aligned countries) struggles and larger political and economic outworkings.

As Robert G. Picard wisely distinguishes, there are several types and degrees of terrorism.[31] He further notes that many of these are poorly reported and misunderstood, if not totally overlooked. Several reasons exist for this low-quality and relatively low-quantity coverage of specific types of terrorism that persists throughout many countries. Some of these reasons are practical and well-known: the proliferation, transience, obscurity, and relatively minute size of small political and religious groups, whether "terrorist" or otherwise, increase the likelihood of inaccuracy, partial igno-rance, and outdated information reported by many journalists. The sheer quantity of languages, cultures, and political platforms of such groups, when taken in toto, requires total immersion of the journalist into in-depth reading about international affairs, world religions, history, and other areas to sur-round and at least superficially understand the weblike subject. Moreover, many terrorist groups, and indeed many national governments, are noted for deliberate misinformation on matters involving strategy, policy, and, in the case of guerrilla-style groups, geographical location.

These and related reasons account for much of the particularly entan-gled, vague, and often inaccurate coverage of certain types of terrorism worldwide. Nevertheless, perspective realism, particularly as modified into the special case of adversarial perspectivism, and the analogy of reciprocal concave-convex worldviews are important and neglected components in ac-counting for the widespread discrepancies in the reporting of so-called ter-rorist events. Specific coverage of Chernobyl, Gorbachev's televised speech following Chernobyl, the KAL airliner downing, and the Berlin disco explo-sion are all useful examples of such perspectivism. Breakthroughs in con-cave-convex rigidities, whether manifested through *glasnost* or through Russian chic (the fascination by Western media with Gorbachev, Pozner, and Soviet culture), are still superficial or nonexistent in many aspects of society and media coverage.

However, the tendencies toward cooperation between and among inter-national journalists are greater than ever before. Moreover, the awareness of perspectivism is dawning in new quarters and deepening in others. Ele-ments of bias and ethnocentrism and media reductionism are more widely reported than in previous decades. Exchanges between and among media professionals from previously isolated countries are consistently on the up-swing. Thus, overall signs toward the melting of rigid worldviews, photocop-ied by mass media, are increasingly positive. A somewhat less superficial caricature of "terrorism" is being drawn, at least in the more thoughtful sectors of society.

Despite these positive tendencies, one may not jump to utopian or any other black-and-white conclusions. Humility is always necessary in scholar-ship, particularly when the subject is multicolored and painted on so large a canvas. Moreover, the better understanding and reporting of terrorism are merely small steps that will have little effect on combatting it, if the underly-ing causes, growth, and ubiquity of terrorism, however defined, remain un-changed.

Finally, the research presented here, albeit current and born of a large and genuine appetite for truth, is necessarily partial and also culture bound. Whether in Harold A. Innis's terms, what he called "the bias of communica-tion," or in Brislin's terms relating to difficulties in cross-cultural methodol-ogy, no research is without limited and inherited frames of reference.[32]

However, the limits of perspective are of a different order from the limits of perspectivism. The latter constructs reality, closes channels of perception, restricts journalism, and reduces awareness of truth. This research aims toward the detection of reality, the opening of channels, the unfettering of journalism, and the discovery of truth.

NOTES

1. "CIA Engineered Berlin Disco Explosion," *Moscow News*, English Edition, May 13–16, 1986, p. 5.
2. "CIA Engineered Berlin Disco Explosion," p. 5. The exact wording of the article as published in the English-speaking edition is: "ANA points out that the parties immediately involved in the attack are the American CIA and the Israeli special service Mossad. . . . The police established that the bomb, filled with US-made explosives, was delivered to the disco club by an American soldier belonging to the drug syndicate."
3. "U.S. Sees Methods of Libya in Attack," *New York Times*, April 6, 1988, p. A1; John Tagliabue, "2 Killed, 155 Hurt in Bomb Explosion at Club in Berlin," *New York Times*, April 6, 1988, p. A1.
4. "Bomb in Berlin Club Kills 2, Hurts 155." *St. Petersburg Times*, April 6, 1988, p. A1. Exact wording reads: "The first call, to a news agency in London, said the bombing was the work of the Holger Meins Commando, a unit of West Germany's Red Army Faction guerrilla group in the 1970s. The Holger Meins group also claimed responsibility for the Feb. 28 assassination of Swedish Prime Minister Olof Palme.

"Another caller, in West Berlin, said an Arab group calling itself Insahllah, or 'God Willing,' was responsible.

"And a second caller in West Berlin said it was the work of the Red Army Faction, one of Western Europe's most notorious far-left gangs. The attack was an 'action against imperialist crime,' the caller said."
5. See, for example, "U.S. Sees Methods of Libya in Attack"; John Tagliabue, "West Germany to Investigate Role of Other Countries in Berlin Blast," *New York Times*, April 7, 1986, p. A1; John Tagliabue, "West Germany Steps Up Watch on Libyans After Berlin Bombing," *New York Times*, April 8, 1986, p. A1; "The U.S. Sought to Link Qadhafi Loosely to Two Terrorist Attacks," *The Wall Street Journal*, April 7, 1986, p. 1; and coverage of the same story in virtually all major U.S. newspapers with international coverage. The story ran primarily April 6 and 7, with follow-up references primarily from April 8–13, 1986.
6. "CIA Engineered Berlin Disco Explosion," p. 5. Contains this rebuttal version of the story: "the message allegedly intercepted by the Americans ascribed to Libya is a forgery. It was in fact transmitted by American Army Sergeant [sic] nicknamed Colonel. In order to transmit the message, he used a special car driven to the capital of the GDR for this purpose." The counterpart story by ABC News is alluded to in "U.S. Aides Think Libya Was Linked to at Least One Bombing Last Week," *New York Times*, April 8, 1986: "An ABC news report quoting United States intelligence sources as saying the United States had intercepted a message from Colonel Qadhafi to the Libyan Embassy in East Berlin after the bombing that 'in essence offered praise for a job well done.' ABC News said the message 'indicated clear knowledge of details of the terrorist attack.' "
7. "Twelve Months of Terror: The Mideast Connection," *New York Times*, April 8, 1987, p. A7.
8. See, for example, E.R. McGilvary, "Perceptual and Memory Perspectives," *Journal of Philosophy* 30, (1933): 310ff; and his much larger work, *Toward a Perspective Realism* (La Salle, Ill.: n.p., 1956).
9. See, for example, Roderick Chisholm, "The Theory of Appearing," in Max Black, ed., *Philosophical Analysis* (Ithaca, N.Y.: Cornell University Press, 1950); H.A. Prichard, *Kant's Theory of Knowledge* (Oxford: Oxford University Press, 1909), chapter 4; H.H. Price, "Illusions," in H.D. Lewis, ed., *Contemporary British Philosophy* vol. 3 (London: n.p., 1956). For

a more concise reference-style discussion, see Paul Edwards, ed., *Dictionary of Philosophy* vol. 7 (New York: Macmillan, 1967).

10. Friedrich Nietzsche, *On the Genealogy of Morals* (New York: Vintage Books, 1967).

11. Friedrich Nietzsche, *The Will to Power* (New York: Viking, 1967). In Walter Kaufman's 1967 English translation, entry 481, p. 267, Nietzsche's words read:

In so far as the word "knowledge" has any meaning, the world is knowable; but it is *interpretable* otherwise, it has no meaning behind it, but countless meanings—"Perspectivism."

It is our needs that interpret the world; our drives and their For and Against. Every drive is a kind of lust to rule; each one has its perspective that it would like to compel all the other drives to accept as a norm.

12. Spartak Beglov, "Poisoned Cloud of Anti-Sovietism," *Moscow News,* English Edition, no. 19, May 11, 1986, as continued from page 1.

13. The interview with Beglov immediately followed publication of his editorial and was held in his Moscow office at APN news agency. Conversation demythified Beglov from "hardened propagandist," the image he is often given abroad, to avuncular senior editor (a Walter Cronkite type) who genuinely believes his own material, not unlike William F. Buckley or other U.S. political columnists. Nicholas Daniloff is reciprocally depicted as a clever and dangerous U.S. spy in the Soviet Union, by comparison, however, like Beglov, disarming in person. Daniloff genuinely strikes the impression of being a well-educated, kind, but hard-nosed reporter, who genuinely regrets the inflated figures (two thousand being the most widely reported) of Western journalists who "made mistakes." But Daniloff does not suspect sleight of hand or fabrication by U.S. journalists, but rather points out, as an experienced Moscow correspondent, the difficulty of obtaining valid information about news stories such as Chernobyl. Like Beglov, he sincerely believes the *primary* fault is with the adversary.

V. Bolshakov, "Senseless Zeal," *Pravda* April 30, 1986, was perhaps the first and most widely read newspaper article to deliver the theme expounded by Beglov, although Gorbachev himself and many party leaders had publicly condemned the West for sensationalist and inhumane coverage. Follow-up articles by Zhukov and Shainev were respectively entitled "Accidentally Dropping the Mask: Who Is Fueling the Ballyhoo and Why," *Pravda,* May 6, 1986, and "Custom-Made Slander," *Sovetskaya Kul'tura,* May 6, 1986.

14. Tom Gervasi, "Charting the Double Standard in the Coverage of Chernobyl," *Deadline* 3, no. 3 (July-August 1986): 1–5.

15. Ellen Jones and Benjamin L. Woodbury II, "Chernobyl and Glasnost," *Problems of Communism,* November-December, 1986, pp. 28–39.

16. Timothy W. Luke, "Chernobyl: The Packaging of Transnational Ecological Disaster," *Critical Studies in Mass Communication* 4, no. 4 (December 1987): 351–76.

17. The lead story, which fills most of the front page of *Pravda,* May 15, 1986, is a transcript of the televised speech. A three-column by four-inch mid-shot of Gorbachev seated at a desk facing the camera is placed between two columns of text to the left and three columns of text to the right under two-inch title and subtitle headlines.

18. Conversation with Yassen Zassoursky took place in his office and at other locations when the author was guest lecturer at the Moscow State University School of Journalism, May 5–15, 1986.

19. U.S. and English newspapers included in the study, many of which have been mentioned earlier in the text, are the *New York Times, The Times of London, The Wall Street Journal, The Financial Times, The Christian Science Monitor, The Guardian,* the *Boston Globe,* the *St. Petersburg Times, The Sun,* the *New York Post, The Daily Mail,* the *Boston Herald,* and *USA Today.* The comparative study was from the May 15, 1986, first edition of each paper, although later editions of the same paper and follow-up stories of May 16–22, 1986, have also been consulted. The U.S. overseas paper, *The International Herald Tribune,* was also scrutinized, but not included within the data of the study, although its pattern of reporting Soviet affairs, or specifically the Gorbachev speech, is not atypical.

20. As reported by Harvard Soviet analyst Bruce Allyn, Kennedy School fellow, who observed the broadcast first-hand, and observed reactions of Soviet citizens fascinated to see Reagan's animated face at such length and had, in some reported cases, a greater sense of the humanity of the U.S. leader during the address.

21. Manny Paraschos and Jo Ann Stewart, "News Source Utilization: A Case Study in Foreign News Coverage," unpublished paper, abstract frontispiece.

22. Douglas M. McLeod and Bob Craig, "Understanding Discrepancies in International News Coverage of the KAL 007 Airline Incident," as presented at the Annual Conference of the Association for Education in Mass Communication and Journalism, San Antonio, Texas, August 5, 1987, p. 22.

23. V.M. Tepluk, *The Responsibility of the Journalist* (Moscow: Mockba, 1984), will be available in English (excerpts only) in Thomas Cooper, Clifford Christians, Fran Plude, and Robert White, *Communication Ethics and Global Change* (New York: Longman, 1988), although most journalistic guidelines are not yet available in English. Although the *Guidelines of the Communist Party* and many other state documents imply or specify the *role* and overall *social* responsibility of the press in a Communist society (as did Lenin's specific writing on the subject), Tepluk's is perhaps the most important Soviet text written for and about the Soviet *professional* journalist's ethical duties (or journalism deontology as it is often called in European and Soviet-aligned countries).

24. Soviet broadcaster Vladimir Pozner of Gosteleradio and *Los Angeles Times* editor Jack Burbee are representative of the U.S. and Soviet journalists who met in Moscow for several days to discuss alternative means for determining news accuracy in foreign affairs. One suggestion for improvement was that Soviet journalists would be invited to critique U.S. news reports for accuracy while U.S. reporters and editors critiqued Soviet reports, like teachers grading and returning term papers.

25. The series of Spacebridges featured different audiences, some mixed, one all women, from different locations such as Seattle, Boston, Leningrad, Moscow, and other cities, with live broadcasts simultaneously taped in the United States and the Soviet Union for cooperative editing by Americans and Soviets and delayed broadcast in both countries wherever possible. In various ways ABC-TV and Gosteleradio coproduced the series using creative catalysts such as Kim Skencer and Evelyn Messenger. Similar Spacebridges among children, teenagers, and other groups, albeit less issue-oriented, have also exposed mass, if not massive, audiences to less stereotypical views of the "other side."

26. When Vladimir Pozner filed a live counterpoint statement following a presidential address on ABC News, White House spokespersons were angered and contacted ABC. Shortly thereafter, ABC executives issued a statement that the choice of timing, if not spokesperson, was unwise. However, Pozner has been given almost countless invitations, both official and otherwise, to represent the Soviet Union on major television programs such as ABC's "Nightline" and PBS specials since the incident.

27. The one-hour broadcast aired at 11:30 P.M. Eastern Standard Time Friday, January 8, 1988, on ABC-TV. Koppel had interviewed Arafat earlier that day for the daily broadcast news/interview format program "Nightline." The live interview had obviously been recut for commercial interruption and book-ended by later commentary by Koppel, who introduced the interview in segments.

28. Michael Parenti, *Inventing Reality* (New York: St. Martin's Press, 1986); see particularly pp. 156–60.

29. Fyodor Burlatsky, "Two Views on the International Journalist," *Sovetskaya Kul'tura* in *The Current Digest of The Soviet Press*, May 21, 1987, p. 6. Part of Burlatsky's introduction to the more specific discussion lays out the broader subject: "We journalists—I make no exceptions here for any of the various fields—bear responsibility to Soviet society for a number of "gaps" in providing information about the international environment in which our society lives."

30. Robert L. Stevenson, Hoyt Childers, Peter West, and Susan Marschalk, "Soviet Media in the Age of Glasnost," as presented at the International Communication Division, Annual

Conference of the Association for Education in Journalism and Mass Communication, San Antonio, Texas, August 5, 1987, abstract.

31. Robert Picard, lecture, Emerson College, Boston, Massachusetts, December 11, 1987, in the Division of Mass Communication.

32. Harold A. Innis, *The Bias of Communication* (Toronto: University of Toronto Press, 1951), p. 64, noted how each tool of communication has a tendency to bias, or change the sensory ratio or perception of the user, or even the time-space orientation of a civilization:

> The character of the medium of communication tends to create a bias in civilization favourable to an overemphasis on the time concept or the space concept and only at rare intervals are the biases offset by the influence of another medium and stability achieved.

Richard Brislin, in *Cross-Cultural Encounters* (Elmsford, New York: Pergamon Press, 1981), and in many other works is among the leadership of scholars (e.g. Doob, Hall) who note the more obvious form of bias, usually called cultural bias, ethnic bias, or similarly (but not identically) national bias, and attempt to include adjustment factors in research to allow for different languages, customs, mindsets, and hidden cultural assumptions.

REFERENCES

Books and Articles

"About the Chernobyl Nuclear Plant Accident." *Moscow News*, No. 36, May 9–12, 1986 p. 1.

Beglov, Spartak. "Poisoned Cloud of Anti-Sovietism." *Moscow News*, No. 19, May 11, 1986, pp. 1, 6.

Bohlen, Celestine. "Soviet Leader Talks of Disaster." *Boston Globe*, May 15, 1986, pp. 1, 13.

Bolshakov, V. "Senseless Zeal." *Pravda*, April 30, 1960.

"Bomb in Berlin Club Kills 2, Hurts 155." *St. Petersburg Times*, April 6, 1986, pp. A1, A16.

Brislin, Richard. *Cross-Cultural Encounters*. New York: Pergamon Press, 1981.

Burlatsky, Fyodor. "Two Views on the International Journalist." *Sovetskaya Kul'-tura*, in *The Current Digest of the Soviet Press*, May 21, 1987, p. 6.

"The Chernobyl Accident." *Moscow News*, No. 37, May 13–16, 1986, p. 1.

"Chernobyl: The Main Danger Is Over, But There Is Still Much to Do." *Moscow News*, no. 42, May 18, 1986, p. 1.

Chisholm, Roderick M. "The Theory of Appearing," Max Black, ed. *Philosophical Analysis*. Ithaca: Cornell University Press, 1950.

"CIA Engineered Berlin Disco Explosion." *Moscow News*, May 13–16, 1986, p. 6.

Cockburn, Patrick. "Gorbachev Calls for N-Accident Warning System." *The Financial Times*, May 15, 1986, p. 1.

Cooper, Thomas; Clifford Christians; Fran Plude; and Robert White. *International Media Ethics and Global Change*. New York: Longman, 1988.

Dickie, John. "Gorbachev Offers to Meet in Hiroshima." *The Daily Mail*, May 15, 1986, p. 10.

Edwards, Paul, ed. *Dictionary of Philosophy*, vol. 7. New York: Macmillan, 1967.

Fialka, John J. "Gorbachev Calls for Stronger U.N. Unit to Monitor Nuclear Power-Plant Safety." *The Wall Street Journal*, May 15, 1986, p. 3.

Gelb, Leslie H. "U.S. Aides Think Libya Linked to at Least One Bombing Last Week." *New York Times*, April 8, 1986, p. A6.

Gerbner, George, and Marsha Siefert, eds., *World Communication*. New York: Longman, 1984.

Gertner, Sharon. "Prophets in an Alien Land" *The Quill,* January, 1988, pp. 22–25.

Gervasi, Tom. "Charting the Double Standard in the Coverage of Chernobyl." *Deadline* 3, no. 3, (July-August 1986): 1–5.

"Gorbachev Tells Soviets Worst Is Over." *USA Today,* May 15, 1986, p. 1.

Innis, Harold A. *The Bias of Communication*. Toronto: University of Toronto Press, 1951.

Jones, Ellen, and Benjamin L. Woodbury II. "Chernobyl and Glasnost." *Problems of Communism,* November-December, 1986, pp. 28–39.

"Kremlin Chief's 'Sorry' to Nuke Victims." *The Sun,* May 15, 1986, p. 1.

Lewis, Paul. "Europeans to Press U.S. on Third World." *New York Times,* April 5, 1986, p. A6.

Luke, Timothy. "Chernobyl: The Packaging of Transnational Ecological Disaster." *Critical Studies in Mass Communication* 4, no. 4, (December 1987): 351–76.

MacBride, Sean. *Many Voices, One World*. New York: Unipub, 1980.

Martin, John C., and Anjy Chadbury. *Comparative Mass Media Systems*. New York: Longman, 1983.

McGilvary, Bradley. "Perceptual and Memory Perspective." *Journal of Philosophy,* Vol. 30 (1933): 310–44.

McGilvary, Bradley. *Toward a Perspective Realism*. La Salle, Ill.: n.p., 1956.

McLeod, Douglas M., and Bob Craig. "Understanding Discrepancies in International News Coverage of the KAL 007 Airline Incident." As prepared for the Annual Conference of the Association for Education in Journalism and Mass Communication, San Antonio, Texas, August 5, 1987.

"Mikhail Gorbachev Addresses People." *Pravda,* May 15, 1986, p. 1.

Miller, Judith. "France Expelling 2 Libyans, Citing Terrorist Links." *New York Times,* April 6, 1988, p. A8.

Mosgovsky, A. "Shameless." *Sovetskaya Rossiya,* May 6, 1986, p. 22.

Nietzsche, Friedrich. *On the Genealogy of Morals*. New York: Vintage Books, 1967.

Nietzsche, Friedrich. *The Will to Power*. New York: Vintage Books, 1967.

Parenti, Michael. *Inventing Reality*.New York: St. Martin's Press, 1986.

Picard, Robert. "Anti-Communism in the New York Newspaper Guild 1935–1955." Paper presented to the North American Labor History Conference, Wayne State University, Detroit, Michigan, October 22–24, 1987.

Price, H.H. "Illusions," H.D. Lewis, ed. *Contemporary British Philosophy* 3 (1956).

Prichard, H.A. *Kant's Theory of Knowledge*. Oxford: Oxford University Press, 1909.

"Radiation Test Shock for Kiev Britons." *The Times* (London), May 2, 1986, p. 1.

Schmemann, Serge. "Gorbachev, on TV, Defends Handling of Atom Disaster; He Breaks 18-Day Silence." *New York Times,* May 15, 1986, pp. A1, A10, A11.

_____ "West German Woman Arrested in 1986 Disco Bombing." *New York Times,* January 10, 1988, p. A4.

Shainev, A. "Custom-Made Slander." *Sovetskaya Kul'tura,* May 6, 1986, p. 22.

Stafford, Charles. "The Plan: Psychology, Then Guns." In "Terrorists: They Will Come," sixth Installment. *St. Petersburg Times,* April 6, 1986, p. 1.

Stevenson, Robert L., Hoyt Childers, Peter West, and Susan Marschalk. "Soviet Media in the Age of Glasnost." As presented at the International Communication Division, Annual Conference of the Association for Education in Journalism and Mass Communication, San Antonio, Texas, August 5, 1987.

Tagliabue, John. "2 Killed, 155 Hurt in Bomb Explosion at Club in Berlin." *New York Times,* April 6, 1986, pp. A1, A18.

Taglibue, John. "West Germany Steps Up Watch on Libyans After Berlin Bombing." *New York Times,* April 8, 1986, pp. A1 A8.

Tagliabue, John. "West Germany to Investigate Role of Other Countries in Berlin Blast." *New York Times,* April 7, 1986, pp. A1, A6.

Tepluk, V.M. *The Responsibility of the Journalist.* Moscow: Mockba, 1984.

"The U.S. Sought to Link Qadhafi Loosely to Two Terrorist Attacks," *Wall Street Journal,* April 7, 1986, p. 1.

"U.S. See Methods of Libya in Attack," *New York Times,* April 6, 1988, p. A1.

Walker, Christopher. "Soviet Leader Admits Rising Chernobyl Toll." *The Times* (London), May 15, 1986, p. 1.

Walker, Martin. "Gorbachev Links Chernobyl with Nuclear Test Freeze." *The Guardian* (London), May 15, 1986, p. 1.

"What's New." *The Wall Street Journal,* April 7, 1986, p. 1.

Williams, Carol. "Chernobyl Toll Climbs to 13; U.S. Doctor Says Worst Is Over." *The International Herald Tribune,* May 17–18, 1986, p. 1.

Zhukov, Yurily. "Accidentally Dropping the Mask: Who Is Fueling the Ballyhoo and Why." *Pravda,* May 6, 1986.

Nonprint

Allyn, Bruce. Tutoring in Soviet Studies. January–May, 1986.

Arafat, Yassīr. ABC News, "Nightline," Ted Koppel interview, January 8, 1989.

Beglov, Spartak. Interview, APN news agency headquarters, Moscow, May 12, 1986.

Daniloff, Nicholas. Panel and conversation, Boston University, Soviet Studies program, October, 30–31, 1987.

Mickiewicx, Ellen. Panel discussion, Annual Conference of the International Communication Association, Chicago, Illinois, May 23, 1986.

Paraschos, Manny, and Jo Ann Stewart, "News Source Utilization: A Case Study in Foreign News Coverage," unpublished paper (1985), frontispiece.

Picard, Robert. Lecture, Emerson College, Mass Communication Division, Boston, Massachusetts, December 11, 1986.

Pozner, Vladimir. Interviews, panels, and personal conversation, Moscow, May 8, 10, 12, Harvard, May 17, 1986, Chicago, May 22, 1986.

The U.S. Vs. Salin Ajimi. CBS made-for-television movie, (aired January 10, 1988).

Zassoursky, Yassen. Lectures, Discussion, Journalism School, Moscow State University, May 6–15, 1986.

CHAPTER 3

Sacrifice and the Body on the Tarmac: Symbolic Significance of U.S News About a Terrorist Victim

by Jack Lule

ON JUNE 14, 1985, members of the Shiite Muslim group the Islamic Holy War commandeered a TransWorld Airlines (TWA) jetliner with more than one hundred and fifty people aboard. The gunmen forced the plane to make repeated flights from Athens to Beirut and to Algiers. In Beirut, a passenger, U.S. Navy diver Robert Dean Stethem, was severely beaten and then killed, shot in the head, his body pushed from the plane onto the runway.

Holding American passengers as hostages, the hijackers demanded the release of seven hundred Shiite Muslims jailed or detained by Israel. After seventeen days of negotiations, with agreements reached for the release of hundreds of detainees by Israel, the hostages were released.

The hijacking and murder are part of a series of international terrorist attacks that have rocked the political scene in the 1970s and 1980s and gripped world attention. It is the nature and significance of that attention— especially the unblinking, undying attention of the U.S. news media—that is the subject of this chapter.

Some questions have dominated discussion about the relationship between terrorism and news. Does news give terrorists the platform they seek? Does the promise of news coverage somehow cause terrorism?

CRITICAL APPROACH

Less often asked are questions posed from a critical perspective on news, questions that probe the relationship between news reports on terrorism and cultural life. Simply, what might U.S. news reports on terrorism mean in the context of U.S. culture?

Rather than focusing on the relationship between terrorists and news, a critical approach would study the relationship between news reports and culture. Rather than emphasizing the use of media by terrorists, a study would emphasize that U.S. media select and present certain terrorist acts, especially involving the death of an American, as a means of enacting powerful, complex dramas. It is not assumed that the news media are crucial to terrorism, but that media are crucial to society, and that U.S. news on terrorism can be understood in this broad social context.

From this perspective, news reports are seen as symbolic acts in cultural context, acts that shape and are also shaped by that context. The reports are seen as a site to engage questions of social and cultural life.

Of particular interest are reports of terrorist victims. The victim is a symbol used by terrorists to represent a people. News reports, recognizing and affirming the symbol, use the victim as a vital dramatic link with readers.[1] The terrorist victim in the news represents a people to a people, and thus should be an important focus for a critical study.

NEWS AND MYTH

In coverage of the TWA hijacking, the victim played an extremely prominent role. Early accounts focused on unconfirmed reports that a passanger had been beaten and killed. Then, when the body had been pushed out of the plane, before the Red Cross was allowed to approach, reports speculated on the identity of the body on the tarmac. Still later, when the body had been identified and returned to the United States, news reports recounted the life of the victim and provided lengthy coverage of his ceremonial burial, one befitting a national hero.

A story thus was told of an innocent one who was slaughtered and sacrificed to evil. Such stories are the stuff of myth. Different from popular usage that refers to myth as a false or fabulous tale, myth here is seen as an integral aspect of culture, a symbolic narrative that attempts to explain and give meaning to events and beliefs.

This study will look to myth to provide insights into news coverage of terrorism. A critical analysis, which interprets news in the context of social and cultural forces, the study will focus on coverage of the TWA hijacking, specifically on reports of the killing of Robert Dean Stethem. The killing was one of the "big stories" on terrorism, selected from the many that fall outside what Todd Gitlin calls the media spotlight, and given extensive and dramatic coverage. As such, coverage of the killing may yield insights into the relationship among terrorism, news, and social life.

The purposes of this study then are to examine the nature of news coverage devoted to Stethem's killing; to analyze the portrayals of the victim; and—through myth—to suggest the possible significance for social and cultural life of news reports about the murder of a terrorist victim.

METHOD

News and Drama

Drawing from interpretive methods of the humanities, including literary and philosophical studies, critical approaches would explore individual news reports about terrorism as symbolic narratives in the context of culture. Attempting to give meaning to the brutal murder of Robert Dean Stethem, journalists may have turned to mythic drama.

Drama is no metaphor. Reporters focus on compelling terrorist incidents, select details, arrange them in story form, and present them as drama to a news audience. News reports about terrorism can be studied as dramas that invite and invoke the participation of readers.

Walter Lippmann saw news this way. He said, "The audience must participate in the news, much as it participates in the drama, by personal identification."[2] The philosopher George Herbert Mead also saw news as drama. The media "report situations through which one can enter into the attitude and experience of other persons," he wrote. "The drama has served this function in presenting what have been felt to be important situations."[3]

More than any writer, the literary and social critic Kenneth Burke has pursued the implications of drama. In many works, Burke has offered a notion of people as symbol-using animals who *act* on the basis of meanings that symbols hold.[4] He has built around this concept a method of study, dramatism, and interpretive analysis, carefully framed in social theory, which offers great potential for a critical study of news reports. This study will use the dramatistic method of Burke to analyze news reports of the TWA hijacking and the murder of Robert Dean Stethem.

Dramatism

Although Burke can be understood as a theoretician of drama, he affirms that drama offers an important method of study. "Dramatism is a method of analysis," he states, "and a corresponding critique of terminology designed to show that the most direct route to the study of human relations and human motives is via a methodological inquiry into cycles or clusters of terms and their functions."[5]

Burke's pentad—act, scene, agent, agency, and purpose—is the primary tool of inquiry.[6] It probes the structure and content of symbolic acts and addresses five questions: "What was done (act), when or where it was done (scene), who did it (agent), how he did it (agency), and why (purpose)."[7] Burke later acknowledges the pentad could be seen as a hexad if "attitude" is viewed as incipient action.[8]

The pentadic method has been examined in many contexts, including studies by Brock[9] and Ivie.[10] Briefly, pentadic criticism analyzes texts by providing a "chart" of dramatic aspects. Such charts are flexible and fluid; the pentadic terms, essentially ambiguous, overlap with one another. Burke seeks *"not terms that avoid ambiguity, but terms that clearly reveal the strategic spots at which ambiguities necessarily arise."*[11]

Despite such ambiguity, an analysis often finds that one term dominates a text. Burke calls it the ancestor, the logically prior, the term of terms.[12] It can coordinate and organize an entire text. For example, a powerful scene, such as a shipwreck, affects agents, their acts, purposes, and agencies. Charting a text's pentadic alignment, and finding the root term and its relationship (or ratio) with other terms, critics can put forth a coherent and persuasive interpretation.

Validation of dramatistic analysis is what the philosopher Paul Ricoeur calls "an argumentative discipline, comparable to the juridical procedures of legal interpretation."[13] A critic presents evidence for and against an interpretation, "and the final interpretation appears as a verdict to which it is possible to make appeal."[14]

Dramatism provides an excellent tool for the critical analysis and interpretation of news reports on terrorism. Burke's pentad may be particularly apt for news analysis, bearing interesting similarities to news's traditional five *W*'s and *H*—who, what, where, when, why, and how.[15] Through the pentad, dramatism provides a framework in which a news report can be studied as a dramatic act, in the context of culture.

PAST RESEARCH

News and Terrorism

Researchers from many disciplines have responded to questions and challenges raised by international terrorism. The literature is voluminous, cutting across many fields. Two books offer excellent bibliographies: *Terrorism, the Media, and the Law* and *Violence as Communication*.[16] A more recent bibliography, with special emphasis on news, is the *Terrorism and the News Media Research Bibliography*.[17] And an annual series on terrorism captures recent work in many fields.[18]

News and Myth

Interesting work can also be found on news and myth. In the 1950s, McLuhan[19] and Barthes[20] contributed exploratory essays. Other studies include a discussion by Sykes[21] of how news and myth communicate abstract ideas in concrete form; studies by Smith[22] of mythic narratives in television news; and an analysis by Bennett[23] of myth, ritual, and political communication.

Tuchman[24] discussed news and myth in terms of their legitimizing functions. Hall[25] argued that news and myth reproduce and maintain dominant ideological codes of culture. Recent dissertations include a study by Campbell[26] on mythic forms in the television program "60 Minutes" and research by Lule[27] on mythic narratives in U.S. news about the Soviet Union.

Four studies have used myth to study news and terrorism. Lawrence and Timeberg[28] suggested that selection and presentation of terrorist events by reporters are governed by mythic paradigms. Knight and Dean[29] stated that news accounts legitimize violence against terrorists, but not the violence of terrorists. Paletz, Ayanian, and Fozzard[30] concluded that myth in television news provides attention but not legitimization for terrorists. Davis and Walton[31] found mythic aspects of consensus and closure informing news coverage of the terrorist killing of Italian Premier Aldo Moro.

Comparisons with myth can add to understanding of news reports about terrorism. Through analysis of news portrayals of a terrorist victim, this study hopes to contribute to that important work.

RESEARCH QUESTIONS

The following research questions will be addressed:

1) What was the nature of news coverage about the terrorist victim Robert Dean Stethem? What general themes can be discerned? Did photographs accompany the accounts? If so, what was the nature of the photographs?

2) In dramatistic terms, what were the acts, agents, scenes, agencies, and purposes of news reports about Robert Dean Stethem? How are pentadic terms linked in individual reports? What root terms organize the reports?

3) To what extent can the news reports be understood as myth, defined as a symbolic narrative that attempts to explain or give meaning to events and beliefs? What might possible mythic portrayals say about the relationship among terrorism, news, and culture? What might be the possible social significance of mythic portrayals of terrorism in the news?

For this study, *New York Times* stories are analyzed. One of the world's elite newspapers,[32] the *Times* is the most widely read newspaper within the U.S. government,[33] the most widely quoted,[34] and is invaluable for research of U.S. news and international affairs.

The time period examined is June 14, 1985, the date of the hijacking, to July 5, when the hostages had been freed and returned to the United States. Each report, editorial, and photograph devoted to the hijacking will be examined for references to the victim, and the images, symbols, and context used to represent the victim.

The approach is microscopic, analyzing one aspect of one newspaper's coverage. It is the strength and limitation of interpretive research. Clifford Geertz says, "The aim is to draw large conclusions from small, but very densely textured facts; to support broad assertions about the role of culture in the construction of collective life by engaging them exactly with complex specifics."[35]

This study engages the complex specifics of *New York Times* reports about the murder of Robert Dean Stethem to explore the role of such news in social life. To what extent can the news reports be seen as dramatic enactments that shape and are shaped by the context of culture, which draws from and gives to social order and cohesion?

DRAMATISTIC ANALYSIS

Day One

VICTIM AS SCENE On June 15, 1985, the first reports of the TWA hijacking appeared in the *Times*. The front-page story was headlined, "Gunmen Seize Jet in Mideast Flight; Passenger Killed." Two subheads preceded the report: "104 Americans on Board—During Odyssey, T.W.A. Plane From Athens Goes Twice to Beirut and Algiers." (Surely purposeful was the word *odyssey* to describe an incident originating in Athens. The word recurs throughout *Times* coverage of the hijacking.)

The report carried the byline of Joseph Berger and no date line, which in the *Times* usually means the story was compiled and written in New York. Accompanied by a large, three-column photograph of the grounded jet, the report attempted to capture the chaotic events and whirl of locations. The lead stated:

> Gunmen commandeered a Trans World Airlines jetliner with 104 Americans aboard yesterday and forced it to fly on a twisting course from Athens to Beirut to Algiers, then back to Beirut, where one passenger was shot to death, and again to Algiers.

Scene was the determining dramatic principle. This initial report attempted to situate and fix the stages on which the action took place. Even in terms of the victim, scene played a crucial role. That is, in the first *Times* account of the hijacking, the unidentified passenger was made part of the stage on which others acted. In dramatistic terms, the victim was depicted not as an agent—one who acts—but as an element of scene, part of the situation.

The lead suggested the influence of victim as scene. It stated that the jet was forced to fly "back to Beirut, where one passenger was shot to death." Later, describing the beating, the report said that the pilot made a frantic appeal.

> "They are beating the passengers! They are beating the passengers!" he said. "They are threatening to kill them now! We want the fuel now! Immediately!" Cries and groans that sounded as if someone was being beaten *could be heard in the background* [italics added].

Elsewhere, the report stated, "The odyssey was filled with moments of terror," but no one was injured until the second landing in Beirut. "*There* [italics added] the pilot radioed the control tower and said of one of the hijackers: "He just killed a passenger! He just killed a passenger!" " [italics added].

The report showed a marked interest in the body's whereabouts. It said, "The body of the slain man was taken from the plane and put aboard an ambulance accompanied by three militia jeeps." The body was "reportedly" brought to the morgue at American University Hospital, but "reporters were not permitted into the morgue." Where the body was *in Beirut* does not seem particularly pertinent; the presence of the body *in the story* appears to be the decisive factor.

Other stories that day also portrayed the victim not as agent but scene. A report quoted State Department spokesman Bernard Kalb and said he "spoke before the plane landed for a second time at Beirut, Lebanon, where one passenger was reported killed." Interviews with released passengers, American Embassy spokespersons, and Mideast officials also used the victim as background for events.

Burke notes, "Political commentators now generally use the word 'situation' as their synonym for scene, though often without any clear concept of its function as a statement about motives.[36] By incorporating victim as situation or scene, the *Times* made a statement about motives. For the *Times,* the victim was part of the "situation," necessary for understanding and reacting to events.

Surely the *Times*'s emphasis on the victim makes sense. The murder of a passenger heightened the intensity and urgency surrounding the hijacking. But as an elite newspaper of political power and influence, the *Times* helps shape and is shaped by cultural context. Its insistence on the victim as scene assured that the symbolic power and emotional drama of the victim would become part of the cultural context for understanding the hijacking.

Days Two Through Five

THE BODY ON THE TARMAC   In the next days, the hijackers released many passengers. Remaining hostages were American men. Some with "Jewish-sounding names" were taken off the plane in Beirut where the original hijackers had been joined by more than twenty other men. The *Times* offered at least ten stories a day.

Although still depicted as part of the scene, the victim, unidentified until the fourth day of coverage, played another prominent role: agency. With released passengers providing information, reports focused on how the hijackers had acted. Scene and agency were balanced, in references about the victim, to portray the brutality of the hijackers.

In Burke's terms, the reports established a ratio between terms. The ratio, "a formula indicating a transition between one term and another,"[37] extended victim as scene to agency, providing a complex, dramatic narrative.

Many versions of the beating and killing were printed. On day two of coverage, June 16, the lead account summarized the "tortuous odyssey," and reiterated that in Beirut "a passenger who was described by the hijackers as a United States Marine was shot in the left temple and his body was thrown out on the tarmac." The phrase *on the tarmac,* essentially scenic, recurred throughout *Times* coverage; it also implied agency—showing the terrorists' disregard for human life.

In another report, a released hostage offered a gripping account.

"We heard the beating, we knew somebody was hurt and pretty badly," the woman said. When leaving the plane, she saw two men "crumpled on the floor." One had "a mask over his face, like they did to the hostages in Iran, with blood on the mask, so we knew somebody was badly hurt."

The *Times* accompanied its accounts with a dramatic centerpiece, a two-column photograph captioned: "Body of the slain American lies in morgue of American University Hospital." The photograph showed a white-coated man gesturing with a pointer to the body, which lay on a white table in darkness and shadows.

On the following day, the *Times* offered more details about the victim's death. The purser of the plane told the *Times* that "one marine was singled out for a brutal beating." She said he was shot dead and "thrown to the tarmac in Beirut." The article continued: "She thought his name was Robert Stetson, although no such name appeared on the list supplied by the airline."

Another report, from Madrid, noted that the victim's body had been sent to a nearby American air force base for identification. Beaten beyond recognition, the body was being examined for clues from dental work and fingerprints.

The most graphic, intense account in the *Times* was filed by Reuters in London. An Australian girl freed by the hijackers told Reuters she had been sitting next to an American serviceman, "a Navy diver and not a marine, as has been reported." The hijackers dragged him out of his seat, tied his hands and then beat him, the girl said.

I watched as they kicked him in the head. They kicked him in the face and knee caps and kept kicking him until they had broken all his ribs.

Then they tried to knock him out with the butt of a pistol—they kept hitting him over the head but he was very strong and they couldn't knock him out. . . . Later they dragged him away and I believe shot him.

These references to the victim are stirring and potent, rousing sadness and sympathy for the victim, anger at and revulsion for his attackers. In dramatistic terms, the ratio between agency and scene effected a powerful portrait of events.

"DEAD MAN IDENTIFIED." On Tuesday, June 18, day four of the coverage, the victim was identified. The front-page story, beneath a subhead "Dead Man Identified," noted that "in Washington, the passenger who was killed by the hijackers Saturday was identified today as Robert D. Stethem, 23 years old, a Navy diver."

Inside the paper, on page A9, a report by Richard Halloran, filed from Washington, provided details. "Slain Passenger Was a Navy Diver," the headline read. Atop the headline was a photograph and caption: "Victim Identified: : [*sic*] Robert Dean Stethem, the slain Navy diver, as pictured in the 1980 high school yearbook." The photograph showed an unsmiling, cleanshaven young man with thick hair, surprisingly long, reaching down to his collar.

The second paragraph once again noted the brutality of his death. "The young man's face had been beaten beyond recognition and his body dumped from the aircraft onto the airfield." Positive identification had been made from medical records and fingerprints, the report said. Friends of the family had flown to Spain to identify the body but were unable to recognize him.

There was conflicting information on his naval duties. One source said Stethem was working on a sewer project at a naval communications station in Greece. Another said Stethem was a Navy commando trained in underwater demolition. The report said "a call to Mr. Stethem's family residence in Waldorf was answered with a request that no questions be asked at this time."

Biographical information was given. Stethem graduated from high school in 1980. He played on the varsity football team, was a weight lifter, and "enjoyed the beach and diving." A friend said Stethem "had enlisted in the Navy after high school because he wanted to travel."

The report ended with a friend's cliché about Stethem, a sad and flat commentary in contrast to the drama and emotion of the previous days. "Mr. Meisinger, who played on the football team with Mr. Stethem, said, 'He wasn't a great athlete but he always gave a hundred percent.'"

VICTIM AS PURPOSE. The *Times*'s portrayal of the victim had progressed in detail and complexity. From unidentified part of the scene, the portrayal of the victim then was used to comment on the actions of the hijackers. After identification, on June 18, the victim took on a new role in the *Times*. He was included in a *Times* editorial that called for retaliation and prevention by the United States. The victim now was called to be part of the national purpose. In "The Hostage Tangle," the *Times* editorial said:

> There are crimes aplenty here. The hijackers are guilty of murder as well as kidnapping. The authorities in Greece are guilty of incredible laxity in letting them board the plane and in their supine negotiations. The United States itself is guilty of having failed to punish Iran for sheltering the killers of two Americans in a hijacking last year. But the necessary retaliation and preventive measures must wait until the current victims are safe.

The *Times* assumed that "the United States" must retaliate for the hijacking and murder. Robert Dean Stethem's murder was summoned as justification, part of the purpose of the nation.

The next day's reports, June 19, day five of news coverage, offered a complementary perspective. Reports cited Stethem as an American hero whose murder would not go unanswered. A front-page account reported President Reagan's call for "antihijacking steps." The President framed his call and opened his press conference by invoking the memory of Stethem as a hero. The *Times* provided a transcript of his words:

> Please be seated. One hour ago, the body of a young American hero, Navy diver Robert Dean Stethem was returned to his native soil in a coffin after being beaten and shot at point-blank range.

His murder and the fate of the other American hostages still being held in Beirut underscore an inescapable fact: the United States is tonight a nation being attacked by international terrorists who wantonly kill and who seize our innocent citizens as their prisoners.

A front-page photograph also offered a view of Stethem as hero. The photograph showed the flag-draped coffin of Stethem, carried by a Navy honor guard, being received at Andrews Air Force Base by the Stethem family and public officials, including then Vice President George Bush and his wife Barbara. Stethem's return home was treated with pomp and ceremony befitting a national hero.

As if to remind readers of Stethem's fate, a report provided yet another account of Stethem's killing. Headlined "Freed Hostage Tells of Sailor's Death," the report quoted a released passenger who said that before the plane landed for the second time in Beirut "one of the stewardesses told the group of hostages 'not to pay attention to the sound we we [sic] were going to hear.' The sound, said the 62-year-old retired corporate executive, was a gunshot. A 23-year-old Navy diver, Robert Dean Stethem, was killed." The accounts, photograph, and the president's words offer up the victim as a hero whose death gave the nation renewed purpose.

Days Six and Seven

June 20 offered more news about terrorism. Four U.S. Marines and nine other people were killed by gunmen at a café in San Salvador. The *Times*'s front page still was given over to photographs and reports of the TWA hijacking. Accounts focused on relatives of hostages. President Reagan, after a speech in Indianapolis, met with the family of a hostage. In other reports, families expressed both support and frustration with the President. In no report was Robert Dean Stethem mentioned.

VICTIM AS HERO. On Friday, June 21, the front page of the *Times* was marked by a four-column photograph of a news conference attended by five hostages and many Shiite Muslim gunmen. Slightly below was a smaller photograph showing a somber Navy man folding the U.S. flag above the casket of Robert Dean Stethem. In the lower corner of the photograph was Stethem's father. The caption read: "Burial With Honors—Richard Stethem, right, watching folding of the flag that draped the casket of his son, Robert, slain in hijacking of Flight 847. Page A10."

Page A10 was dominated by a large, four-column photograph of the Stethem family at Arlington National Cemetery accepting the U.S. flag from Navy Commodore Frederick G. Kelley. The presence of the flag in both photographs denoted the national status of the victim.

Headlined "Hijacking Victim Buried at Arlington Cemetery," the accompanying report was a long, dramatic tribute. The victim was portrayed as a hero of almost mythic status. Previous themes were repeated. A subhead quoted President Reagan's description of Stethem as "A 'Young American Hero.' " The phrase was also repeated in the text. The circumstances of death were also restated. "He was beaten and shot to death June 14 by the hijackers," the report said, "who dumped his body from the aircraft onto the tarmac of the Beirut airfield."

And the victim was depicted as having sacrificed his life for the nation. In the fourth paragraph, the report selected from the eulogy the theme of sacrifice: " 'Robert Stethem has not died in vain,' the Rev. Wendell Cover said in the memorial service. 'He gave us an example of courage, bravery and love.' " The closing paragraphs too used words of sacrifice. Stethem's brother Patrick said, "He gave his life not for one individual or two, but for every single person in the free world today."

The portrayal by the *Times* elevates Stethem to almost mythic status. The death of a terrorist victim had been transformed by the *Times* into a mythic drama of heroic sacrifice.

Days Eight through Sixteen

Through the second week of the crisis, the hijacking still dominated the *Times*'s front page. Few reports mentioned Stethem. Accounts that did mention the victim merely recycled phrases, quotations, and photographs from previous days. On June 22, for example, the *Times* summarized events, using the pilot's frantic broadcast, "He just killed a passenger!" It also mentioned that after the killing, "his body was dropped on the tarmac." On Sunday, June 23, the *Times* stated the president had telephoned the Stethem family on Tuesday. No details were provided about the call. Another report was accompanied by a large photograph of the Navy honor guard carrying Stethem's coffin.

On June 26, the *Times* editorialized for retaliation against offending nations. In "Yes, There is Something We Can Do," the paper suggested that the United States boycott the airports of those who shelter "kidnappers and murderers," implicitly summoning Stethem as purpose.

Excerpts from interviews with released hostages continued to refer to Stethem's murder. On June 30, the second paragraph of a front-page interview with a hostage mentioned Stethem. "He was my friend," the hostage said. "It was kind of sad. They thought we were marines, combat types." A summary of "key moves" in the crisis again used the photograph of Stethem's coffin being carried by the navy honor guard.

Days Seventeen through Twenty-One

On June 30, after seventeen days in captivity, the thirty-nine American hostages were freed. The headline for July 1 stretched across all six columns: "39 American Hostages Free After 17 Days; Go From Lebanon to Syria and Head Home." In the many reports that filled the paper that day and in the days following, as the hostages triumphantly returned to the United States, Robert Dean Stethem reemerged on the front page of the *Times*. Indeed, already buried, the victim still dominated reports about the conclusion of the hijacking.

Resurrecting its theme from the previous week, the *Times* used Stethem

as purpose. The lead paragraph of the lead story on July 1 selected words
from the president's speech and emphasized that the national celebration
over the return of the hostages should be tempered: "President Reagan wel-
comed the release of the American hostages today, but said the United
States 'will not rest until justice is done' in Beirut as well as El Salvador."
The same report used the more explicit words of Secretary of State George
Shultz. " 'We want to find who in particular beat and shot Robert Stethem,'
Mr. Shultz said."

Interviews with hostages and relatives repeatedly focused on the victim.
A report on the joy of hostages' families noted that "still in mourning was
Patricia Stethem, the mother of Robert Dean Stethem, a 23-year-old Navy
diver who was pistol-whipped and shot point-blank aboard the hijacked
flight by his Shiite Moslem captors."

The president and the *Times* both framed the return of the hostages with
reference to Stethem, and Stethem was used to call forth a national purpose
of retaliation and revenge. The president's statement, cited in a number of
reports, said that the "murderers of Robert Stethem and of our marines and
civilians in El Salvador must be held accountable." The *Times* too editorialized that "the drama of sentimental reunions should not obscure some pain-
ful truths. One American passenger on the T.W.A. plane was savagely mur-
dered and his killers remain at large in Beirut."

Reports on the following days continued to center on Stethem. A front-
page report on July 2 gave yet another account of his killing. Another report
was devoted to the administration's attempts to locate the killers: " 'We
want Stethem's killers brought to justice,' " an official said.

On July 3, a front-page story about the President greeting the ex-hostages
was preceded by the subhead: "While Voicing Joy, He Focuses on Hijackers' Murder of Seaman." The report quoted the president:

> "Our joy at your return is substantial," Mr. Reagan said. "But so is our pain at
> what was done to that son of America. I know you care deeply about Robbie
> Stethem and what was done to him. There will be no forgetting. His murderers
> must be brought to justice."

The same report noted that "Mr. Reagan spent much of the day praising
Mr. Stethem, calling his brother, Patrick, and saying that the slain seaman
was an 'American hero.' " A photograph accompanied the report; it showed
the president and his wife placing a wreath on Stethem's grave as the victim's sister watched.

On Friday, July 5, a *Times* report again probed the death of Stethem, in
a long report, "T.W.A. Pilot Tells How Diver Died." Stethem was severely
beaten in the cockpit, the pilot said. " 'They would support themselves by
holding onto the door to keep their balance and jump up and down on him,
landing solidly with their heels,' the captain said." The *Times* devoted more
than half a page to the new details.

Through three weeks, the *Times* pursued the story of the TWA hijacking
and the death of Robert Dean Stethem. From an unidentified body on the

tarmac, Stethem became for the *Times* an American hero, the leading role in a mythic drama of sacrifice and retribution. The following section discusses the significance of such portrayals in the context of U.S. culture.

DISCUSSION

Victimage

Robert Dean Stethem's killing certainly was newsworthy; it was not surprising that the *New York Times* provided long, intense converage of the hijacking and murder. But what might such reports *mean* in the context of culture? Though this study has been small in scope and exploratory in approach, some responses to this question can be offered. Dramatistic analysis has illuminated *Times* portrayals of Stethem, offering opportunities for insights into news reports about terrorism and their possible significance for social life.

An intriguing progression was seen in *Times* coverage. Early in the crisis, the victim was a prominent part of the scene. Before the body was identified, the *Times* assumed the victim was essential for understanding a tense, international situation. After identification, Stethem became part of a call for national purpose. He died representing his nation, the *Times* said, and coverage of his ceremonial burial suggested he was a national hero who had sacrificed his life for his country.

After his burial, few reports mentioned Stethem. But upon return of the hostages, the victim was returned to the public stage, commanding the attention of government officials and the front page of the *Times,* and becoming the central figure in cries for justice and retribution.

Such a portrayal has links suggestive of mythic tragedy. An ordinary man in extraordinary conditions is proven to be a hero by suffering and dying for his people. Through the pentad, the creation of a mythic hero is revealed in the *Times* reports, a hero whose sacrifice offered readers a compelling drama of victimage.

What is the significance of victimage in the news? Burke sees the process of victimage as central to social life. Through the shared sacrifice of victims, Burke says,[38] individuals achieve identification and integration within groups. He asks "whether human societies could possibly cohere without symbolic victims which the individual members of the group share in common," and calls victimage "the very centre of man's social motivation."[39]

The sociologist Hugh Duncan, a disciple of Burke, worked to extend the implications of Burke's work for social life. He said, "The sociology of our time must begin in anguished awareness that victimage is the means by which people purge themselves of fear and guilt in their relations with each other."[40] In this view, victimage is the ritual unburdening of a people that takes place through great social dramas of purgation and purification, sacrifice and salvation.

Yet victimage accomplishes more. It not only purges a people of guilt and fear, it unites them. In the sharing of sorrow and anger, in the sharing of enemies and victims, a group can come into being. People can achieve, in symbolic acts of victimage, the communion and consensus necessary for social order, identification, and integration.

This study suggests that U.S. news reports on terrorism, at least as seen in *New York Times* coverage of Robert Dean Stethem's killing, may serve as symbolic acts of victimage. That is, the news reports, through portrayals of the terrorist victim, offer readers a social drama of sacrifice and salvation that may help shape and sustain social life.

A complex drama of victimage can be discerned in the *Times* reports. Stethem was portrayed as "a young American hero" who "gave us an example of courage, bravery and love" and who sacrificed his life "for every single person in the free world today." In their brutal murder of the young man, the terrorists come to personify evil powers that destroy such virtue and threaten modern community order.

More important, the victim—not necessarily purified before sacrifice, but in sacrifice—is elevated and transformed into a powerful charismatic figure, a tragic, mythic hero. Burke sees this as a key strategy of sacrificial dramas. The victim is made "worthy by a subtle kind of poetic justice," that makes "the sacrificial vessel 'too good for this world,' hence of the *highest* value, hence the *most perfect* sacrifice."[41]

Thus, in the drama of news reports, Robert Dean Stethem, the mythic hero, was sacrificed. And here, in victimage, might lie the meaning and social significance of news reports about terrorism. In their gripping portrayals of the victim's sacrifice to terrorism, the news reports offer the community the opportunity to participate in a great drama of hope, despair, purpose, and pain, and in that drama, and in that participation, community can be created and confirmed.

Victimage may provide insights into the relationship among terrorism, news, and society. From the many terrorist incidents that flare around the world, reporters and editors perhaps react to and select those that address conscious and unconscious social needs for victimage. Rather than suggesting implications for the overworked ground of terrorist "use" of the news media, this study suggests that U.S. media may select, present, and use a very few terrorist acts, especially involving the killing of a U.S. citizen, as a means of enacting a social drama of victimage. Duncan noted[42] that people do not so much need information about, but identification with, community life. News portrayals of terrorism might be an integral means by which people find identification with community life through victimage.

Thus, rather than retaining a narrow perspective on terrorists and the news media, this study suggests a focus on a much larger process, the creation and maintenance of community through social dramas of victimage, of which news on terrorism is just one part. The larger context contains portrayals of terrorism and violence in television news, prime-time programs, novels, feature films, magazines, comic books, textbooks, and myriad other symbolic forms.

This larger context raises the darker side of victimage. Both Burke and

Duncan recognize that symbolic dramas of victimage have been used to shape and mold community life in perverse, monstrous ways. The genocide of the Jews in Nazi Germany is the most extreme example, thus far, of the terrible power of victimage in society.

Duncan wrote eloquently that "we cannot become humane until we understand our need to visit suffering and death on others—and ourselves. We *need* to socialize in hate and death, as well as in joy and love." He continued, "We do not know how to have friends without, at the same time, creating victims whom we must wound, torture, and kill. Our love rests on hate."[43]

Through its stories on Robert Dean Stethem, the *New York Times* offered readers a mythic drama of love and hate. News reports on terrorism perhaps can be studied and understood as part of a larger process of purification and degradation, a social drama of victimage in which the death of the terrorist victim becomes an opportunity for a people to acknowledge and affirm community life.

NOTES

1. Jack Lule, "The Myth of My Widow: A Dramatistic Analysis of News Portrayals of a Terrorist Victim," *Political Communication and Persuasion* 1, no. 2 (1988): 101–120.

2. Walter Lippmann, *Public Opinion* (New York: Macmillan, 1922), p. 355.

3. George Mead, *Mind, Self, and Society* (Chicago: University of Chicago Press, 1934), p. 257.

4. See Kenneth Burke, *A Grammar of Motives* (Berkeley: University of California Press, 1969); Kenneth Burke, *Dramatism and Development* (Barre, Mass.: Clark University Press, 1972); Kenneth Burke, "Dramatism," in James E. Combs and Michael W. Mansfield, eds., *Drama in Life* (New York: Hastings House, 1976); and Kenneth Burke, *Permanence and Change,* 3rd ed. (Berkeley: University of California Press, 1984).

5. Burke, *Drama in Life,* p. 7.

6. See Burke, *A Grammar of Motives* and Burke, *Drama in Life.*

7. Burke, *A Grammar of Motives,* p. xv.

8. See Burke, *Dramatism and Development* and Burke, *Drama in Life.*

9. Bernard L. Brock, "Political Speaking: A Burkeian Approach," in W. Rueckert, ed., *Critical Responses to Kenneth Burke* (Minneapolis: University of Minnesota Press, 1969), pp. 444–55; Bernard L. Brock, "Epistemology and Ontology in Kenneth Burke's Dramatism," *Communication Quarterly* 33 (Spring 1985): 94–104; and Bernard L. Brock and Robet L. Scott, eds., *Methods of Rhetorical Criticism: A Twentieth Century Perspective* (New York: Harper & Row, 1985).

10. Robert L. Ivie, "Presidential Motives for War," *Quarterly Journal of Speech* 60 (October 1974): 337–45.

11. Burke, *A Grammar of Motives,* p. xviii (author's emphasis).

12. Burke, *A Grammar of Motives,* p. 127.

13. Paul Ricoeur, *Interpretation Theory* (Fort Worth: Texas Christian University Press, 1976), p. 78.

14. Paul Ricoeur, "The Model of the Text," in P. Rabinow and W. Sullivan eds. *Interpretive Social Science* (Berkeley: University of California Press, 1979), p. 93.

15. Burke, *A Grammar of Motives,* p. 228.

16. Abraham Miller, ed., *Terrorism, the Media, and the Law* (Dobbs Ferry, NY: Transnational Publishers, 1982); and Alex P. Schmid and Janny de Graaf, *Violence as Communication:*

Insurgent Terrorism and the Western News Media (Beverly Hills, Ca.: Sage Publications, 1982).

17. Robert G. Picard and Rhonda Sheets, *Terrorism and the News Media Research Bibliography* (Boston: Terrorism and the News Media Research Project, Emerson College, 1986).

18. Yonah Alexander, ed., *The 1986 Annual on Terrorism* (Hingham, Mass.: Kluwer Academic Publishers, 1987).

19. Marshall McLuhan, "Myth and Mass Media," *Daedalus* 88 (1959): 339–48.

20. Roland Barthes, *Mythologies,* trans. by A. Lavers (London: Jonathan Cape, 1972).

21. A.J.M. Sykes, "Myth in Communication," *Journal of Communication* 20 (March 1970): 17–31.

22. Robert R. Smith, *Beyond the Wasteland* (Falls Church, Va.: Speech Communication Association, 1976); and Robert R. Smith, "Mythic Elements in Television News," *Journal of Communication* 29 (Winter 1979): 75–82.

23. W. Lance Bennett, "Myth, Ritual and Political Control," *Journal of Communication* 30 (Autumn 1980): 166–79.

24. Gaye Tuchman, "Myth and the Consciousness Industry," in Elihu Katz and Tomas Szecsko, eds., *Mass Media and Social Change* (Beverly Hills, Ca.: Sage Publications, 1981), pp. 83–100.

25. Stuart Hall, "The Rediscovery of Ideology," in Michael Guerevitch, Tony Bennett, James Curran, and Janet Woolacott, eds., *Culture, Society, and the Media* (London: Methuen, 1982), pp. 56–90.

26. Richard A. Campbell, "Narrative, Myth and Metaphor in '60 Minutes': An Interpretive Approach to the Study of Television News" (Ph.D. Dissertation, Northwestern University, 1986).

27. Jack Lule, "News as Myth: A Hermeneutic Approach to U.S. News of the Soviet Union" (Ph.D. Dissertation, University of Georgia, 1987).

28. John S. Lawrence and Bernard Timberg, "News and Mythic Selectivity," *Journal of American Culture* 2 (Summer 1979): 321–30.

29. Graham Knight and Tony Dean, "Myth and the Structure of News," *Journal of Communication* 32 (Spring 1982): 144–58.

30. David L. Paletz, John Z. Ayanian, and Peter A. Fozzard, "Terrorism on TV News," in William C. Adams, ed., *Television Coverage of International Affairs* (Norwood, N.J.: Ablex Publishing, 1982), pp. 143–65.

31. Howard H. Davis and Paul Walton, "Death of a Premier: Consensus and Closure in International News," in Howard David and Paul Walton, eds., *Language, Image, Media* (Oxford: Basil Blackwell, 1983), pp. 8–49.

32. John C. Merrill, *The Elite Press* (New York: Pitman, 1968).

33. Carol H. Weiss, "What America's Leaders Read," *Public Opinion Quarterly* 38 (Spring 1974): 1–22.

34. Craig H. Grau, "What Publications Are Most Frequently Cited in the Congressional Record?" *Journalism Quarterly* 53 (Winter 1976): 716–19.

35. Clifford Geertz, *The Interpretation of Cultures* (New York: Basic Books, 1973), p. 28.

36. Burke, *A Grammar of Motives,* pp. 12–13.

37. Burke, *A Grammar of Motives,* p. 262.

38. Burke, *Permanence and Change,* p. 284.

39. Burke, *Permanence and Change,* p. 285.

40. Hugh Duncan, *Symbols in Society* (New York: Oxford University Press, 1968), p. 39.

41. Kenneth Burke, *The Philosophy of Literary Form,* 3rd ed. (Baton Rouge: Louisiana State University Press, 1973), p. 40.

42. Burke, *Symbols in Society,* p. 34.

43. Burke, *Symbols in Society,* p. 39.

PART II

Perspectives on Journalism and Terrorism

CHAPTER 4

Tuned-in Narcissus:
The Gleam in the Camera's Eye

by Richard M. Pearlstein

WE ARE ALL ACQUAINTED with the myth of Narcissus, the legendary Greek youth whose obsessive fascination with his own exquisite, pond-reflected image ultimately culminates in varying forms of self-destruction. And we are all aware that most political terrorists desire, and seek to ensure, the very existence of their own media-reflected images. What we may yet not fully grasp, however, is that the political terrorist is a kind of "tuned-in Narcissus" who possesses profound political, ideological, tactical, *and* psychological concern for the very nature of that media-generated image.

Psychological and other studies of the terrorism–news media nexus have previously focused upon unilateral relationships between terrorists and news media, terrorists and governments, governments and terrorists, and terrorists and victims. The purpose of this brief chapter is to examine the hitherto neglected psychodynamic interrelationship between the news media and the terrorist. First discussed are those specific psychological types of individuals who perpetrate terrorist incidents. Second, those psychodynamic rewards, which appear to be highly attractive to such individuals and inherent in political terrorism itself, are examined. The chapter shall lastly consider how minor modifications of a specific such psychodynamic reward—frequently sensationalistic, and obliquely laudatory, news media attention—might help to attenuate the psychological, if not political, ideological, and tactical allure of terrorism.

This work is based largely upon my recent study *Armed Narcissus: An Inquiry Into the Mind of the Political Terrorist*. That study, itself an outgrowth of my doctoral dissertation, seeks to consider the individual psychological dimensions of political terrorism. More specifically, *Armed Narcissus* attempts to analyze the psychological backgrounds and motivations of a reasonably large, diverse, and representative case study sample of individuals who volunteered to become political terrorists. That sample is comprised of the following ten individuals: Susan Stern, Diana Oughton, Donald DeFreeze, Nancy Ling Perry, Patricia Soltysik, Zvonko Busic, Ilich Ramírez Sanchez, Giorgio Panizzari, Ulrike Meinhof, and Renato Curcio. I am also in the process of expanding and further diversifying my case study sample to include other, more recent terrorists as Abu Nidal, Victor Gerena, and certain American, right-wing, "survivalist" terrorists.

Before discussing my theory of what psychological factors appear to help motivate individuals to become, and remain, political terrorists, I would like to address what is after all one of the most problematic and critical aspects of political terrorism: defining it. For this chapter's purpose, "terrorism" shall be defined as *a specific form of civil rebellion, or civil insurgency, in which the use or threatened use of unacceptable violence is imposed* from below *against certain symbolic victims or objects in order to coerce a primary target to accept a demanded outcome due to the effectuation of intense fear or anxiety*.[1] Such "unacceptable" acts of political terrorism are typically manifested as assassinations, kidnappings for ransom and/or propaganda effect, hostage-takings, torture, bombings, and threats of the above.

"Terror" is defined here as *a form of intimidation in which the use or threatened use of violence is inflicted* from above, *rather than imposed from below*, thus differing from terrorism in that it represents *an official or quasi-official*, as opposed to a rebellious, *act*. Both terrorism and terror may be considered authentically "political" in nature only if calls for a "demanded outcome" are a) somehow articulated or otherwise conveyed to a primary target and b) couched in distinctly political terms.[2]

In attempting to analyze those psychological factors that appear to help motivate otherwise highly diverse individuals to become, and remain, political terrorists, considerable attention is paid here to the fundamental concept of narcissism, or the "psychology of the self."[3] Suggestions of an interrelationship between the psychology of narcissism and the practice of political terrorism have been superficially raised by a growing number of observers.[4] Yet despite the clear presence of a rather well-defined body of literature on the relation of narcissism to aggression, broadly construed,[5] a systematic investigation into the narcissism–political terrorism nexus had never been previously undertaken. Following is an essential outline of my theory regarding the political terrorist qua psychological entity.

First, as a general matter, "narcissism" is defined as a range of psychoanalytic orientations, impulses, and/or behavioral patterns either wholly or overwhelmingly subject to ego-concern, as opposed to object concern. More specifically, and for the purpose of this chapter, "narcissism" shall be defined as *the mode or manner in which an individual relates to the external, object world either solely or predominantly upon the latter's potential capacity to provide that individual with ego reinforcement, compensation, and/or satisfaction*. Hence, "narcissism" *itself* is defined in terms of object relations, or "narcissistic object relations." One clear such manifestation of narcissistic object relations is what may be termed "narcissistic object manipulation."

Based upon the case study evidence, it appears that the external, psychological determinants, bases, or sources of political terrorism lie in what are termed *narcissistic injury* and *narcissistic disappointment*. For our purposes, the term *narcissistic injury* shall be defined as *massive, profound, and permanent damage or harm to an individual's self-image and/or sense of self-esteem*. The term *narcissistic disappointment* shall be defined on two levels of analysis. As an internal, intrapsychic phenomenon, narcissistic disappointment is defined as *a psychological disturbance* whereby: a) the ego, or self, is unable to "measure up" to the ego ideal, or positive and desirable standards of conduct, and is, consequently, "punished" by the superego, or conscience; or b) the ego is veritably "tyrannized" by an overly grandiose ego ideal. On an external, interpersonal level, narcissistic disappointment is defined as: a) profound disappointment in the self prompted by an individual's pronounced inability to measure up to what he or she perceives as positive and desirable standards of conduct; or b) harsh disillusionment with individuals and/or groups that represent or advocate those standards of conduct, and a resultant disappointment in the self *for ever having embraced* those standards. In brief, in no fewer than nine out of ten political terrorist case studies, narcissistic injury or narcissistic disappointment play central psychobiographical roles.

Why might the practice of *political terrorism itself* be psychologically attractive to victims of narcissistic injury or narcissistic disappointment? In responding to this key question, we must first recall that theoretical definition of narcissism employed in this chapter. Narcissism has therefore been construed in terms of (narcissistic) object relations. Given furthermore the myriad grossly and obviously manipulative interpersonal relationships initiated by the political terrorist, political terrorism might be interpreted as, among other things, a superb exemplification of narcissistic object manipulation.

Friedrich Nietzsche once observed that "nothing on earth consumes a man more quickly than the passion of resentment." And indeed, the apparent ease and spontaneity with which the political terrorist qua victim of narcissistic injury or disappointment so "defends" him- or herself from profound psychic wounds merely serve to reflect that psychological "journey" typically "taken" by such individuals. I refer here first to an overall regression, or return to an earlier stage, of (normal) childhood development. In his discussion of the child's "grandiose self," Heinz Kohut delineates a normal

> phase in which *the gleam in the mother's eye mirrors the child's exhibitionistic display,* and other forms of maternal participation in the child's narcissistic enjoyment *confirm the child's self-esteem* and, by gradually increasing selectivity of these responses, begin to channel it in realistic directions.[6]

It is to this and even earlier and more primary phases of development that the victim of narcissistic personality disturbances retreats. This psychological manifestation has thus been aptly termed *secondary narcissism*.

Important too are the direct and indirect aftermath of narcissistic injury and disappointment: narcissistic rage, narcissistic defense, and all too typically, some form of narcissistic aggression. Taken as a whole, these manifestations of secondary narcissism may be termed the *narcissistic rage-aggression-defense nexus*. And again, for our purposes, political terrorism may be regarded as an outstanding example of narcissistic aggression.

Lastly, political terrorism offers its practitioners certain distinct and powerfully alluring psychic benefits, or "rewards." These psychodynamic rewards may be classified into two fundamental categories. One is the syndrome of political terrorism as "auto-compensatory violence," itself an interrelated "cluster" of psychological and psychopolitical factors. These include what I have termed: a) the political terrorist's clearly manifested, psychic sense of omnipotence; b) the political terrorist's establishment, assumption, and maintenance of a "new," "as-if other" pseudo-identity; and c) the indubitable psychological utility of political terrorist group membership. Another class of psychic rewards, which springs from the contextual justification of political terrorism, actually enables the political terrorist to assume the "mask of omnipotence" yet *eschew* the "mask of villainy," i.e., the role of political terrorist as a "negative identity." These latter, indirect psychic rewards may be realized: a) through the contemporary sanctification of political terrorism as a mode of "personal liberation"; and b) after reading the seminal writings of German philosopher Max Stirner and Russian anarchist Sergei Nachaev, the brutally "egoistic" rationalization of contemporary terrorism.[7]

For the most part, these are reasonably straightforward, even nominal theoretical concepts. It is useful to spend a brief moment on one, somewhat less conceptually self-evident psychodynamic reward in the rather fascinating psychopolitical process: the political terrorist's establishment, assumption, and maintenance of a "new," "as-if other." pseudo-identity.

One practical way through which the political terrorist is able to achieve a psychic sense of omnipotence is through the establishment, assumption, and maintenance of a "new" pseudo-identity. In his discussion of the "as-if image mode" of object relations, psychoanalyst Warren M. Brodey addresses the concomitant development of this pseudo-identity. As Brodey states:

> The image of himself seen reflected at a distance is called *an as-if other*. . . . An identity grows that is supported from within. The process of externalization [i.e., the projection of one's own psychological processes onto the environment] verifies this pseudo identity, this *as-if* total person.[8]

In many respects, the fateful decision to become a political terrorist constitutes the firm rejection of an individual's "old," weak, and psychically discredited self or identity through the establishment, assumption, and maintenance of a "new," omnipotent, "as-if other" self. By resorting to an auto-compensatory act of behavior like political terrorism, the victim of narcissistic personality disturbances is therefore able to create not only an as-if reality but also an as-if pseudo-*identity,* which is in effect *defined by* that process of externalization and self-validation. Hence in "acting out" his or her own narcissistic personality disturbances through the creation, adoption, and preservation of a specific, direct action, as-if other pseudo-identity, the political terrorist might be said to don a "mask of omnipotence." In toto, the violent defense of the self that is, psychologically speaking, political terrorism constitutes not a mere narcissistic *defense* of the "old" self but, rather, the veritable *displacement* of an old, feckless identity by a "new," grandiose, and seemingly omnipotent one.

What specific role might the news media play in delivering these psychodynamic rewards to the political terrorist qua victim of narcissistic personality disturbances? Based upon both the above theoretical considerations and the relevant case study data, it appears that what recent news media coverage of specific terrorist events accomplishes is three-fold in nature. First, the massive and uniquely intense news media coverage of political terrorism serves to "recertify" the political terrorist's clearly manifested, psychic sense of omnipotence. Moreover, the verbal and visual content of political terrorism news coverage frequently conveys an explicit aura of omnipotence to its news audience. That audience includes, of course, both present and would-be terrorists. Some familiar examples of these points are below.

Second, recent news media reports of political terrorist activity have also served to recertify, *and perhaps even actualize,* the political terrorist's attempt to maintain a "new," as-if other pseudo-identity. Hence the news media have actually helped the terrorist, who has already "donned" a "mask of omnipotence," to *wear* that mask! These points are further expanded upon, and exemplified, below.

Lastly, recent news media coverage of political terrorism has provided the terrorist with an ideal forum for the contextual justification of his or her acts. Thus the news media have in part enabled the terrorist to assume the "mask of omnipotence" rather than the "mask of villainy." Again, these points are considered below.

It has already been asserted that the verbal and visual content of political terrorism news coverage frequently suggest an explicit aura of terrorist omnipotence to the news audience. This observation may be applied to both the electronic and print media. And indeed, as Robert Picard states, the news media's "excesses in coverage" have frequently been "unduly sensationalistic."[9]

Picard and Paul D. Adams note in their recent study of the print media that reported government characterizations of terrorist acts and perpetrators tend to be "judgmental, inflammatory, and sensationalistic." Hence terrorist incidents may be characterized as "brutal acts," and terrorist perpetrators may be described by government officials as "evil, brutal, and/or as criminals." And, as Picard and Adams note, print media personnel and witnesses do "tend to use terms that are generally more neutral than those used by government officials."[10] However, how often have *other* elite, and nonelite, print and electronic media personnel *also* utilized such descriptive terrorist act characterizations as "daring" and "spectacular," and such nominal terrorist act characterizations as "spectacular," "raid," and the like? And to load the equation even further, what effect might the usage of such sensationalistic, and obliquely laudatory, characterizations have as psychodynamic rewards delivered to the political terrorist qua victim of narcissistic personality disturbances?

Also asserted here is that recent news media coverage of political terrorist activity has served to "recertify," and perhaps even helped actualize, the political terrorist's attempt to maintain a "new," as-if other pseudo-identity. One practical means through which the print and electronic news media have enabled the terrorist to "wear" the "mask of omnipotence" is in the news media's usage of political terrorist *pseudonyms*. In fact, these pseudonyms—e.g., Carlos the Jackal, General Field Marshal Cinque, and so forth—actually serve as *the terrorist's own characterization* of his or her "new," as-if other, omnipotent pseudo-identity. It is certainly true that news media personnel frequently share, in Picard's words, "uncertainty of the perpetrator's identity"[11] during unfolding terrorist incidents. In a number of instances, however, news media personnel are indeed aware of a terrorist's true, or "old," identity. If so, the news media should reveal and continue to report the true identity of a terrorist, and refrain from rendering psychodynamic rewards to the political terrorist.

News media coverage of political terrorism in the 1970s and 1980s has provided the terrorist with an ideal propaganda forum for his or her political and other views. As Picard has pointed out,

> the publicity provided through interviews *has the effect of putting the terrorists on an equal footing with government officials,* since news reports tend to play one interview off against the other, allowing officials to respond to a terrorist's messages. *This type of legitimization is another desire of those engaged in such violence.* Another problem results from the fact that interviews and the publication of statements and demands *often provides terrorists unedited access to the media that makes the media handmaidens to propaganda efforts. Other groups operating within the normal constraints of society do not enjoy the opportunity of unfettered access to the public via the media. Unedited access to the media is rarely given by the media under normal circumstances (except for live interviews with major government figures).*[12]

By thus placing terrorists on an "equal footing" with major government officials and providing terrorists with "unedited access" to their own channels, the news media have helped: a) enable the political terrorist to assume the "mask of omnipotence" and b) provide the terrorist with an unrivaled medium through which a contextual justification or legitimization of his or her acts might proceed. This process provides the terrorist with political, tactical, ideological, *and* psychodynamic rewards. Therefore, precisely how the news media might alter the common practice of providing terrorists with unedited access to their own channels must be considered. Another issue to ponder is the manipulative process whereby political terrorist groups are allowed contextually to justify and legitimize their own unquestionably savage actions. For in toto, the media and its audience must never hesitate to allow the terrorist to assume the mask of villainy and the negative identity that he or she so richly deserves.

The psychodynamic rewards that the "gleam in the camera's eye" offer to this "tuned-in Narcissus" may be illustrated by a number of case studies. Consider, for example, former Weathermen member Susan Stern's own recollections of her terrorist experiences in her autobiographical journal *With the Weathermen*. Upon learning of her status as an unindicted co-conspirator in the Chicago Weathermen "Days of Rage" case in 1970, Stern recalls that she was "flattered" by the news. As she puts it, "I was threatening. Someone was taking me seriously."[13] At the "Seattle 7" trial, which was held to try a "Seattle Liberation Front" attack upon a Marine recruitment office, a now-indicted Stern portrays herself as

> someone. I knew I was someone because there were so many people hanging around me, asking questions, looking to me for answers, or just looking at me offering to do things for me, *to get some of the glow from the limelight.* . . . Wherever I went the people loved me. . . . Everybody was mightily impressed with me. . . .[14]

During her jail term, Stern wrote a letter to a close friend, summarizing her personal motivations toward political terrorism:

> Still, I am unhappy in my role as revolutionary, because it is not enough for me; I want to stand out in the history I am trying to make. *My existence will have meaning only if lots of others know about it.* Call it fame, immortality, call it what you will, until I have it, I will always be unhappy. . . . *My desire for immortality, my need for fame is perhaps the essence of my life;* it alone can give meaning to my existence.[15]

The case of Symbionese Liberation Army member Donald DeFreeze is even more instructive as an exemplification of the "tuned-in Narcissus." On February 17, 1974, thirteen days after the SLA's kidnapping of newspaper heiress Patricia Hearst, the terrorist group sent an audio cassette to the Hearst family. DeFreeze, who had already adopted the rather revealing nom de guerre "General Field Marshal Cinque," was aroused that his true, "old" identity had been disclosed through the news media. Patricia Hearst's former fiancé, Steven Weed, recalls that, in the February 17 tape, "fired with hatred and rage,"

> *Cinque* assaulted us directly. He said he knew us and we knew him. His hood had been removed, his picture plastered across the front page of every newspaper in the country, and now, listening to this tape, we were face to face with him. . . . "Greetings to the people," the communiqué began. "General Field Marshal Cinque speaking."[16]

And then, in a "voice now betraying his self-righteous rage,"

> Cinque began reading what was apparently his own writing, his bitter response to his unmasking by the press: "You do, indeed, know me. You have always known me. I'm the nigger you have hunted and feared night and day. I'm that nigger you have killed hundreds of my people in the vain hope of finding. I'm that nigger that is no longer just hunted, robbed, and murdered. I'm the nigger that hunts you now. Yes, you know us all. You know me, I'm the wetback. You

know me, I'm the gook, the broad, the servant, the spik. Yes, you know me. You know us all and we know you—the oppressor, murderer, and robber. And you have hunted and robbed and exploited us all. Now we are the hunters that will give you no rest."[17]

A raw craving for media attention is also manifested in the case of another SLA member, Patricia "Mizmoon" Soltysik. Like Susan Stern and Donald DeFreeze, Soltysik's earlier existence had been ravaged by a long string of profound narcissistic injuries and disappointments. In a prophetic conversation with Mary Maillot, the daughter of a famous World War II Belgian resistance fighter, Jacques Maillot, Soltysik declared:

> Remember this well. I am going to become famous. I, Pat Soltysik, I shall be known over the entire world. They will speak of me in the newspapers.[18]

It would be possible to cite other relevant case studies, such as that of Ilich Ramírez Sanchez ("Carlos the Jackal"), but the main points have already been made. These are that: a) the "gleam in the camera's eye" does indeed help deliver certain compensatory psychodynamic rewards to the political terrorist qua victim of narcissistic personality disturbances; and b) the electronic and print news media might consider making certain minor corrective, albeit pertinent, modifications in their generally superb political terrorism news coverage. In closing, I stress that I do not want to criticize but rather to help and advise the news media of what is after all a hitherto neglected aspect of political terrorism—of "tuned-in Narcissus."

NOTES

1. See Richard M. Pearlstein, "Lives of Disquieting Desperation: An Inquiry into the Mind of the Political Terrorist" (Ph.D. Dissertation, University of North Carolina, 1986); Andrew M. Scott, *Insurgency* (Chapel Hill: University of North Carolina Press, 1970); Robert Taber, *The War of the Flea* (New York: Lyle Stuart, 1965); Martha Crenshaw Hutchinson, "The Concept of Revolutionary Terrorism," *Journal of Conflict Resolution* 16 (1972):383–96; Frederick J. Hacker, "Terror and Terrorism: Modern Growth Industry and Mass Entertainment," *Terrorism* 4 (1980):144; and Jordan J. Paust, "Some Thoughts on 'Preliminary Thoughts' on Terrorism," *American Journal of International Law* 68 (1974):502.

2. for discussions of the nature of terrorism, see Harold Lasswell, "Terrorism and the Political Process," *Terrorism* 1 (1978):255–63; F. Gentry Harris, "Hypothetical Facets or Ingredients of Terrorism," *Terrorism* 3 (1980):240; G. Green, *Terrorism: Is It Revolutionary?* (New York: Outlook, 1970); C.A. White, "Terrorism: Idealism or Sickness?" *Canada and the World* 39 (1974):14–15; Flora Lewis, "The Terrorist: Less a Sign of Revolution Than Decay," *New York Times,* April 30, 1978, p. 2; V.I. Lenin, "Left-Wing Communism: An Infantile Disorder," in *Selected Works of V.I. Lenin,* vol. 3 (Moscow: Foreign Languages Publishing House, 1961), pp. 371–460; and Leon Trotsky, "Terrorism in War and Revolution," in Isaac Deutscher, ed., *The Age of Permanent Revolution* (New York: Dell, 1964), pp. 110–16.

3. See Heinz Kohut, *The Analysis of the Self* (New York: International publishers, 1971); Heinz Kohut, "Thoughts on Narcissism and Narcissistic Rage," *Psychoanalytic Study of the Child* 27 (1972):360–400; and Andrew P. Morrison, ed., *Essential Papers on Narcissism* (New York: New York University Press, 1986).

4. See Robert Liebert, *Radical and Militant Youth: A Psychoanalytic Inquiry* (New York: Praeger, 1971); Christopher Lasch, *The Culture of Narcissism: American Life in the Age of Diminishing Expectations* (New York: Norton, 1979); Lawrence Z. Freedman and Yonah Alex-

ander, eds. *Perspectives on Terrorism* (Wilmington, Del.: Scholarly Resources, 1983); and Jerrold M. Post, "Notes on a Psychodynamic Theory of Terrorist Behavior," *Terrorism* 7 (1984):245–46, 248.

5. See Gregory Rochlin, *Man's Aggression: The Defense of the Self* (Boston: Gambit, 1973); Kohut, "Thoughts on Narcissism"; and Natyhan P. Segel, "Narcissistic Resistance," *Journal of the American Psychoanalytic Association* 17 (1969):944.

6. Heinz Kohut, "The Psychoanalytic Treatment of Narcissistic Personality Disorders," *Psychoanalytic Study of the Child* 23 (1968):96.

7. See John Carroll, ed., *Max Stirner: The Ego and His Own* (New York: Harper and Row, 1971) and Sergei Nachaev, "Catechism of the Revolutionist," in M. Confino, ed., *Daughter of a Revolutionay* (London: Alcove Press, 1986).

8. Warren M. Brodey, "On the Dynamics of Narcissism: Externalization and Early Ego Development," *Psychoanalytic Study of the Child* 20 (1965):167–68.

9. Robert G. Picard, "News Coverage as the Contagion of Terrorism: Dangerous Charges Backed by Dubious Science," *Political Communication and Persuasion* 3 (1986):393.

10. Robert G. Picard and Paul D. Adams, "Characterizations of Acts and Perpetrators of Political Violence in Three Elite U.S. Daily Newspapers," *Political Communication and Persuasion* 4 (1987):1–9.

11. Robert G. Picard, "The Conundrum of News Coverage of Terrorism," *University of Toledo Law Review* 18 (1986):146.

12. Picard, "Conundrum," pp. 148–49; author's emphasis.

13. Susan Stern, *With the Weathermen: The Personal Journal of a Revolutionary Woman* (Garden City, NY: Doubleday, 1975), p. 249; author's emphasis.

14. Ibid., pp. 252, 262.

15. Ibid., pp. 354–55.

16. Steven Weed, *My Search for Patty Hearst* (New York: Crown, 1976), pp. 137–38.

17. Weed, *My Search*, p. 137.

18. Fred Soltysik, *In Search of a Sister* (New York: Bantam, 1976), p. 1.

CHAPTER 5

Media Victims:
Reactions to Coverage of
Incidents
of International Terrorism
Involving Americans

by Louise F. Montgomery

A SPECIAL SEGMENT of the American population, people who have been so involved in coverage of incidents of international terrorism that they can be called media sophisticates, offers much advice for television, radio, newspaper, and magazine reporters and editors. Most of this special audience—the victims of terrorism and their families—want the mass media to improve coverage and change obviously inexcusable behavior, but they would say yes to interview requests if they were involved in another newsworthy incident. The respondents to a survey were clear in indicating that their relationship with the mass media was affected by the ordeal: 9 percent more said their trust in the media decreased than those who said it increased.

This particular section of the American public has a love-hate relationship with the media; many of the people who complained that the media would not leave them alone praised certain journalists. In many cases, respondents to this survey lived for extended periods with the media camping in their driveways and shoving microphones in their faces whenever government officials suggested that hostages were about to be released. Other respondents in the study survived a harrowing ordeal as hostages, only to be met at the end of a long trip home by demanding, rude journalists inquiring, "How do you feel?"

Of all responses to an open-ended question about how journalists should change the way they cover incidents of international terrorism, the most common was a suggestion that the "How do you feel" question be eliminated. In general, the findings in this study support critics' pleas that reporters follow their own rules for good journalism in covering terrorism. A majority of respondents in this study endorse the position taken by Grant Wardlaw in the 1982 book, *Political Terrorism:* the mass media have been remarkably insensitive to the feelings of hostages and their families and have displayed a marked lack of taste in the way they have presented personal suffering.[1]

In addition, these data indicate a preference of a substantial number of respondents for television; accuracy ratings for print publication fell behind those of radio and television. Details follow in the discussion of the survey.

The survey includes sixty-one respondents—twenty-one victims of incidents of international terrorism, thirty-four family members, and six others involved in the incidents—and reveals how profoundly they were affected by the mass media. From hosting a gaggle of reporters in their driveways, sometimes on their roofs, to being the media's guests for short helicopter rides just for fun, the respondents in this study were intensively involved with local, national, and international radio, television, newspapers, and magazines for periods of a few days to the 444 days hostages were held in the American embassy in Teheran.

Questionnaires were mailed to about two hundred persons whose names were gleaned from stories in various national news periodicals on international terrorism incidents in the 1980s in which Americans were victimized. Periodicals read for names and hometowns including the *New York Times, Newsweek,* and *Time.* When addresses could not be obtained from telephone books, local newspaper editors were asked to help. Many undeliverable questionnaires were returned by the postal service; fifty-six completed questionnaires were returned by mail; and telephone interviews were completed with five.

Incidents in which the 61 respondents were involved are:

Achille Lauro ship hijacking	9
Seizure of the American embassy in Teheran	13
Killing of American servicemen in El Salvador	7
Hijacking of a Pan Am airliner in Karachi	1
TWA Flight 847 hijacking that landed in Beirut	26
Other incidents	5

Most respondents—fifty, or 86 percent, of the fifty-eight who had been interviewed by some medium—were interviewed by a variety of media, but five (9 percent) were interviewed only by television and radio, and three (5 percent) were interviewed only by print media. Three respondents had not been interviewed.

The first "credibility" question (see Table 5.1) asked respondents to evaluate the completeness of overall coverage of the terrorism incident. Only six, 11 percent, said coverage was "totally complete," and five (9 percent) said it was somewhat or greatly incomplete. The majority of the fifty-

Table 5.1. Evaluation of Completeness of
Coverage[*]

	PERCENT OF THOSE RESPONDING
Totally complete	11
Mostly complete	61
Neutral	19
Somewhat incomplete	7
Greatly incomplete	2
Total	100
Number of respondents = 57	

[*]The question was, How do you view the overall reporting of the
incident in which you were involved?

seven persons who answered this question—thirty-five, or 61 percent—said
coverage was mostly complete.

In an attempt to determine what behavior on the part of the journalists
pleased or bothered the terrorism victims and their families, we asked the
respondents to describe behavior that they considered particularly professional or particularly unprofessional. Many respondents answered both
parts; overall 75 percent of the sample listed one or more journalists whose
behavior they considered "particularly professional," while 43 percent
listed journalists who were "particularly unprofessional."

Behaviors described as professional focused on the sensitivity of the
journalist to the families' anxieties and their willingness to provide information the families could not obtain from other sources, particularly the U.S.
government. Respect for the privacy of the family, respect for their wishes
to delay interviews until they had rested, and other "sensitive" behavior
were listed by many respondents.

Unprofessional conduct cited by the respondents focused on pushiness
and failure to respect the families' privacy. Many criticized journalists for
sensationalizing the story, for being more interested in tears and grief than
in the substance of the story, and for going to any length—even invading
homes by posing as family members—to get the story.

A disturbing number of respondents, to one degree or another, faulted
journalists for being unprepared, for not knowing the story they were reporting. This complaint was voiced primarily about local newspaper and radio
reporters; the main complaint about television journalists was their obtrusiveness. Several respondents got tired of journalists camping in their driveways, but it is particularly interesting that some families who had a family
member in Teheran did not complain about journalists being a part of their
lives for 444 days. The Sickman family of Marine guard Rodney (Rocky)
Sickman was besieged by as many as one hundred journalists who de-
scended on their small-town Missouri home whenever government officials

Table 5.2. Accuracy Rating by Medium*

MEDIUM	TV	NEWSPAPER	RADIO	MAGAZINE
Accurate	81%	75%	72%	77%
Neutral	13	7	23	4
Inaccurate	2	8	3	19
Number of respondents	50	48	38	26

*Data reported in this table came from questions asking respondents to indicate which media interviewed them and how accurately their own remarks were reported by each medium.

indicated that a break might occur in the siege. Yet the three members of the family who completed questionnaires gave high marks to journalists for completeness, accuracy, and fairness. The aggressiveness of reporters as the hostages' release neared irritated one family member. Mrs. Toni Sickman, Rocky's mother, wrote that "when things were getting close to the end, they [journalists] were like wild dogs."

Particularly disturbing were reports from two respondents that newspaper reporters took revenge on them because the victim refused to be interviewed the moment he or she arrived after a two-day flight home. In one case, the reporter refused to give the family copies of a picture, and in another, the reporter refused to provide a copy of the newspaper story, explaining that she would have if the victim had cooperated by being interviewed. Some respondents said that journalists came to the story with a preconceived notion of what the families or victims would say. The journalists asked questions but did not listen to the answers, they complained.

However, despite complaints of unprofessional and rude behavior on the part of some journalists, overall, in response to a question of whether journalists were sensitive and mannerly or insensitive and rude, 80 percent of the respondents said they were sensitive and mannerly.

In several ways, the questionnaire asked respondents to differentiate between media (see Table 5.2). Television got higher marks than print media; in response to a question of whether the respondent's remarks were reported accurately, 81 percent said their remarks were reported accurately on television, and only one person said TV reported his remarks inaccurately. The remainder of those interviewed by television chose a neutral response.

Newspapers got only a 75 percent accuracy rating on reporting remarks of the 48 persons interviewed by newspapers, with 8 percent saying their remarks were reported inaccurately.

Radio got ratings of 72 percent from the thirty-eight persons interviewed by this medium, while magazines were said to have reported their remarks accurately by 77 percent of the respondents. Interestingly, however, magazines drew the largest number of inaccurate responses—five respondents (19 percent of the twenty-six interviewed by magazines) chose "greatly inaccurate" when asked to rank how magazines reported their remarks.

To determine whether the respondents' trust of the media grew or was diminished by their personal encounters with the media, the questionnaire asked the respondents whether their trust increased, decreased, or stayed the same.

Overall, the media lost more than they gained: 22 percent said their trust increased, while 31 percent said it decreased, and 46 percent said it remained the same. Questionnaires were studied to determine whether persons who got their news predominantly from electronic or print media seemed to differ on this item; it appears the broadcasting media lost more than print. Of the fourteen persons who listed only electronic sources of news on the terrorism incident, six—or 43 percent—said their trust decreased, while of the thirty-two who relied on a variety of print and electronic media, eleven, or 34 percent, said their trust decreased. No respondents listed only print sources of news.

To measure whether those intensively involved with media coverage of terrorist incidents got tired of the story, respondents were asked to evaluate the quantity of coverage. Only six—11 percent—said coverage was inadequate, while thirty-two—57 percent—said it was excessive. Another eighteen—32 percent—said the quantity of coverage was right.

However, the negative responses to media coverage and reporters' behavior are not reflected in answers to the question of whether the respondents would, in the future, agree to be interviewed by the media. Eighty-one percent would agree to be interviewed again by television, compared with 78 percent by newspaper. To determine whether the respondents had closer and better relations with their hometown media than with national or international, we posed the same question in those terms. The responses were the same for national and local—64 percent said yes—but the yes answers dropped to 61 percent for interviews by international media.

Do these highly interested and highly involved respondents blame the media for terrorism or the terrorism incident in which they or their families were involved? A majority of our respondents said no, but not by very comfortable margins. Forty-four percent said the media are "partly responsible" for terrorism, while 74 percent said media coverage helped the terrorists.

Similar questions were asked about media treatment of hostages and the terrorists: Do you think treatment of the hostages (or treatment of the terrorists) by the media was fair? To the questions concerning the hostages, forty-two, or 69 percent, of the sample said yes, while eleven, or 18 percent, said no. The remaining eight respondents did not answer this question. Responses to the questions regarding the terrorists were similar; 69 percent said treatment was fair, while 23 percent said it was not. Five failed to answer the question.

Another troublesome finding for the media occurred in response to this question: Did coverage help or hinder the release of hostages? Of the fifty-four persons responding to this question, thirty (55 percent) said it helped, while fifteen, or 28 percent, said it neither helped nor hindered and nine (17 percent) said it hindered.

In summary, respondents in this study reinforce the conventional wisdom offered by critics who say journalists should follow the rules of good journalism in terrorism coverage. In general, journalists who fake interest just to get a story are fooling no one. Those who demonstrate sincere interest in families and share information not available through official channels are rewarded with the trust and cooperation of those involved in incidents. Journalists who shove and push and show up for interviews ill-prepared draw the wrath and mistrust of sources.

Some respondents played special roles as managers of coverage of incidents in which they were involved, such as the brother of TWA hostage Ralf Traugott and the Illinois man who managed the media for the twenty parishioners from his church who were on TWA Flight 847. In these two cases, the respondents devoted many hours to media management and got from the media what they wanted; both ranked all media high on accuracy and the trust in the media of each remained the same throughout the ordeal.

The respondents' recommendations for improving media coverage of incidents of international terrorism mirror the media's self-criticism. Points the sixty-one media sophisticates made are:

- Report only important information, don't trivialize, don't report rumor.
- Be sensitive to families, respect privacy, don't hound.
- Be patriotic; do not ask us what the government should do.
- Do not put words into our mouths; listen to answers.
- Do not show personal events like the government informing parents of a child's death.
- Do not let the hostages be forgotten; work with government officials to find a solution.
- Look at terrorism in depth.
- Do not keep asking, "How do you feel?"

One aspect of this study that remains to be pursued is to speak with those who did not return questionnaires. In some cases, the researchers spoke briefly by telephone with victims or family members to confirm addresses, but questionnaires were not returned. In this study, more than in others, the potential for skewing of data because of nonresponse seems higher than usual. It may be that many of the people who were most repulsed by media behavior failed to return questionnaires; for instance, the parents of Robert Dean Stethem, the young military man killed on TWA Flight 847, agreed by telephone to complete questionnaires but did not return them. When follow-up attempts were made, the family had changed to a new and unlisted number. Similarly, the pilot of the TWA Flight 847 resisted all efforts to be interviewed.

In addition, letters and lengthy comments many respondents returned with the questionnaire need to be systematically analyzed for guidance in follow-up research.

NOTE

1. Grant Wardlaw, *Political Terrorism: Theory, Tactics, and Counter-Measures* (London: Cambridge University Press, 1982).

CHAPTER 6

Journalists as Targets and Victims of Terrorism

by Robert G. Picard

MANY OBSERVERS OF TERRORISM have laid part of the blame for such violence on journalists and their employing organizations, arguing that terrorism would not exist without coverage and that journalists assist terrorists in carrying out their objectives.[1] Some terrorists clearly consider the potential impact of media coverage when planning some operations, and they carry out actions designed to manipulate coverage by creating incidents that will receive coverage because of social norms and common media industry practices. This type of manipulation can be considered a type of victimization of media that makes journalists unwilling and, sometimes, unwitting accomplices of terrorists.

The television, radio, and print news media are tools terrorists use to accomplish their goals, just as are weapons and explosives, aircraft and ships, and other items and persons who can be used by or become targets of terrorists. When journalists and media are not the direct targets of terrorists, they are victimized by actions that force coverage of terrorist operations. Laying blame for terrorism on media is clearly a case of blaming a victim for the acts of the perpetrator.

This type of victimization, however, can be avoided or counteracted by media personnel through awareness of their roles in terrorist activities and implementation of practices designed to reduce the potential harm of media coverage. Most major news agencies and television networks have guidelines and suggestions for coverage that deal with such difficulties.[2]

This chapter will not focus on journalists as the victims of manipulation, however, but rather on attacks in which journalists or their employing media organizations are directly targeted for violence. Journalists face a variety of problems when trying to cover political violence, including language and cultural barriers, the distances required to travel to reach locations of events, the difficulties of transmitting reports back to their employers and audiences, the inadequacy of available information sources, and the manipulation of the communication process by perpetrators of the violence, government officials, and other interested parties. In carrying out their reporting duties, many correspondents have been injured and died in areas of conflict and war zones when they were caught in the crossfire of combatants. Others have been attacked as a result of misidentification or misunderstandings. Most journalists consider such casualties as acceptable although undesirable hazards of the occupation. These threats posed to journalists in war zones and areas of conflict have concerned journalists' and humanitarian organizations for many years, and efforts have been made to reduce them.

The result of such concern was the establishment, in the 1970s and 1980s, of educational programs designed to help journalists protect themselves from injury and death and the development of internationally recognized identification cards for journalists to help avoid misidentification and charges of being enemy agents.[3] Such efforts, however have little impact when journalists are specifically targeted for terrorism.

This chapter concerns the intentional targeting of journalists for attack. It explores the real problems of intimidation, extortion, injury, and death that media employees face at the hands of those who engage in such attacks. When terrorist groups target specific nongovernment civilians or business enterprises for attack, journalists and media organizations are second only to executives of major firms in military goods and international trade as the targets of choice. During the past decade, an average of two dozen journalists have been killed annually in terrorist attacks.

Journalists are regularly the targets of terrorists for nearly every type of terrorist act from shooting and bombings, to kidnappings and hostage-takings, to the forced broadcast and publication of messages. This aspect of the media relationship with terrorism is ignored in the existing literature but plays a very real role in the way journalists cover and relate to terrorist groups.

Part of the difficulty of preventing attacks on journalists evolves from the fact that attacking journalists guarantees coverage. Media organizations attempt to reduce violence against journalists—particularly state-sponsored violence—by reporting and widely publicizing attacks on journalists through print and broadcast media and professional organizations. This policy has been shown to be useful in getting some governments to end attacks on journalists. The policy, however, can have the opposite effect on groups and individuals who wish to use coverage as a means of gaining recognition for their group or cause.

Journalists are also seen as an institutional target for terrorism because they and their employing organizations are viewed by many groups as an integral part of the social structures that terrorist groups oppose or are viewed as adjuncts to the governments of nations that groups consider enemies. This view is not without basis because media serve the social and political interests of whatever type of society in which they exist and the legitimacy of mass society is established and maintained through media.[4]

In 1987 at least twenty-five journalists were killed worldwide and ten more had been kidnapped or disappeared without a trace.[5] Those deaths resulted from about eight hundred separate attacks on journalists throughout the world during the year.[6] Many were victims of state terrorism or state-supported terrorism as elites attempted to maintain control or silence opponents.

Attacks on journalists occur for four main reasons: 1) to stop coverage that is under way, 2) to punish media for previous coverage, 3) to punish or threaten the government of the nation from which the reporters originate, and 4) to gain a forum for expression of views. This chapter reviews examples of such attacks and their implications for the abilities of news organizations to carry out their informational roles.

ATTACKS DURING NEWS-GATHERING

Journalists are regularly targeted for attack when they cover incidents or issues in ways that anger interested individuals and groups. Attacks occur to halt news-gathering, particularly photography, during incidents that individuals do not wish covered or in an effort to halt ongoing coverage.

When civilians protested actions of the government of Haiti that were interfering with the election process in the summer of 1987, for example, government troops and Tontons Macoutes, terrorists linked to the Duvalier regime, began indiscriminate attacks on civilians in which scores of persons died. On July 3, at a rally during which military units attacked civilians, foreign journalists taking photographs were deliberately fired upon. Reporters and camera crews scrambled for cover and managed to avoid being hit, but some suffered minor injuries and equipment was damaged in the attack.[7]

Such attacks on journalists continued as the promised election approached. On election day, November 29, a television cameraman for a station in the Dominican Republic was killed, and journalists from the United States, Mexico, El Salvador, and Great Britain were wounded in deliberate attacks by armed gangs and solders. A New York–based independent human rights group, the Committee to Protect Journalists, reported that "journalists did not merely get caught in crossfire: the gunmen targeted them repeatedly, terrorizing both the local press and hundreds of foreign journalists who had flocked to Haiti to cover the vote."[8]

ATTACKS FOR PAST COVERAGE

Previous news coverage can also result in the targeting of journalists for attack. This occurs when subjects of news reports dislike the coverage carried in news media and then single out critical journalists as enemies and targets for attack.

This type of targeting of journalists occurred in Colombia in August 1987 when the names of nine well-known journalists were found on a list apparently compiled by death squads linked to that nation's military forces. One of those named has since been slain and six others have fled the nation. Journalists on the list had been actively covering the nation's so-called dirty war against the Patriotic Union, a Communist political party that has had about five hundred of its leaders and members killed since 1986, and had linked death squads to the nation's military forces.[9]

In September 1986, José Carrasco Tapia, an editor of the Chilean weekly news magazine *Análisis,* was dragged from his home by armed men in civilian clothes and later found dead, having been shot a dozen times. Carrasco was a severe critic of the military dictatorship in the country and had once gone into exile after being detained by government forces. Opponents of General Augusto Pinochet blamed the attack on government security forces, noting that Carrasco was taken from the scene in a van like those used by state security agents, that the country was under a curfew at the time of the attack, and that no one but police and military authorities were allowed on the streets at the time the attack took place.[10]

ATTACKS TO PUNISH CERTAIN NATIONS

Other attacks are carried out not for what the journalists or their employing organizations have reported, but because terrorist groups wish to punish or coerce behavioral changes by the governments of the nations from which the journalists originate.

This occurred in Lebanon in 1987, when gunmen linked to groups supported by Iran kidnapped French journalists Roger Auque and Jean-Louis Normandin. The two were kidnapped after Georges Ibrahim Abdallah, the alleged leader of the Lebanese Armed Revolutionary Faction, was ordered to stand trial on charges of killing a U.S. military officer and an Israeli diplomat in France in 1982, and after France and Iran clashed about the rights of a bombing suspect who was trapped in the Iranian embassy in Paris. The seizure of the journalists was not a new tactic for Lebanese terrorists but followed earlier kidnappings of Cable News Network correspondent Jeremy Levin, who has since escaped, and Associated Press Beirut bureau chief Terry Anderson, who, after many years, is still in capitivity, as well as journalists from European nations.

Anderson was kidnapped by Islamic Jihad on March 16, 1985, and has been held hostage longer than any other American currently being held in Lebanon. His kidnappers indicated that they seized the bureau chief as an attack on the United States and its citizens, rather than for specific coverage directed by the journalist.

ATTACKS TO GAIN FORUMS

At times journalists and their media organizations are attacked by terrorist groups in order to communicate with the public in a direct fashion. This often occurs when the coverage that is given does not provide the exposure they wish or because these groups are unable to gain coverage because of government control of or self-censorship by media.

On October 23, 1987, for instance, armed men entered the Agence

France-Presse offices in Lima, Peru, captured journalists and technicians working at the bureau, and forced them to transmit a statement on the wire service criticizing the economic policies of the Peruvian government. The intruders, who represented the Tupac Amaru Revolutionary Movement, then painted the group's symbol on the walls and floors and departed. At about the same time, a group of seven men armed with automatic weapons seized Radio Onda Popular and forced its staff to broadcast a tape calling on citizens to overthrow the Peruvian government; then they, too, withdrew from the scene. The journalists working at the wire service and radio station were not physically harmed in the attacks.[11]

A similar occurrence took place in Ecuador in January 1987 when members of the group Alfaro Lives, Damn It! seized at gunpoint the Quito radio stations El So and Musical near the presidential palace. The group broadcast a statement demanding the release of a group member held by authorities and the resignation of President León Febres Cordero Rivadeneira before departing.[12]

Such occurrences are not confined to unstable nations. On February 1, 1988, two Native Americans entered a newspaper office in Lumberton, North Carolina, and took more than a dozen journalists, editors, and other employees hostage. The armed men, who demanded an investigation of alleged racism against blacks and Native Americans by local law enforcement authorities, held the newspaper employees hostage until government authorities agreed to launch outside investigations. During the incident, television, radio, and print coverage of their act and demands was carried throughout the nation.[13]

In August 1987 a gunman walked onto the set of KNBC-TV, Los Angeles, during a live newscast and forced at gunpoint consumer reporter David Horowitz to read a statement about CIA activities. The statement was not broadcast live, however, because station managers managed to take the program off the air. The weapon used by the gunman was later found to be a toy replica of a handgun.[14]

IMPLICATIONS FOR JOURNALISTS

Intentional attacks on journalists leave media organizations with few options to protect their employees. In most cases, media are faced with the choice of continuing their reporting despite the risks or ending or reducing coverage. Most large news organizations, such as wire services and television networks, are reluctant to end coverage altogether because of their ideological beliefs in the importance and necessity of information flow.

Where conditions for journalists have deteriorated significantly, organizations will generally attempt to find alternatives to ending completely such coverage. In Lebanon, for instance, most U.S. news organizations have withdrawn American citizens from their bureaus and rely upon native journalists to handle day-to-day coverage. This reduces the daily exposure of their U.S. employees to attack because of their American citizenship. Most of the wire services and networks have shifted the bases of American crews assigned to Lebanon to Cyprus where they can fly into Beirut for short, hopefully safer, periods when major events occur that warrant the presence of American correspondents on the scene.

In determining which regions of the world are particularly dangerous for journalists, some news organizations are using the analyses of risk management companies. The majority, however, have chosen to use their own information and rely upon the judgment of their correspondents. The organizations must weigh the local histories of attacks on journalists, whether such attacks were on local or international journalists, and the types of journalists most often attacked. These decisions also involve understanding local reactions to the foreign policies of the nations from which the journalists originate and weighing the potential for attacks on a given news organization's employees at any given time.

When journalists remain in regions or countries known to be dangerous to them, many are borrowing the security measures and techniques recommended for diplomats and businessmen. Some are increasing security at their offices and learning defensive techniques to avoid being kidnapped or shot. These measures may reduce the incidents of journalists being attacked by some terrorists, but those who are determined to attack specific journalists will not be swayed because the nature of the occupation forces journalists into meetings with various parties in conflicts and into localities where those who can provide protection are often not in full control.

The National Association of Broadcasters has recommended that broadcast stations plan ahead of time how they would deal with domestic demands for air time by individuals holding hostages. Legal counsel for the association advises that "one is to go along with the demand, but only after receiving *official* requests from law enforcement authorities" or that one should go along with the demand, but only to the limits of editorial judgment and good taste"[15]

Most journalists' groups advise correspondents to give up stories rather than risk their lives. The InterAmerican Press Association, for instance, tells journalists, "You are more important than the story. No story is worth your life."[16] The same message is conveyed by most journalistic employers, but many correspondents still report subtle pressures from editors and producers and competitive pressures to get news even when terrorist groups threaten them.

In the end, however, most journalists view the potential for terrorist attack as part of the risks of the job. Associated Press executive news editor Walter R. Mears notes,

> Basically, the simple answer is that you can't be a reporter and be protected. All you can do is ask people to exercise some judgment about their own safety and not to take risks where the risks are avoidable. We put people in places where they are taking a risk just being there. They know it, and we know it.[17]

NOTES

1. See, e.g., M. Cherif Bassiouni, "Problems in Media Coverage of Nonstate-sponsored Terror-Violence Incidents," in Lawrence Z. Freedman and Yonah Alexander, eds., *Perspectives on Terrorism* (Wilmington, Del.: Scholarly Resources, 1983), pp. 177–200; Rudolf Levy, "Terrorism and the Mass Media," *Military Intelligence* (October-December 1985):34–38; Alex P. Schmid and Janny de Graaf, *Violence as Communication: Insurgent Terrorism and the Western News Media* (Beverly Hills, Calif.: Sage Publications, 1982); and *Terrorism and the Media* (Washington, D.C.: American Legal Foundation, n.d.).

2. See "Chicago Sun-Times Standards for Coverage of Terrorism," *Presstime* (March 1982):29; *Coverage of Riots and Other Civil Disorders,* ABC News Guidelines, mimeo; *Coverage of Terrorist Acts,* ABC News Guidelines, mimeo; and Margaret Genovese, "Special Report: Terrorism," *Presstime* (August 1986):26–33.

3. Louise Montgomery, ed., *Journalists on Dangerous Assignments: A Guide for Staying Alive* (London: International Press Institute, 1986).

4. J. Herbert Altschull, *Agents of Power: The Role of the News Media in Human Affairs* (New York: Longman, 1984).

5. "Death Toll for Journalists Rises to 34 in '87," *Presstime* (January 1988):41; see correction in letters, *Presstime* (February 1988):75.

6. Committee to Protect Journalists, *Attacks on the Press 1987* (New York: Committee to Protect Journalists, 1988).

7. Joseph B. Treaster, "Calls Grow, Amid Violence, for Ouster of Haiti's Rulers," *New York Times,* July 4, 1987, p. A4.

8. Susan Benesch, "Haiti: Gunmen Sought to Kill Press Freedom along With Elections," *CPJ Update* (January-February 1988):1.

9. Merrill Collett, "Hazards Mount for Colombian Press," *CPJ Update* (January-February 1988):4.

10. Shirley Christian, "Chilean Editor and Two Others Are Found Slain," *New York Times,* September 10, 1986, p. A1.

11. "Peruvian Guerrillas Invade Media Offices," *Boston Globe,* October 25, 1987, p. 55.

12. "Radio Takeovers, *Insight,* January 26, 1987, p. 40.

13. "9 Hostages Held at a Newspaper," *New York Times,* February 2, 1988, p. A19.

14. "Newsroom Ordeal," *Broadcasting,* August 24, 1987, p. 97.

15. *When Hostages Are Taken: What Should You Do?* National Association of Broadcasters, Counsel from the Legal Department, Memo L-303, January 1983.

16. *Surviving Dangerous Assignments* (Miami: Inter American Press Association, 1985).

17. Genovese, "Special Report: Terrorism," p. 33.

PART III

Evaluating Media
Performance

CHAPTER 7

The Voluntary Guidelines' Threat to U.S. Press Freedom

by Robert Terrell and Kristina Ross

TERRORIST ATTACKS against U.S. citizens and symbols of U.S. governmental authority during recent years have produced a critically important controversy for the U.S. news media. At the heart of the controversy is the escalating debate about the propriety of the U.S. press adopting "voluntary" guidelines with regard to the manner in which it reports on terrorists and terroristic episodes. Much depends on the outcome of the voluntary guidelines debate, including the fate of press freedom in the United States.

At this point, most journalists and their employers are opposed to voluntary guidelines for the coverage of terrorism. But the guidelines' advocates, aided by some units of the federal government and presidential administration spokespersons, gained support. As a result, there is a strong possibility that a major portion of the U.S. news media will be forced to "voluntarily" establish guidelines for reporting about terrorism.

Administrative spokespersons focused major attention on terrorism since President Reagan assumed office in 1980, cajoling citizens, journalists, and foreign allies to join their crusade.

"Terrorism is war," proclaimed then Secretary of State George Shultz in a 1987 statement before the Senate Armed Services Committee. "It's a shadow war involving direct and brutal assaults on the lives of our citizens, on our national interests overseas, and on our basic values.

"It's vital that we win that war."[1]

Less than six months after Secretary Shultz made the above declaration, Reagan administration representatives coordinated the issuance of a similar warlike pronouncement by the leaders of the six nations most closely allied with the United States:

> We, the heads of state of government of the seven major democracies and the representatives of the European Community assembled here in Venice, profoundly aware of our people's concern at the threat posed by terrorism . . . commit ourselves to support the rule of law in bringing terrorists to justice. Each of us pledges increased cooperation in the relevant fora and within the framework of domestic and international law and the investigation, apprehension and prosecution of terrorists.[2]

One of the fronts focused on most often by those who are convinced that the United States and its allies are involved in a war with "international terrorism" is news media coverage. Using cold war–style rhetoric, they repeatedly warn that media coverage of terrorism should be supportive of U.S. and other Western interests.

"The real danger facing the free world today is underestimating the total across-the-board war that is being waged against our society," proclaimed Morris I. Leibman, former chairman of the American Bar Association's Standing Committee on Law and National Security, in a 1984 meeting on terrorism and the media. Leibman, who is also a member of the Executive Board of Georgetown University's Center for Strategic and International Studies, was awarded the Presidential Medal of Freedom by Ronald Reagan in 1981.

"Terrorism, assassinations, and guerrilla warfare are tools being used to achieve definite ends," continued Leibman: "We need to understand that terrorism is now accepted by our enemies as a specialized profession and is being interwoven with propaganda and disinformation as part of the war for the minds of men and women. . . . We need to develop new understanding, skills, and abilities to cope with this new assault on freedom's terrain."[3]

One of the most important participants at the meeting where Leibman made the above remarks was Senator Jeremiah A. Denton, then chairman of the Subcommittee on Security and Terrorism. Senator Denton, who was a prisoner of war in North Vietnam for almost eight years, provided comments representative of the consensus of those who are dominating the voluntary guidelines discussion.

"As chairman of the Subcommittee on Security and Terrorism, one of the characteristics of terrorists that has impressed me is their dependence upon the news media as an indispensable part of their strategy," said Senator Denton.[4]

Another keen observer, Charles Fenyvesi, a journalist and a former hostage (held in the Hanafi takeover of the B'nai Brith building in Washington, D.C., in 1977), asserted:

> Terrorist incidents involving hostages should be handled by the news media in ways analogous to kidnapings and wars. In a kidnaping, police and reporters usually have an agreement on what can be published and what must be withheld until the victim is safe. In war, there is censorship of one type or another, the objective being to deny the enemy information it may use.[5]

One of the most unfortunate implications of recommendations of the sort being proposed by spokespersons such as Leibman, Fenyvesi, and Senator Denton is the fact that they would require journalists to consider terrorists "the enemy." Wholesale adoption of such guidelines, whether voluntarily or otherwise, would almost certainly produce dangerous consequences for U.S. journalists—and the credibility of the U.S. news media.

For rather obvious reasons, police departments and branches of the military responsible for counterinsurgency operations are key participants in the voluntary guidelines debate. But unlike political figures, who tend to be somewhat indirect in their appeals and threats for press adoption of voluntary guidelines, spokespersons for these units of government tend to be direct about their desire to enlist press support for their antiterrorist objectives.

The widely distributed guidelines for press coverage of terrorist episodes formulated by Washington, D.C.'s former Chief of Police Maurice Cullinane are representative of the thinking of law enforcement personnel.[6] Chief Cullinane's guidelines, which he called "raw" and "flexible," were formulated after his department's negotiated release of hostages to end a terrorist episode in the late 1970s. They recommend that during terrorist episodes journalists report only those facts released by the police and refrain from identifying groups claiming responsibility for bombings in order to avoid providing "how to" information to other terrorists.

Dr. Preston Horstman, a police psychologist who has also developed a set of widely distributed guidelines, recommends that journalists refrain from reporting terrorist demands and information about the reasons why particular terrorist episodes occur. In addition, Dr. Horstman recommends that terrorists' tactics be depicted by journalists as "despicable acts committed by losers." His guidelines also urge journalists to make the point in their stories that no hostage situation has ever been successful for the hostage-taker.[7]

Most notably absent from guidelines of the sort proposed by Police Chief Cullinane, Dr. Horstman, and some journalists are recommendations pertaining to the responsibility of journalists to present the reasons *why* particular terrorist episodes are launched. In any event, the publicly available documents that the U.S. goverment's counterterrorism experts have produced on the subject of the press and terrorism tend to be more comprehensive and direct than those produced by individuals such as Chief Cullinane and Dr. Horstman.

One of the most comprehensive government documents on the subject was produced in 1985 by a team charged with responsibility for examining worldwide low-intensity conflict issues with a focus on Central American conflicts in order to "develop a common low-intensity conflict data base, develop 'lessons learned,' and identify the implications for national strategies and their impact on military operations for low-intensity conflicts."[8]

Chapter 15 of the book-length government report sets forth the military's perception of the reasons why government-media cooperation is desirable:

> The need for government agencies, particularly the military, to understand the role and functions of the media is increased in low-intensity conflict, where the media has the potential either to hamper or to enhance chances for success. The military must recognize the crucial part the media plays in gaining popular support for the military mission in all categories of low-intensity conflict. The role of the media in counterterrorism and counterinsurgency is especially critical.
>
> Since the media can be expected to function during all forms of low-intensity conflict, the government agencies and departments must establish close, cooper-

ative relationships in which both the media and the agency or department benefit and are mutually supportive. In the case of the military, it must recognize that it cannot control the media. Moreover, an antagonistic relationship with the press must be conscientiously avoided. A working cooperation between public affairs officials and the media can go far in ensuring that essential security restrictions on news dissemination are understood and complied with by the media. Mutual respect will be especially helpful in establishing and enforcing reasonable essential censorship in guidelines, as well as media self-restraint without censorship in controversial situations. These comments are not intended to infer that the press is obligated to be supportive. Indeed, it is the role of the press to criticize, if necessary, or to be supportive, if appropriate.[9]

In the section of the *Joint Low-Intensity Conflict Project* report titled "Keeping the Public Informed," the authors present the U.S. military's strategy with regard to developing a cooperative relationship with the news media:

> One problem may be that untimely or inaccurate information published or broadcast by the news media can interfere with resolution of an incident, foreclose options for dealing with it, or unwittingly provide intelligence to an enemy. This is especially true in a terrorist incident with "live" or frequent news media coverage. It can result in the perception that the military is not supportive of basic First Amendment rights, with the consequence being an "us versus them" adversary mentality. Preconceptions such as this, once formed, are difficult, if not impossible, to dislodge. Consequently, if one waits until the decision is made to employ military force before formulating public information plans, it will be too late to provide first-hand news reports on the military activity to the American people.
>
> We need, therefore, to explore new ways to work closer with the news media and to solve these problems long before the conflict breaks out. This is particularly true in a fragile world filled with violence and terrorism which threatens public order, human lives, and international and national interests. The military and the media must reduce the adversarial nature of their relationship and cooperate within mutually agreed-upon ground rules.[10]

Military planners are particularly concerned about "real time" press coverage by journalists intent on keeping the public informed about fast-breaking terrorist episodes. According to the authors of the *Joint Low-Intensity Conflict Project* report, such reportage can compromise security. Their conclusion with regard to the manner in which this potential conflict between traditional journalistic objectives and those of the military might be cooperatively resolved is instructive:

> Military and news media planners have not yet come to grips with this modern phenomenon and they must. It may be necessary to have some kind of on-scene military security review procedure, before video transmission, to maintain operational security. This should, of course, be clearly spelled out in the agreed-upon ground rules. . . .
>
> An additional factor is the profound effect of "two-dimensional" or "multidimensional" press coverage of terrorist actions or low-intensity warfare situations as we have seen particularly in the Middle East. The United States press now has the technological capability and the means to cover *both* sides—the terror-

ists' and the victims of the various factions' engaged in a war such as in Lebanon. Meanwhile the "other side," be it a terrorist or insurgency group, sees the media—particularly television— as a propaganda means to convey its threats or message. This on-the-scene, real-time coverage does dais [sic] the issue of censorship (or as some prefer—security review), an issue the military has been able to avoid since World War II. Can separate ground rules be worked out for the broadcast-telecast media? Should separate ground rules be established to avoid compromising security of United States forces and operations? Additionally, the press now has the means to get to the place of conflict without being taken by the United States forces. Should ground rules be developed to control press access in those situations? All these questions require resolution.[11]

Although the majority of U.S. journalists are opposed to the adoption of a collaborative relationship of the sort recommended in the *Joint Low Intensity Conflict Project* report, many of them concede that cooperation may be necessary and appropriate. Moreover, during the past decade or so, a notable number of news organizations have voluntarily formulated codes and procedures for coverage of terrorism. But in every instance where such guidelines have been adopted, those responsible have asserted that government pressure did not significantly influence the decision. This may be true in some cases, but it is clearly apparent that the relentless pressure for the adoption of guidelines is having substantive impact.

The long-range implications of this move toward voluntary censorship are troubling for many reasons, the most important of which is its implication for press freedom. The unavoidable truth is that the basic nature of the U.S. press, particularly its watchdog function, is in the process of being fundamentally altered. The full significance of this can probably be best understood within context of the history of the relationship between the U.S. media and various forms of domestic terrorism.

HISTORICAL OVERVIEW

Although the topic of press coverage of terrorism has become the subject of public controversy in recent years, the roots of censorship pertinent to terrorism can be traced back to the colonial era. During the period in which the nation was formed, few newspapers focused public attention on the terrorist attacks which successive waves of European immigrants waged against Native Americans. Furthermore, journalists tended to ignore the genocidal nature of the terroristic settler attacks, which were frequently aided by government officials.

Prior to the Civil War, Southern journalists practiced numerous forms of censorship designed to protect the system of black slavery upon which the region's economy was largely dependent. This included the maintenance of a code of silence with regard to the terrorist methods used to enforce black subjugation. Quintus C. Wilson, former dean of the School of Journalism at West Virginia University, described the situation in a 1965 article on pre–Civil War censorship:

To some extent slavery played a part in the establishment of these controls. In the pre-war years in the South, constant pressure was exerted by the vested interests to prevent any criticism of slavery in the Southern press. Economic reasons alone were sufficient to deter many editors. In communities where anti-slavery sentiment was frowned upon, editors soon discovered that condemning slavery resulted in cancellation of subscriptions. One Virginia editor was killed in a duel fought because of his "abolitionist sympathies."

During this period, the press in the South was widely controlled by politicians of the small but wealthy group in the slave-holding class and was almost everywhere subservient to their will in the promulgation of false teachings.[12]

Although many Southern journalists were forced to practice censorship with regard to the terrorist tactics used to maintain slavery, many others willingly practiced such censorship. And even though a proportionately large number of Northern journalists attacked slavery, the majority practiced censorship with regard to the numerous forms of terrorism used in their communities to enforce black exclusion from white schools, neighborhoods, churches, and workplaces.

After the Civil War, journalists from all sections of the nation, the overwhelming majority of whom were white, adhered to an informal system of censorship with regard to white-on-black lynchings. And lynching is terrorism: nothing more, nothing less. Furthermore, the mainstream press has historically tended to avoid providing full and complete coverage of the bombings, beatings, maimings, and general intimidation exercised by the white terrorists who comprised the bloodthirsty lynch mobs.

Curtis D. MacDougall, a former professor in the School of Journalism at Northwestern University, described the thinking of white journalists who engage in this particular form of voluntary censorship:

> When I was a reporter for the *St. Louis Star-Times,* the managing editor once spent a full hour soliciting the opinions of about everyone in the newsroom regarding the propriety of using a picture of a lynching. The picture, obtained through one of the press associations . . . showed a dead man in a heap at the bottom of a tree on which he had been hanged. No facial expression was visible. Nevertheless, the decision was made to black out the body and substitute an artist-drawn 'X' to mark the spot.
>
> This conservatism was typical of editors through a century of brutal torture and murder of hapless Negroes, mostly in the South. Plenty of photographs were available, but if they even reached the newsroom, they were relegated to the paper's morgue [files] or wastebasket. Almost none ever were printed.[13]

Representatives from organizations such as the National Association for the Advancement of Colored People regularly petitioned the mainstream press to report lynchings and other atrocities during the early decades of this century with little success. They were considered biased pleaders, supporters of highly suspect political philosophies such as equal rights for blacks and equal protection for blacks by law enforcement authorities. On those occasions when mainstream newspapers condescended to print stories about lynchings and other forms of domestic terrorism, they tended to do so in a manner which might best be described as lurid.

The following excerpt, taken from the October 19, 1933, edition of the *New York Times,* is representative:

> In the wildest lynching orgy the state has ever witnessed, a frenzied mob of 3,000 men, women and children, sneering at guns and tear gas, overpowered state troopers, tore from a prison cell a Negro prisoner accused of attacking an aged white woman, and lynched him in front of the home of the judge who had tried to calm them.
>
> Then the mob cut down the body, dragged it through the main thoroughfares for more than half a mile, and tossed it onto a burning pyre.[14]

Ralph Ginzburg, who has experienced numerous disagreements with the mainstream press and government representatives because of his comparatively liberal attitude toward publishing, estimated that nearly two thousand blacks were lynched in the United States between 1900 and 1964. The gruesome deaths of the overwhelming majority of those who were lynched were never written about in the mainstream press. Nonetheless, some journalists objected to this practice of censoring the news regarding the systematic acts of terror being perpetrated against blacks. Ernest L. Meyer was such a journalist. He recorded his thoughts on censorship of stories about lynchings in a 1934 column printed in the Madison (Wisconsin) *Capital Times:*

> There has been a good bit of criticism of the *Capital Times* for printing on page one of last Tuesday's edition actual photographs of the two victims of the San Jose lynching bee.
>
> The pictures of the man dangling from the tree were described as "shocking and unnecessary."
>
> So was the crime. The grim butchery deserved a grim record. And those photographs were more eloquent than any word-picture of the event. They were calculated to cool any sympathy for the San Jose mob. . . .
>
> They may be morbid fare for nice people. But it is better to be sickened by brutality than to be seduced by it.[15]

Opinions of the sort presented in the above excerpt have been sufficient during the balance of U.S. history to get any white person who had the temerity to write or utter them branded a traitor to his or her race. This was particularly true of journalists, who simply were not expected until recent times to address nonwhites as if they deserve equal rights.

One of the most important things to be understood about the traditional form of censorship practiced by the mainstream press with regard to domestic white terrorism is the fact that it was voluntary. Excepting the situation that existed in the South before the end of the Civil War, there was surprisingly little government pressure on the press to practice such censorship. Segments of the press were subjected on occasion to pressure from white citizens irate *because* of coverage of domestic white terrorism. But it would be difficult to prove that such pressure could not have been responded to by means other than racially biased censorship. The situation began to change in the 1960s, a period during which blacks were once again at the center of a struggle destined to fundamentally alter the national balance of power.

VOLUNTARY PRESS CENSORSHIP IN THE 1960s

The turbulent decade of the 1960s ushered in a new era for U.S. race relations. Determined to escape the restrictive bonds of the apartheid-like system known as segregation, blacks mounted a major protest movement. Their tactics were frequently novel and quite often dangerous. White America, including the mainstream press, was taken by surprise by the breadth and intensity of the new movement. This was largely due to the fact that white Americans had been systematically prevented from acquiring information about their black counterparts by the press and other mass communications mediums.

The expanding vibrance of the Civil Rights movement was such that it was more or less immediately apparent that it was going to be historically significant. Thus people wanted to know what was going on and why. They wanted to know more about the ministers, students, and previously docile working-class blacks who were leading the movement. They also wanted to know more about the terrorist tactics employed by various white groups to crush the movement.

After an initial period of denial during which editorial writers generally admonished blacks to calm down and stop demanding the impossible (racial equality), the mainstream press began to provide substantive coverage of some aspects of the Civil Rights movement. But shortly thereafter, Southern politicians began to criticize press coverage of the freedom rides, sit-ins, demonstrations, and voter registration campaigns. They charged that the movement was essentially a series of staged events being played out for newspaper reporters and television cameras. For the most part, these initial calls for censorship were rejected. But similar charges by those intent on preserving a way of life built on systemic racial oppression began to generate second thoughts by the mid 1960s.

The source of the second thoughts was described by C.A. McKnight in a 1965 speech at a meeting of the American Society of Newspaper Editors. McKnight, then editor of the *Charlotte Observer,* told his listeners the Civil Rights movement was being covered comprehensively, accurately, with good balance and perspective. Nonetheless, he said, the movement was presenting the mainstream news media with certain problems:

> One problem is the disquieting fact that our reporters and photographers, by their very presence on the scene, have at times tended to incite or to aggravate disorder and violence, and at other times to become the objects of violence. . . .
>
> A second professional problem involves editorial judgments. When is a demonstration legitimate? And when is it staged just to get attention in the press?

We all know that the impact of a Birmingham or a Selma flows not so much from the event, per se, but from the newspaper, radio and television coverage the event produces.

This is a fact that every successful Negro leader understands very well. The best ones are very adept at "using the press" to mobilize national and international support for their objectives. A certain amount of editorial judgment must be exercised in covering the Civil Rights movement.[16]

Attorney General Nicholas Katzenbach provided an authoritative government assessment of the amount and kind of "editorial judgment" the nation's journalists should exercise with regard to their coverage of the Civil Rights movements in a 1965 statement to a group of government officials, academicians, and press representatives assembled at a three-day conference on violence at Brandeis University. The attorney general, who began by claiming that news coverage of the Civil Rights movement had constituted a powerful deterrent to racial violence in the South, raised what he called "negative questions" about the overall character of such coverage. He said he was specifically thinking about indiscriminate interviews with demonstrators and leaders of such events.

"To proffer a citywide or even nationwide audience to persons with such self-serving interests runs the risk of turning conscious news coverage into unconscious propaganda," charged Attorney General Katzenbach.[17]

Discussion of press coverage of the Civil Rights movement and other forms of "public disorder" heated up substantially with the deadly social explosion that came to be known as the Watts Riot. As angry blacks in cities across the nation torched their communities with cries of "Burn, baby, burn!" journalists began to seriously question the propriety of their coverage. Two factions emerged as journalists engaged in tense discussions in city rooms, broadcasting studies, and professional meetings. One faction claimed that the most important shortcoming in press performance was too little coverage of the reasons why the nation's black ghettos were being burned. The other faction claimed that the problem was too much coverage of ghetto blacks.

John Gregory Dunne presented the consensus of the latter group in an article wherein he criticized television coverage of the Watts Riot:

No one wants to impugn the coverage, ingenuity, and virtuosity of the broadcast journalists in Watts. But the very nature of television, with its pressing need to fill the gaping maw of dead air, mitigates against reasoned analysis of a running civil disturbance. Consciously or not, electronic journalism is essentially show business, and show business demands a gimmick. With its insatiable appetite for live drama, television turned the riots into some kind of Roman spectacle, with the police playing the lions, the Negroes the Christians. The angle, in this case, was that the Christians were winning.[18]

Those who disagreed with spokespersons such as John Gregory Dunne and Attorney General Nicholas Katzenbach frequently claimed that the racial biases of the mainstream media were the primary sources of inadequate press coverage of the civil rights movement. They argued, therefore, that

instead of implementing guidelines for censorship the press should develop
a more balanced approach to the racial crisis that had now moved out of the
Southern states and engulfed much of the rest of the nation. Margaret Halsey presented a cogent statement consistent with this perspective in a 1965
article titled "White Papers and Negro Readers":

> The white press obviously aspires to influence thought, for it employs besides its
> regular editorial writers whole coveys of commentators, syndicated columnists,
> writers or "think-pieces," pundits, political experts, etc. But over and over these
> opinion-makers unwittingly reveal that they write from the white community's
> point of view and not as spokesmen for the whole Republic. . . .
>
> Negroes are adjured by Caucasian journalists to obey "the law of the land,"
> no matter what their grievances, and respect for the law is held up to them by
> these writers as an obligation which takes precedence over any injury, however
> lasting or however mortal. . . .
>
> "The law of the land" rhetoric impresses white readers. But must it not con-
> vince Negroes that American journalism, insofar as it tries to influence opinion,
> is basically dedicated to the status quo and the continuing comfort and conve-
> nience of white people? . . .
>
> The Press is an established institution and as such is not by nature friendly
> to the idea of drastic social change. . . . It is with "the power of the press" to
> make Negroes feel less like voices crying in the wilderness and make more like
> people who are being listened to. It is within the power of the press to open the
> eyes of white people to their own insularity.[19]

Although they were listened to and heeded in some ways, journalists
who shared Margaret Halsey's opinions were not able to dissuade most of
those who favored the adoption of guidelines for coverage of racially oriented disorders. Thus by the beginning of 1966, U.S. journalists were being
urged to adopt a fifteen-point list of guidelines for reporting such disorders.
The list was formulated at a meeting held under the aegis of the School of
Journalism and the Department of Telecommunications of the University of
Southern California. It reflected the consensus of the journalists, college
professors, wire service personnel, and media executives who attended the
meeting. The list, which was broadly distributed via trade publications, recommended that journalists covering disorders "emphasize efforts by law
enforcement officials to restore order."[20]

National attention was focused on the voluntary censorship issue during
the summer of 1967 when Senator Hugh Scott recommended that representatives from the press confer with government and civic leaders to develop
a code of emergency procedures for reporting racially oriented disorders.
Senator Scott attempted to rally support for his recommendation by charg-
ing that the television networks were focusing their riot coverage on "sensational aspects of the situation."[21] He also charged that the nation's television
stations had broadcast "frequent appeals to riot by extremists."[22]

Spokespersons for the national television network were quick to refute
Senator Scott's charges. Frank Stanton, president of CBS, using terms essentially identical to those of his counterparts at the other two networks,

said the senator was mistaken. He pointed out the fact that from the week of the Newark rebellion to the Milwaukee rebellion one month later, the overwhelming number of blacks permitted on CBS news programs were moderates like Martin Luther King, Roy Wilkins, and the governors of New Jersey and Michigan. According to Stanton's tally, the number of moderates permitted to address the nation via CBS broadcasts during the period in question outnumbered militants sixty-six to fifteen.

There are numerous indications that mainstream print journalists were employing similar forms of censorship at the time. Moreover, during the months immediately after Frank Stanton revealed that CBS was tailoring its new broadcasts such that moderate spokespersons were provided dominant access to the public, officials from the Justice Department conducted a series of meetings with press representatives. The meetings, which were similar to those held between government officials and press representatives during World War II to coordinate censorship measures, were intended to articulate an essentially unified strategy for reporting racially oriented civil disorders.

"Our basic mission is to cover the story, but we're supposed to be observers, not participants," said a CBS spokesman in defense of his organization's compliance with the Justice Department's recommendations.[23] As is the case today, representatives from CBS (and their mainstream counterparts in other sections of the news media) accepted the government's assertion that neutral coverage of racially oriented civil disorders was inflammatory. Thus they agreed to provide limited coverage designed to minimize public awareness of the size, intensity, and location of such disorders. One of the most important results is that the public was given a distorted impression of the disorders and their primary sources.

There is little indication that the public, with the possible exception of blacks, was aware of the breadth and character of the censorship system employed by the mainstream news media during the 1960s. Nonetheless, the censorship was apparent to those active in the movement and to many of those who studied press performance with regard to the Civil Rights movement. Some of those who understood what was being done were extremely critical. Jeannette Hopkins, author of the comprehensive study *Racial Justice and the Press,* was one of them.

"The emphasis on responsibility of the press to avoid incitement suggests that it conceived its mission not only in the classic observer role, but . . . in a participatory role, for to be involved as an influence for order, even though an unobtrusive one, *is* to participate," wrote Hopkins. "The press has become part of the scene itself," she charged, "its role on the street stage is a factor to be taken into account."[24]

The most important report during the 1960s on the subject of press coverage of blacks and the Civil Rights movement was produced by the National Advisory Commission on Civil Disorders. The book-length report, which was commissioned by President Lyndon Johnson, presented the news media with a Catch-22 set of recommendations.

On the one hand, the report charged that the press had traditionally practiced racism with regard to its coverage of blacks and other minorities. Therefore, it recommended that the press broaden its traditional white perspective and incorporate nonwhites into every level of the news profession in order to ensure fairer, more balanced coverage. On the other hand, the National Advisory Commission's report advocated the establishment of a comprehensive system of censorship managed by journalists and government officials:

We recommend that every news organization that does not now have some form of guidelines—or suspects that those it has are not working effectively—designate top editors to (a) meet with its reporters who have covered or might be assigned to riots, (b) discuss in detail the problems and procedures which exist or are expected and (c) formulate and disseminate directives based on the discussions. Regardless of the specific provisions, the vital step is for every newsgathering organization to adopt and implement at least some minimal form of internal control. . . .

What is needed first is a series of discussions, perhaps a combination of informal gatherings and seminar-type workshops. They should encompass all ranks of police, all levels of media employees, and a cross-section of city officials. At first these could be get-acquainted sessions—to air complaints and discuss common problems. Working reporters should get to know the police. . . . Police and city officials should use the sessions for frank and candid briefings on the problems the city might face and official plans for dealing with disturbances.

Later sessions might consider procedures to facilitate the physical movement of personnel and speed the flow of accurate and complete news. Such arrangements might involve nothing more than a procedure for designating specific locations at which police officers would be available to escort a reporter into a dangerous area. In addition, policemen and reporters working together might devise better methods of identification, communication, and training. . . .

In some cases, if all parties involved were willing, planning sessions might lead to the consideration of more formal undertakings. These might include: (a) agreements on specific procedures to expedite the physical movement of men and equipment around disorder areas and back and forth through police lines, (b) general guidelines on the behavior of both media and police personnel and (c) arrangements for a brief moratorium on reporting news of an incipient disturbance. The Commission stresses once again its belief that though each of these possibilities merits consideration, none should be formulated or imposed by unilateral government action. Any procedure finally adopted should be negotiated between police and media representatives and should assure both sides the flexibility needed to do their respective jobs. Acceptance of such arrangements should be frankly based on grounds of self-interest, for negotiated methods of procedures can often yield substantial benefits to each side—and to the public which both serve.[25]

The *Report of the National Advisory Commission on Civil Disorders* had a significant impact on the nation's mainstream news media. By focusing attention on their racist practices, it provided authoritative support for those individuals and organizations committed to hiring and promoting blacks and other non-Caucasians. It also provided support for those who had been advocating that nonwhite communities be provided more balanced press coverage.

But the most important impact of the report is probably the fact that it sanctioned the adoption of broad-scale censorship with regard to reporting civil disorders. Therefore, by the end of the 1960s, most of the nation's major news organizations had established formal or informal guidelines and contingency plans for reporting racially oriented civil disorders. Furthermore, most of the guidelines and plans contained specific instructions with regard to the kinds of information that should be censored and directions for working closely with police and other government officials.

PREPARING FOR WAR: THE 1970s AND 1980s

The contemporary phase of the controversy generated by the movement to get the U.S. news media to implement guidelines for coverage of terrorism began inauspiciously. By the beginning of the 1970s, the black ghetto rebellions that rocked the nation during the 1960s were waning, and the specter of terrorism from abroad had not yet emerged as a dominant source of concern. Thus the news media's white, middle-class hegemony was essentially unchallenged. For the most part, journalists were confident and secure in their widespread assumption that they were unbiased practitioners of a brand of reportage that deserved the respect of fair-minded people the world over.

The first indications that the press was headed for one of its most important confrontations in history began to emerge during the middle 1970s because of a series of attacks launched by terrorist groups from the Middle East. As the hijackers, kidnappers, and bombers began to dominate the attention of U.S. government officials, pressure began to mount on the press to censor its coverage. For example, in 1977 Ronald Reagan was already urging the nation's news media to stop all live coverage of terrorist events.[26] Former President Gerald Ford was issuing calls at the same time for an end to the "lavish attention" that the news media were allegedly bestowing on terrorists.

Ronald Reagan was particularly irate about television's alleged excesses. He wanted censorship and was not above saying so. "If the nation's television assignment editors and radio news directors would take a collective deep breath and declare a moratorium on live coverage of terrorist events during the commission of the crime, they would be cutting off the source of inspiration for an untold number of loose nuts who harbor similar crazy ideas,"[27] proclaimed Reagan in an article printed in *The Quill,* an influential trade magazine subscribed to by many journalists.

The year 1977 was a good one for those who advocated censorship of press coverage of terrorism. Several of the nation's most influential organizations, including CBS and United Press International (UPI) announced that they were implementing guidelines for covering terrorists. Most such announcements included vague assurances that the organizations were still committed to press freedom. The *Chicago Sun-Times* and *Chicago Daily News* hosted a conference on the media and terrorism during which at least one participant claimed that guidelines were necessary because proper handling of terrorist events had not become second nature to journalists. Furthermore, 1977 was the year in which spokespersons from the National News Council (now defunct) announced that they had voted to act as a forum for the collection and distribution of guidelines for press coverage of terrorism. This was just five years after the organization was founded amidst promises that it would not be used to impede the right of the press to report the news.[28]

Despite the growing popularity of the guidelines bandwagon, many journalists continued to resist. Walter Cronkite expressed the opinion of a sizable segment of them in a 1979 comment printed in *Broadcast* magazine. "We can't be asked to abstain from journalistic practices because a story will complicate diplomatic practices," said Cronkite.

> That's a diplomatic problem; it's not our problem. We have to be responsible, of course. But within that ethical framework of responsibility, we have to pursue the story. It would be terrible, if through self-interest or government interest, we didn't get a clear picture. . . . How terrible it would be if we [the media] didn't have clear channels to the people, and the people thought that what they were getting was controlled by the government.[29]

The protestations of prominent spokespersons like Walter Cronkite notwithstanding, the advocates of guidelines continued to press their case. Censorship advocates frequently advocated negative coverage of terrorists or none at all. Zbigniew Brzezinski, former national security adviser for President Carter, expressed a representative opinion in a 1979 article in the *Washington Post*. In response to an interview with the Ayatollah Ruhollah Khomeini broadcast by CBS's "60 Minutes," Brzezinski charged that the press was "catering to the enemies of this country." Claiming that he was agitated by the interview, Brzezinski asserted, "There ought to be some way to control the press. The press in this country should be controlled."[30]

Real-time coverage of terrorist episodes emerged as a major issue in the guidelines controversy toward the end of 1977. Public discussion of this aspect of press coverage of terrorism tended initially to focus on the problems such reportage creates for police and military personnel. Critics of real-time reportage of terrorist episodes, which are frequently multinational episodes involving hundreds of people, charged that the press had begun to assume responsibilities traditionally reserved for political leaders and diplomats.

This assertion was and is partially true. Real-time interviews with hostages and hostage-takers clearly have diplomatic ramifications. But the most important aspect of this new and dramatic dimension of press capability is the fact that it provides terrorists unprecedented opportunities to communicate directly with the individual citizens whose opinions and behavior they seek to change. Furthermore, it provides the same citizens unprecedented opportunities to form opinions *before* politicians and diplomats have opportunities to organize and interpret the facts in accordance with their objectives.

Late 1970s discussions of the best, and most appropriate, ways for the news media to respond to terrorist episodes were complicated by a pervasive sense of urgency—and deep-felt fears of future horrors perpetrated by hooded men and women seemingly unafraid of death. The nation's editorial pages clearly reflected the anger and confusion coursing through the ranks of mainstream journalism. J. Bowyer Bell, a senior research associate at the Institute of War and Peace Studies at Columbia University, was one of the few persons with access to a mainstream media forum who possessed real insight into the situation. In a 1978 *Columbia Journalism Review* article titled "Terrorist Scripts and Live Action Spectaculars," he advocated a calm, reasoned response to terrorism:

> There has been a tendency to forget the long, bloody history of Western political violence: the assassin's toll, bombs tossed into theatres, landlords murdered, factories burned, lynch mobs, and urban riots. Instead, the public and the media perceive the dramatic slaughters of recent years, the machine gunning of innocents, the no-warning bombs, the murdered diplomats, and the extended hijacking odyssey, as novel and dread threats that must be met with novel and effective responses to defend the freedom and liberty of the West, now so inexplicably threatened. . . .
>
> Terrorism in its manifold forms will remain with us. Sometimes such violence is significant as a real threat, but mostly it is not. The enemy is us. Indignation is expensive; outrage is dear. Make the best of a troubled world. . . . Perilous as matters seem, if open, democratic societies in the West cannot protect the liberty of us all from a handful of gunmen, accommodate legitimate dissent, and repress the politics of atrocity under the law—if we cannot tolerate the exaggerated horror flashed on the evening news, or the random bomb, without recourse to the tyrant's manual—then we do not deserve to be free.[31]

Such sentiments were unpopular when Bell made them, and they remain so today. The tendency of a significant percentage of those who dominate the news media coverage of the terrorism controversy is to advocate reprisals, to hurl forth dire threats at faceless, nameless enemies. The cumulative impact by the latter portion of the 1970s was a transformation in the language used to portray the threat of terrorism. Journalists and major political figures began to use the language of war: terrorists were perceived to be deadly enemies of the United States and its supporters. They were, therefore, regularly portrayed in the press as depraved, questionably sane human beings who had forfeited the right to receive unbiased coverage.

The following excerpt, taken from a 1978 issue of the *Indiana Law Review,* provides a representative example of the manner in which the press was pressured to suspend commitments to fairness where terrorists were concerned

> The problem lies in journalism's moral and neutrality posture, which prohibits the development of an ethic oriented toward the maintenance of community, its standards, values and culture. Traditions that prescribe an inflexible "watchdog"

role for the press, or emphasize the publication of terrorist rhetoric when the community feels intimidated, appear self-defeating. Clearly judgements must be made by journalists that differentiate between wars of ideas fought within legitimate institutions of the community, and struggles fought outside these institutions and which rely upon violence rather than verbiage, intimidation instead of intellect.[32]

By the end of the 1970s, the perspective presented in the excerpt above was developing notable credibility with the U.S. news media. Furthermore, it was attracting support from famous and influential journalists. This was particularly the case after the Iranian hostage crisis, a deeply traumatic episode for many U.S. citizens. One of the most interesting comments on the subject of the news media's allegedly inappropriate neutrality was presented by Daniel Schorr, one of the nation's best-known journalists:

The TV-wise Iranian militants certainly managed, by capturing the American hostages, to capture America's attention. . . .
    It was theater—guerrilla theater—on the most stupendous scale yet, but not a new phenomenon. For some 15 years [advocates of] unpopular causes have been learning that violence and the threat of violence, can crash through the barriers of middle class and establishment resistance to TV recognition. . . .
    Not surprisingly, American officials, watching helplessly from the sidelines while TV became the negotiating arena, cried foul. For government, a free one-way TV pass into our living rooms for our adversaries had been a source of pain since at least 1957, when President Eisenhower criticized CBS for its unprecedented interview with Soviet boss Nikita Khrushchev in the Kremlin.[33]

The Carter administration, faced with an unprecedented amount of real-time coverage of the Iranian hostage crisis, was particularly critical of the news media's coverage of terrorism during its last days. President Carter himself focused the criticism on the press during a 1980 press conference wherein he called on U.S. journalists and the organizations for which they work to "minimize as severely as possible their presence and their activities"[34] in Iran. He also announced during the news conference that he was considering cutting off telephone and satellite communications with Iran. Such a move, of course, would have severely limited the capacity of the press to provide full and complete coverage of the hostage crisis. It would have also resulted in U.S. journalists becoming far more dependent U.S. government spokespersons for information about events in Iran.

Pressures on the press to adopt censorship measures with regard to its coverage of terrorism escalated after President Reagan's election. The new President, determined to project a stronger, more forceful image than his predecessor, immediately let it be known that he intended to be tough on the terrorism issue. The administration sponsored numerous meetings and a considerable amount of research and publishing on the subject of terrorism. One of the threads that ran through it all was criticism of the media. Moreover, the censorship measures being touted were virtually identical to those drawn up to restrict press coverage of the Civil Rights movement of the 1960s:

Media personnel should attempt to cooperate with police and other news organizations in order to minimize abuses arising from unrestrained competition. Reporters and equipment should be pooled when practicable to minimize obtrusiveness and burdens on law enforcement personnel. . . . Media supervisory personnel should make themselves available to law enforcement officials, and public information officers employed, in order to facilitate dissemination of accurate information. . . .

Some of these proposals are not alien to the traditional exercise of self-restraint now practiced by the United States media. . . . Other proposals may require alteration of journalism's traditional role as an impartial reporter of events without regard to their consequences. Such claims of impartiality, however, do not insulate the media from becoming the instrument, though unwillingly, of terroristic crime. . . .

Thus the time is ripe to discuss a more active role for the media in handling terroristic violence coverage. The media's failure to take the initiative would only exacerbate existing conflicts and invite the search for more restrictive alternatives.[35]

The above excerpt, taken from an article produced from a report for the Law Enforcement Assistance Administration, put more emphasis on the threat of government intervention in the press-terrorism controversy than had generally been the case before Ronald Reagan's election. It also included a long list of specific kinds of censorship the press should practice during terrorist crises. Advocacy of such censorship reached a new plateau in 1985 in the wake of the hijacking of TWA Flight 847. Immediately afterward, spokespersons for the Reagan administration took to the nation's airwaves and editorial pages pressing their charge that the news media had "trampled on national security"[36] in their haste to cover the crisis. Such charges were made even though several news organizations withheld some information about the crisis after being asked to do so by government officials.

Henry Kissinger, who urged the Reagan administration to "make it absolutely clear that any harm done to any American by terrorists would lead to very violent reprisals,"[37] said he was particularly upset by the manner in which the nation's press covered the TWA hijacking. "I think what the media ought to consider is not to carry anything [about terrorist events]," said Kissinger, "including the terrorists."[38] Charles Krauthammer, a *Time* magazine essayist, sounded a similar note in a commentary two weeks after Kissinger provided his ill-considered recommendation. Equating terrorism with evil, Krauthammer suggested that terrorists simply be ignored, particularly by television:

Broadcast television imposes limits, strict but self-enforced limits, on explicit sex. Why not on explicit terror? There is no reason why all the news of a terrorist event, like news of a rape, cannot be transmitted in some form. But in the interest of decency, diplomacy and our own self-respect, it need not be live melodrama. . . .

Evil is riveting. From watching Hitchcock we know of the perverse, and fully human, enjoyment that comes from looking evil in the eye. But when the evil is real and the suffering actual, that enjoyment is tinged with shame, the kind of shame one experiences when exposed to pornography.

And like pornography, terrorist television, the graphic unfolding of evil on camera, sells.[39]

It probably did not occur to Charles Krauthammer and his editors that he was advocating the same kind of censorship practiced by leaders of the closed societies *Time* magazine regularly excoriates for violations of press freedom. In any event, less than a week after Krauthammer's recommendations were distributed via *Time* across the United States and throughout much of the rest of the developed world, six thousand members of the American Bar Association (ABA) were provided similar comments on the subject of censorship and terrorism by Prime Minister Margaret Thatcher of Great Britain. Addressing the opening assembly of the ABA meeting in London, Mrs. Thatcher said news organizations should be urged to suppress information that might prove useful to terrorists. She also urged the democratic nations "try to find ways to starve the terrorist and the hijacker of the oxygen of publicity on which they depend."[40]

Mrs. Thatcher, whose comments were made during a discussion of the TWA Flight 847 hijacking, asked a question that has consistently been answered in the affirmative by U.S. media spokespersons during the past two years: "Ought we not to ask the media to agree among themselves to a voluntary code of conduct, under which they would not say or show anything which could assist the terrorists' morale or their cause while the hijack lasted?"[41]

Former U.S. Attorney General Edwin Meese III, who also attended the London meeting of the ABA, spoke in support of the voluntary code of censorship recommended by Mrs. Thatcher. He announced that the Reagan administration was considering beginning talks with the U.S. news media that might result in the media establishing a censorship code for use during future terrorist episodes. Mr. Meese also discussed agreements by the news media to suppress information and bar broadcasts of some kinds of interviews.

Press reports of the 1985 London meeting of the ABA included statements of support for the recommendations of Prime Minister Thatcher and Attorney General Meese from many individuals prominent in the U.S. government and the legal profession. Supporters included the president-elect of the ABA, William W. Falsgraff, who said, "Recent events suggest a voluntary accord could work if the standards are responsible and if the media is convinced it's in the interests of all free nations to abide by it.[42]

Spokespersons for many of the nation's major news organizations criticized the recommendations of Thatcher, Meese, Falsgraff, and their supporters. They were, they said, particularly concerned that the U.S. Attorney General was recommending they work with the government to establish a code of censorship. "The Constitution, with its guarantees supported by the courts, has historically been the best code ever drawn up, and I really don't see any need to tinker with it," said A.M. Rosenthal, executive editor of the *New York Times*. Rosenthal, who remained admirably firm on this particular issue for several years, was expressing sentiments similar to those provided in the wake of the London ABA meeting by spokespersons from the three major television networks.

Despite public statements to the contrary, the threats of censorship are obviously having a major impact on U.S. journalists and the organizations for which they work. Journalists are defensive, and somewhat insecure, with regard to criticism of the quality of their coverage of terrorism. In addition, they are obviously uncomfortable with the critical remarks of those who accuse them of being insufficiently patriotic. Furthermore, they are worried—and with good reason—about the prospect of restrictive legislation. The following excerpt, taken from a special report on terrorism printed in *Presstime*, an influential trade publication for mainstream journalists, conveys much of the unease and resignation (and spirit of compromise) that exists in the ranks of the U.S. press corps at this time where the subject of terrorism is concerned:

> To date, Congress has not made any move to legislate restrictions on press coverage of terrorist incidents. The House Foreign Affairs Committee's Subcommittee on Europe and the Middle East conducted a hearing last summer, following the TWA Flight 847 incident, on the news media and terrorism. The thrust of the hearing was on the need for media self-regulation and self-criticism. In addition, a dozen members of Congress have urged television networks to convene a "summit" to consider coverage guidelines. . . .
>
> But if newspapers have been lukewarm to suggestions that they consider adopting their own guidelines on covering terrorism and downright cold to the notion of industry-wide action, the idea of talking about the subject—with other media people, with experts in the field of terrorism and with government officials—has hit their button.[43]

There is a good possibility that within the next few years the U.S. press will adopt some kind of comprehensive agreement with regard to the manner in which terrorism is reported. Government pressure, both overt and covert, will be influential, but probably not decisive. The objectives of the Reagan administration in the 1980s notwithstanding, there are many people in the U.S. government who absolutely oppose the establishment of a governmentally imposed system of censorship. The decisive factor in the decision to implement a code for coverage, or guidelines, will almost certainly come from the terrorists themselves—and the nature of the war they are conducting for the hearts and minds of people who might help them realize their objectives.

The key point to be understood is that even though terrorism has existed for centuries, the contemporary situation is difficult *because* of the existence of the mass media and the pivotal influence they exert on the ways in which people think and behave. Coping with the challenges and responsibilities the present situation presents to journalists will almost certainly require the establishment of some kind of code of conduct. However, this does not mean that the necessary system should incorporate requirements for the press to suppress information, collaborate with government officials, and abandon the concept of neutrality. Most important, any appropriate system must be based on sophisticated understanding of terrorism, its sources, practitioners, and objectives.

DEFINING TERRORISM

Who and what are terrorists, anyway? Are terrorists "crazies" bent on pointless violence and destruction, partially insane people with no regard for the value of human life? Or are they "freedom fighters" dedicated to the liberation of oppressed groups who have resorted to violence after all alternate channels for justice have been exhausted?

Clearly, when discussing terrorism, careful attention should be paid as to who labels whom a "terrorist" and for what purpose. Whose interests are served by the labeling? Through what channels are the labels carried? More than a game of semantics, the label "terrorist" carries negative political and social connotations that may or may not be appropriate to the accused individual or group. Further, the news media, which are most frequently used for labeling, do not always question the validity of the label.

WHOLESALE TERRORISTS

Identity of Wholesale Terrorists

Most governments would deny they are terroristic. However, the method for determining the validity of such denials is simple: if high- or low-intensity violence and destruction accompany government support of a particular policy, whether at home or abroad, and if that violence is not part of a recognized war maneuver, that government is engaged in wholesale terrorism.

The term *wholesale terrorism* was coined by Edward S. Herman in his article "Power and the Semantics of Terrorism."[44] Wholesale terrorism describes what may also be called regime terrorism, which has its roots in the French Revolution during what was called the Reign of Terror.[45]

Purpose of Wholesale Terrorists

Regime or wholesale terrorism is practiced by governments or powerful elites for the purpose of maintaining dominance over targeted groups. This includes efforts to oppress opponents of their state. Wholesale terrorists also use violence to maintain the subservience or obedience of groups or individuals identified as enemies of the state. Sometimes they use the threat of violence to intimidate a rebelling population.[46]

Exported and In Situ Wholesale Terrorism

Wholesale terrorism need not necessarily be used within the geographical boundaries of the practicing government (as in in situ terrorism) to be classified as wholesale. The motives and goals of in situ or exported wholesale terrorism differ. If a nation's self-interest is promoted by an ally's continued dominance of its populace, a nation with the means (financial, mili-

Table 7.1. Casualties of Wholesale Terrorist Events

STATE	NUMBER KILLED
El Salvador: Río Sumpul, May 14, 1980	600+
South Africa: Kassinga refugee camp, May 4, 1978	600+
Guatemala: Panzos, May 29, 1978	114
Israel: Sabra and Shatila, Lebanon, September 1982 ...	1,900–3,500
Argentina: 1976–82 "disappeared"	11,000
Chile: 1973–85	20,000+
Dominican Republic: 1965–72	2,000
El Salvador: Matanza I, 1932	30,000
El Salvador: Matanza II, 1980–85	50,000+
Guatemala: Ríos Montt pacification campaign, May–June 1982	2,186
Guatemala: 1966–85	100,000+
Indonesia: 1965–66	800,000+
Indonesia: Invasion and pacification of East Timor, 1980–85	200,000+
Soviet Union: Afghanistan, 1979–85	200,000+
Libya: External assassinations of Libyans, 1980–83	10+
Cambodia: Pol Pot era, 1975–80	300,000+
Nicaragua: U.S.—Sponsored contras 1981–85	2,800+
United States: Assault on Indochina, 1955–75	4,000,000+

tary, or both) may aid its ally through exported wholesale terrorism. An example of this type of export could be continuing U.S. financial involvement in South Africa. In addition, if it is in the national self-interest to overthrow or control an enemy government, a nation may export wholesale terrorism in the guise of a civilian revolution on the enemy's soil (as in the Soviet invasion of Afghanistan.)

Further examples of exported wholesale terrorism are abundant in recent history. For a breakdown of estimated casualties resulting from recent wholesale terrorism, see Table 7.1.[47]

Regardless of the political or economic reasons for the actions, the casualty figures or the results of wholesale terrorism evidence that wholesale terrorists can hold the world hostage with greater ease than their small-scale cousins, the retail terrorists. The political "reasons" for such slaughter do not provide an alibi for murder under any other name.

Methods Used by Wholesale Terrorists

Because wholesale terrorists are already powerful, they generally do not need to resort to tactics such as car-bombing or hijacking to make their point. Governments or elites frequently have at their disposal their mili-

tary—corps of trained and skilled police or soldiers with sophisticated arma-
ments against which targeted populations have little hope of defense using
conventional means of retaliation.[48] The members of the police or military
corps are already indoctrinated to uphold government policy as part of their
training. Therefore, governments enjoy the loyalty of large numbers of willing, skilled, and equipped personnel to carry out policy plans with violence.

In addition, wholesale terrorists can also deny the basic human rights of
their opponents by the enactment of repressive laws enforced by state police. They can structure the economy in such a manner that it is nearly impossible for their opponents, or designated enemies, to acquire access to the
necessities for living. They frequently practice cultural imperialism through
oppression of the population's indigenous, ethnic, or cultural expression.
Thus, wholesale terrorism need not only be violent in epic proportions. It
can also consist of covert oppression and manipulation of the social, economic, and cultural support systems of the attacked population.

A classic example of in situ wholesale terrorism employing covert and
overt violence is the white minority government of South Africa. The South
African government routinely uses militarily enforced suppression of free
expression by the black majority. Countless blacks have been killed, impris-
oned, relocated, or reported missing for attempting to express opinions
about their systematic oppression. South Africa provides, therefore, good
examples of the physical and mental violence common to wholesale terrorism.

Media Manipulation by Wholesale Terrorists:
The Blind Media

Wholesale terrorism is practiced on a near daily basis, frequently for
protracted periods of time.[49] Thus, wholesale terrorism does not always at-
tract attention from the media. As the media tend to focus on unique events
for coverage, they frequently overlook commonly occurring wholesale terrorism. This lack of news media attention is not merely a case of temporary
blindness. For example, Western governments engaged in wholesale terrorism are also host nations to the most powerful news media on earth. But the
"free" media in such nations generally acknowledge or report the semantic
games played by government officials when labeling their foreign terroristic
activities. Particularly obvious was the Reagan administration's history of
exporting wholesale terrorism to Central America labeled as "aid to the freedom fighters." Furthermore, the mainstream U.S. media tended to perpetu-
ate the Reagan administration's deception by consistently referring to the
contras as patriotic freedom fighters even though the methods they were
using to overthrow the Nicaraguan government were terroristic.

In nations in which wholesale terrorism is practiced without the benefit
of a free press the situation is worse. Publicity is not an underlying target
for in situ wholesale terrorists unless it is favorable or sympathetic to their
cause. Propaganda organs within the wholesale nation's borders may exist

to further "legitimize" their cause or rally its support, but rarely does true journalism survive within such nations. Media external to the borders of the terrorist nation may acknowledge the wholesale terrorism, but such recognition indeed is not sought. Again, a difficulty external media face in identifying wholesale terrorism is recognizing the propagandistic semantics used to distort reality.

In summary, then, wholesale terrorists are generally governments or powerful elites who employ modern weapons through highly organized military and socially structured means to achieve the obedience, intimidation, and/or compliance of a dissenting populace on their own, their ally's, or their enemy's soil. Wholesale terrorism may occur over years or months until objectives are achieved or until necessary support structures fail. Mainstream journalists rarely acknowledge the actual terroristic activities of wholesale terrorists because they do not consider them news, because they generally do not examine critically the semantics used by officials, or they are not free to print such criticisms.

RETAIL TERRORISM

Identity and Goals of Retail Terrorists

Retail terrorism is practiced by small groups of passionately committed factions who desire recognition of their grievances by the government or politically powerful.[50] Within the category of retail terrorism are two separate groups: nationalistic and revolutionary terrorists.

Nationalistic terrorists share ethnonationalist links such as language, religion, or territory.[51] The IRA and the PLO are examples of such groups. They may be seeking religious hegemony in their state or demanding recognition of their existence through the provision of a representative voice and sanctified territory for their people.

Ethnocentrism is less important for revolutionary terrorists than for their nationalistic counterparts.[52] Such groups may consist of coalitions of differing nationalities, religions, languages, or customs mobilized to force fundamental changes. One of the most notable examples of such a coalition was the revolutionaries from the thirteen American colonies who defeated the British colonialists in the war for independence. Using the relatively unknown and highly unconventional tactic of guerrilla warfare, the revolutionary colonists employed highly effective terrorist tactics. Their successful campaign has served as a model for oppressed groups in many sections of the world during the past two hundred years.

Targets of Retail Terrorism

The targets of retail terrorists may be internal or external to the state or region in which they operate. Such targets may be representatives of local peer groups (here "internal common peer group") or a peer group of the opposing persons or institutions ("internal targeted peer group.") Targets may also be members of an international peer group similar to themselves or to the group opposing (called "external common peer group" and "external targeted peer group").

INTERNAL COMMON PEER GROUP An example of this type of retail terrorist target can be found in the Front de Libération Nationale (FLN), which attacked native indigenous Algerians in order to force them to join the revolution or be considered an enemy of it.[53]

INTERNAL TARGETED PEER GROUP In this example, the African National Congress (ANC) may terrorize a certain group of white South Africans in order to instill fear in all white South Africans.

EXTERNAL COMMON PEER GROUP Retail terrorists may attack a commonly identified enemy and its international peers to inspire sympathy for their cause. For example, Palestinians living in the United States may demonstrate in favor of the PLO after the PLO has attacked one of its identified enemies.

EXTERNAL TARGETED PEER GROUP When Iranian Jihad terrorists target American citizens overseas, they obviously send a message to all Americans to avoid the regions of the world in which the attacks occur.

Methods of Retail Terrorism

Retail terrorism is planned strategically to strike unpredictably, thereby generating a sustained apprehension in the minds of potential targets. Rather than desensitizing their targets to violence, retail terrorists use constant paranoia to create a distinct psychological advantage.[54]

Unlike wholesale terrorists, retail terrorists employ simple, reliable, and efficient weapons that can be easily assembled with commonly available raw materials.[55] They also tend to use materials readily obtainable on the black market. Their weapons need not be capable of mass destruction but rather need be only effective enough to be noticed.

In fact, one of the most useful weapons of retail terrorists is their capacity for "primitive" and, therefore, unexpected behavior. Suicide missions using simple plastic explosives are among the more effective tactics retails terrorists employ. Because the retail terrorists frequently appear irrational, defense against their attacks is difficult.[56]

It is important to note, however, that although the weapons used by retail terrorists are simple, they are frequently highly effective. For example, widely used plastic explosives, such as C-4 or Semtex, are temperature resistant, malleable, odorless, and easily camouflaged. They can damage nearly any common building material.[57] Retail terrorists tend not to have access to their own militia or planes and tanks as do wholesale terrorists. But their goal does not tend to be massive destruction. Simply, the weapons of retail terrorists are parsimonious to their needs.

Additionally, retail terrorists need only a group of three or four individuals to conduct attacks, as opposed to the highly trained and organized armies that wholesale terrorists sometimes employ. Because their groups are generally small and their members maintain civilian identities (and blend into their surroundings), retail terrorists are particularly difficult to identify.

Retail Terrorists and the Media: The Captured Audience

Because the news media are attracted to the kinds of violent episodes characteristic of retail terrorist attacks, terrorists expect media coverage of their events.[58] Publicity draws the attention of international audiences to their grievances and sometimes helps exert compelling influence on such audiences. And in the case of retail terrorists, some publicity is better than none, negative or otherwise. Through media coverage, retail terrorists hope to foster international criticism of their enemies and sympathy for their causes. They frequently do not achieve this. Nonetheless, it is clear that retail terrorists court media attention because the media provide essential opportunities for them to present their grievances.

News media critics accurately point out such evident manipulation by retail terrorists. Furthermore, public officials regularly suggest that the news media suppress coverage of retail terrorists in order to deny them the guaranteed platform they expect.[59]

What is missing from such criticism, however, is the overlooked fact that most media coverage fails to provide information that retail terrorists consider beneficial to their cause. For example, during the Iranian hostage crisis of 1979, in 444 guaranteed days of coverage, the majority of network news coverage focused on issues external to the Iranian situation such as the reaction of the hostages' families to the event, the declining health of the shah, and the health status of the hostages. Little contextual information, such as the internal political and social environments of the hostage-takers, was provided.[60] This missing information could have been used to help U.S. citizens understand Iran and thus possibly help prevent the occurrence of similar crises in the future.

Further, as the world shrinks, it is ever more important that the U.S. news media provide information the nation's citizens can use to really understand the reasons why their nation is involved in so many bloody confrontations with terrorist groups in other sections of the world. There is also a need for more information about the terroristic activities engaged in and supported by various public and private sectors of U.S. society.

GUIDELINES FOR COVERING TERRORISM

We agree that there is a need for the U.S. news media to adopt voluntary guidelines of some sort of reporting terrorism. But we are strongly opposed to most of the systems of censorship that have been touted by various individuals and groups during the past two decades. For example, we strongly urge that any guidelines adopted by the news media be carefully designed to promote accurate, informative, and unbiased reporting. Most important, appropriate guidelines will specifically reject the recommendation that journalists collaborate with police and other government agencies during terrorist episodes. We also urge that all media coverage of any given terrorist episode present the reasons *why* it is taking place.

With regard to the increasingly popular recommendation that the news media censor all news about terrorists, we recommend that a radically different approach be adopted. The press should devote far more attention to the political, racial, religious, class, and historical contexts in which terrorists operate—not less. This is necessary because such factors are essential to understanding why terrorist acts are committed, and what must be done to end them.

The tendency of U.S. journalists to use government spokespersons as primary sources of information during terrorist episodes has numerous political ramifications. It is especially significant with regard to the critically important decision regarding which groups do and do not get labeled terrorists. For example, the United States news media tend to use two governmentally influenced concepts of terrorism that are substantially biased.

The first is the practice of refusing to label groups supported by the U.S. government as terrorist. The second is their practice of defining terrorism as the use of violence to oppose governments favored by the U.S. government.

In light of such practices and in the interest of promoting press performance that will result in better understanding of terrorists, we propose the following guidelines for U.S. news media:

- Report terrorist demands concisely, free from propaganda. When no demands exist, seek to identify the causes of the episode—and the motivations of the terrorists.

- Seek to explain the significance of terrorist demands by focusing on contextual factors such as their political, racial, social, class, religious, and ethnic origins within context of the beliefs, attitudes, and values of the terrorists.

- Maintain the position of neutral observer—unless specifically requested to participate. If participation is elected, take no actions which may jeopardize objectivity. Provide information directly to law enforcement authorities only upon request. Such information should never be covertly surrendered.

- Never lose the perspective that lives are at stake.

- Constantly seek additional sources of information by consulting experts with varying perspectives in order to assure the provision of balanced contextual information. Report such information in moderate terms. Avoid the use of propaganda.

- Know who you are dealing with, and avoid the temptation to engage in careless, biased speculation.

- Never forget that terrorists are also human beings.

- Resolutely oppose any and all attempts to censor, or impose sanctions against, journalists or news agencies that reject these (or any other) guidelines for reporting terrorism.

More and better information about terrorism and its sources is particularly needed in the United States, which—due to the hegemonic, global objectives of the U.S. government—will almost certainly continue to experience deadly confrontations with terrorists for years to come. Assuming the best, our recommended approach to coverage of terrorism will be widely adopted by the U.S. press corps instead of the recommendation for coordinated censorship presently being touted by self-proclaimed protectors of "freedom's terrain."

NOTES

1. George Shultz, statement before the U.S. Senate Armed Services Committee, February 3, 1987.

2. "Venice States on East-West Relations, Terrorism and Persian Gulf," *New York Times,* June 10, 1987, p. 3.

3. Sarah Midgeley and Virginia Rice, eds. *Media and Terrorism in the 1980s* (Washington, D.C.: The Media Institute, 1984), p. viii.

4. Ibid., p. 8.

5. Charles Fenyvesi, "Looking Into the Muzzle of Terrorists," *The Quill* (July-August 1977):18.

6. "Hostage News Guide Proposed by Police Chief," *Editor & Publisher,* December 3, 1977, p. 15.

7. *Southern Newspaper Publishers Bulletin* (October 1977).

8. *Joint Low-Intensity Conflict Project,* Project Directive, Department of the Army, Headquarters, United States Army Training and Doctrine Command, Office of the Commanding General (July 1, 1985), p. B1.

9. *Joint Low-Intensity Conflict Project,* p. 15–1.

10. *Joint Low-Intensity Conflict Project,* p. 15–4.

11. *Joint Low-Intensity Conflict Project,* p. 15–7.

12. Quintus C. Wilson, "Military and Political Censorship of the Press During the Civil War," Publisher's Auxiliary 100th Anniversary Historical Series (January 1965).

13. Curtis D. MacDougall, *News Pictures Fit to Print* (Stillwater, Oklahoma: Journalistic Services, 1971).

14. *New York Times,* October 19, 1933.

15. MacDougall, *News Pictures Fit to Print,* p. 4.

16. C.A. McKnight, "Civil Rights and the Newspaper Editor," *Nieman Reports* 14 (June 1965):7.

17. John H. Fenton, "Katzenbach Asks Aid of Press," *New York Times,* July 23, 1965.

18. John Gregory Dunne, "Heightened Reality," *Columbia Journalism Review* (Fall 1965):17.

19. Margaret Halsey, "White Papers and Negro Readers," *New Republic* (October 16, 1965):18–20.

20. Edmonde A. Haddad, "A Code for Riot Reporting," *Columbia Journalism Review* (Spring 1967):35–36.

21. Hal Humphrey, "Three Networks Reject Riot Code," *Los Angeles Times,* August 21, 1967.

22. Humphrey, "Three Networks Reject."

23. Jeannette Hopkins, *Racial Justice and the Press* (New York: Metropolitan Applied Research Center, September 1968), p. 27.

24. Hopkins, *Racial Justice,* p. 27.

25. *Report of the National Advisory Commission on Civil Disorders* (Washington, D.C.: U.S. Government Printing Office, 1968), pp. 378–81.

26. *New York Times,* June 10, 1977, p. 15.

27. "Terrorism and News Judgments: In Search of Definable Boundaries," *The Quill* (April 1977): 12.

28. David K. Shipler, "Council Is Planned to Monitor the Press," *New York Times*, December 1, 1972, p. 53.

29. "Without Portfolio: Delicate Dilemma of TV Journalism," *Broadcast* (December 24, 1979):24.

30. "Without Portfolio," p. 22.

31. J. Bowyer Bell, "Terrorist Scripts and Live-Action Spectaculars," *Columbia Journalism Review* (May/June 1978):47–50.

32. W.B. Jaehnig, "Journalists and Terrorism: Captives of the Libertarian Tradition," 53 *Indiana Law Journal*, p. 743.

33. Daniel Schorr, "TV and Terrorism: The Ego Trap," *Denver Post*, December 31, 1979, p. 16.

34. Paul Harris, "Carter's 'Go Easy' Statement on Coverage of Iran Could Erupt Into Government-Media Flap," *Variety* (April 23, 1980): p. 52.

35. M. Cherif Bassiouni, "Media Coverage of Terrorism: The Law and the Public," 32 *Journal of Communication* (1985): 140–42.

36. "Does TV Help or Hurt," *Newsweek* (July 1, 1985):32.

37. "King Henry of the Airwaves," *Newsweek* (July 1, 1985):37.

38. Ibid.,

39. Charles Krauthammer, "Looking Evil Dead in the Eye," *Time* (July 15, 1985):80.

40. R.W. Apple Jr., "Thatcher Urges the Press to Help 'Starve' Terrorists," *New York Times*, July 16, 1985, p. A3.

41. Ibid.

42. "Calls for a Code on Terrorist Coverage," *Broadcasting* (July 22, 1985):36.

43. Margaret Genovese, "Terrorism: Special Report," *Presstime* (August 1986), p. 32.

44. Edward S. Herman, "Power and the Semantics of Terrorism," *Covert Action Information Bulletin* 26 (Summer 1986):10.

45. Martha Crenshaw Hutchinson, *Revolutionary Terrorism* (Stanford: Hoover Institution, 1978), p. 2.

46. Huchinson, *Revolutionary Terrorism*, p. 25.

47. Herman, "Power and the Semantics of Terrorism," p. 10.

48. Wayne Biddle, "It Must Be Simple and Reliable . . ." *Discover* (June 1986):22–31.

49. Hutchinson, *Revolutionary Terrorism*, p. 14.

50. Biddle, "It Must Be Simple and Reliable . . .," p. 22.

51. Ibid., p. 23.

52. Ibid., p. 24.

53. Hutchinson, *Revolutionary Terrorism*, pp. 19–39.

54. Ibid.

55. Biddle, "It Must Be Simple and Reliable," p. 25.

56. Ibid., p. 26.

57. Ibid., p. 27.

58. For discussion of retail terrorists' use of media see Ralph Dowling, "Terrorism and the Media: A Rhetorical Genre," *Journal of Communication* 35 (Winter 1986): 12–24; Bassiouni, "Media Coverage of Terrorism", Philip Elliott, Graham Murdock, and Philip Schlesinger, " 'Terrorism' and the State: A Case Study of the Discourse of Television," 5 *Media, Culture and Society* (April 1983):155–77; and Gabriel Weimann, "The Theater of Terror: Effects of Press Coverage," *Journal of Communication* 33 (Winter 1985): 38–46.

59. See Bassiouni, "Media Coverage of Terrorism"; Abraham H. Miller, "Terrorism, Media and the Law: A Discussion of the Issues," in Abraham H. Miller, ed., *Terrorism, Media, and the Law* (Dobbs Ferry, N.Y.: Transnational Publishers, 1982); Patrick V. Murphy, "The Police, the News Media and the Law," in Miller, ed., *Terrorism, Media and the Law;* and Noam Chomsky, "Libya in U.S. Demonology," *Covert Action Information Bulletin* 26 (Summer 1986).

60. David L. Altheide, "Three-in-One News: Network Coverage of Iran," *Journalism Quarterly* 59 (Autumn 1982):482–86.

CHAPTER 8

Media Compliance with Voluntary Press Guidelines for Covering Terrorism

by Timothy Gallimore

INTRODUCTION

THE PURPOSE OF THIS CHAPTER is to measure the extent of media compliance with the voluntary guidelines that news organizations and professional journalism organizations have adopted for covering terrorism. A content analysis was performed on the media's coverage of the 1982 Washington Monument seige and the hijacking of Pan Am Flight 73 in Karachi, Pakistan, in 1986. The study is an attempt to measure how well the media performed based on the common codes and major principles of responsibility that the media themselves have set for the coverage of terrorism.

There is much debate over whether or not the media ought to adopt any guidelines to direct coverage of any kind. The media have said that their professional codes of ethics and the First Amendment protection for the press are sufficient to guide their coverage of terrorism and the like. Some of the controversy over voluntary codes for news coverage is related to media fear of legal enforcement of those guidelines. Without entering that polemic, suffice it to say that the results of this study show that reliance on professional codes of ethics and on rhetoric invoking First Amendment freedoms for the press have not led to the most professional or responsible coverage of terrorism. Some media organizations have adopted specific written guidelines for covering terrorism. But what the media have said in their guidelines did not always match what appeared in their coverage of the terrorist incidents analyzed for this study.

SIGNIFICANCE OF THE PROBLEM

There is a need for the media to self-regulate to avoid possible restrictive legislation on how they will cover terrorism and other potentially explosive stories. Guidelines allow the media to set the criteria for professionally ac-

ceptable and responsible performance. If the media do not continue to promote and comply with standards of acceptable performance, then they will
find themselves acquiescing to responsibility standards set by others—possibly by the government.

The research problem is extremely significant in assessing how well the
media are meeting their responsibility in providing coverage of terrorism. It
is critical to analyze the media's performance under circumstances that present a worst-case scenario for their actions to have detrimental impact. If
the media are to live up to their espoused doctrine of self-policing and responsible individual news judgment, then we should expect these professional principles to be at their height of implementation where the most caution is needed. This type of analysis should demonstrate if the media really
live up to the high ideals of their professional codes of ethics and specific
codes for responsible coverage of terrorism.

The problem is of particular importance to the broadcast industry, which
could be subjected to some form of regulation if self-imposed measures do
not produce responsible coverage and acceptable behavior of journalists
covering terrorism and related issues. The increasing use of mobile satellite
ground stations adds to the importance of having some firm standard of responsible coverage. The new technology now enables local television stations to beam any story—live—to a national audience. The established networks now get information from these local stations, which may not exercise
the same level of caution and journalistic excellence as the national media.
The technology also allows for ad hoc and co-op networks to develop for
sharing, instantly, dramatic footage that might not meet the industry's standard of responsibility.

Despite the general statements of responsibility found in professional
codes of ethics, there is a standard of acceptable performance in covering
terrorism. There are some things that the media do and others that they
refrain from doing when covering terrorist incidents or other news items
requiring special handling. Judy Henry of the Cable News Network (CNN)
in Atlanta said the network "took some serious heat" on its coverage of the
Challenger space shuttle story. That heat came from other news organizations because CNN reported one aspect of the tragedy live. "It was just
coincidental that we happened to be on the McAuliffe family at the time,"
Henry said in explaining CNN's televising of the family's immediate reaction to the explosion.[1] Media actions are being channeled by some criteria
other than those found in the professional codes of ethics. Media organizations, like CNN, that have not adopted written codes are still being evalu-
ated according to some measure of responsibility held by their peers.

RESEARCH QUESTIONS

What then are the present measures of responsible terrorism coverage?
And are the media complying with these voluntary standards of performance? to answer these questions, a survey of media outlets and profes-

Table 8.1. Media and Professional Journalism Organizations
Surveyed for Codes

ORGANIZATION	CONTACT	RESPONSE	CODE
UPI	Pieter VanBennekom	letter	Yes
AP	Walter Mears	letter	No
ABC	Robert Siegenthaler	letter	Yes
CBS	Van Gordon Sauter	letter	Yes
CNN	Ed Turner	letter	No
NBC	Thomas Ross	letter	Yes
ASNE (American Society of Newspaper Editors)	Lee Stinnett	letter	No
ASME (American Society of Magazine Editors)	Robert Kenyon, Jr.	letter	No
Washington Post	Richard Harwood	letter	No
NAB (National Association of Broadcasters)	Edward Fritts	letter	No
NPPA (National Press Photographers Association)	Michael Sherer	letter	No
Christian Science Monitor	Katherine Fanning	letter	No
RTNDA (Radio-Television News Directors Association)	Ernie Schultz	letter	No
SPJ (Society for Professional Journalists)	Russ Tornabene	letter	No
U.S. News & World Report	Henry Trewhitt	phone	No
Newsweek	Maynard Parker	phone	No
Time	Henry Grunwald	none	
Chicago Sun-Times	Ken Towers	none	
Chicago Tribune	James Squires	none	
New York Times	A.M. Rosenthal	none	

sional journalism organizations was conducted to find out what codes and guidelines the media had adopted to delineate the parameters of responsibility. A content analysis was also conducted to judge how well media coverage conformed to the principles and measures of responsibility found in the codes.

Copies of codes were solicited from thirty media and journalism organizations. The organizations listed in Table 8.1 were asked to forward copies of whatever codes they had adopted for covering terrorism. Ten television stations in Indianapolis, Boston, and Washington, D.C., were also included in the guidelines survey. Of the twenty organizations responding, four have written codes for covering terrorism. Another three said they did not have written guidelines specifically on coverage of terrorism but that they did have "general guidelines, statements, or an approach" to covering terrorism and other news items involving violence.

The results of the survey fall pretty much along the lines of the dispute over the need for adopting codes. Only one (UPI) of the professional associations and the print media in the survey has adopted codes. The print media usually advance the strongest First Amendment argument against adopting codes, but the broadcast media, being already subject to some government regulation, seem to be more concerned about self-regulation in covering terrorism. Although the Associated Press (AP) does not have written codes for covering terrorism, it does have "general guidelines drawn from experience" to help direct its coverage.

The codes that were submitted can be categorized into standards for responsible coverage and standards for governing the behavior of journalists at the scene of terrorist incidents. From these various codes, some common themes emerge as the do's and don'ts of covering terrorism. The following list could be said to represent the media's responsibility standard.

1. No reliance on terrorists or authorities as sole sources.
2. Balance the volume of news on the incident so that other news of the day will not be crowded out.
3. Provide context, perspective, background, possible motivation of the terrorists, and causes of the incident.
4. Do not disclose police or rescue plans.
5. Do not use inflammatory catchwords or report rumors.
6. Protect the lives of hostages by withholding their identity if disclosure will result in harm.
7. Report terrorists' demands and deadlines but don't provide a platform for terrorists.
8. Involve top management in tough decisions about coverage.
9. Do not participate in incidents or serve as a negotiator.
10. Respect the privacy of hostages and their families.

The common themes in the guidelines match the common elements in stories about terrorism and represent the problem areas that journalists must be constantly aware of. Journalists walk a tightrope between coverage of a legitimate news story and providing a stage for terrorists. These voluntary guidelines help identify the fine line that they must draw in the reporting process. The major research question for the study is: To what extent did the news media comply with their voluntary guidelines in their coverage of the Washington Monument seige and the Pan Am hijacking terrorist incidents?

METHODOLOGY

The analysis focuses on the first three common themes in the media codes for terrorism coverage—source reliance, volume of coverage, and inclusion of context and background information. These are the responsibility criteria most easily measured. The first criterion addresses the need to report terrorists' demands without giving them free and unedited access to air time. The confirmation of information via a multiplicity of sources is a safeguard against reporting rumor, manipulation by terrorists, and official censorship of the news.

Attention to the volume of coverage given to terrorist incidents is a responsibility measure to put the incidents in the proper perspective of the other important news events of the day. It is also an attempt by the media to make sure that terrorists do not commandeer coverage space and time and turn the media into their authorized propagandists to get sanction for their messages.

Coupled with the proper balance of time and space allotted to terrorist acts, the context-background-causes criterion is aimed at helping the audience correctly interpret the terrorist news event. The measure is also aimed at explaining what the act means without providing a stage for perpetrators. The media must give a reason why they chose to cover the incident and why it is important for the audience to know about the terrorists, their acts, and their purposes.

Coverage of the Washington Monument seige was chosen for analysis because the incident represents a type of potentially recurring domestic story that the media will always have to deal with. The seige incident occurred on December 8, 1982, when Norman Mayer, a long-time nuclear protester, threatened to blow up the Monument with one thousand pounds of explosives he claimed was loaded in a van that he parked at the base of the structure. Mayer held eight people hostage at the monument until a reporter negotiated their release. The ten-hour seige was ended when police sharpshooters killed Mayer as he attempted to drive the van from the scene.

Many news organizations may excuse themselves from the guidelines-responsibility debate by saying that they do not provide first-hand coverage of international terrorism—the popular fare of the day. But no news outlet is insulated from the occasional "gunman on the loose" who takes hostages, threatens to blow up public buildings, or forces disc jockeys and television reporters to air messages live. Whether they want to admit it or not, all media outlets are potential victims of terrorist manipulation, and without forethought, preparation, and a plan of action, their coverage under the pressure of a terrorist event may not reach the highest standard of responsibility and professionalism.

The second incident, the hijacking of Pan Am Flight 73 in Karachi, Pakistan, was chosen for the analysis because it represents a recent media encounter with a major international terrorist incident. On September 5, 1986, four armed men dressed as security guards stormed a Pan Am jet in transit from Bombay to New York. The crew escaped but the terrorists held the 350 passengers on the runway for fifteen hours. When lights in the plane went out, the hijackers opened fire and tossed grenades killing seventeen people and injuring about one hundred others. Two of the hijackers were killed and two captured by Pakistani security forces.

Although the incident was not as prolonged as other hijackings, it does provide an appropriate context in which to examine media coverage. Much of the debate about voluntary guidelines and the evaluations of past performance in the TWA Beirut and *Achille Lauro* hijackings had taken place before the Karachi hijacking, and the media therefore had time to make their own assessments and position themselves for improved coverage of the recurring threat.

The major news magazines *Newsweek, Time,* and *U.S. News & World Report* were chosen for the content analysis because their weekly publication cycle allows for more time between the occurrence of news events and their presentation. It is assumed that the additional time afforded these publications would lead to better, more detailed, and responsible coverage since there is more time to gather information, interview a variety of sources, and to ferret out background and contextual material that would meet the news industry's most rigorous responsibility standards. The magazines, therefore, provide the best opportunity to compare broadcast coverage of the same incidents which was done under shorter deadlines, more pressure, with less complete information, and little chance to get detailed contextual material.

The coverage done by the major television networks—ABC, CBS, and NBC—was also analyzed for the study. It must be noted that the actual broadcasts were not viewed. Measures of source reliance, volume of coverage, and contextual background information were derived from the *Television News Index and Abstracts*. This index describes the contents of network news broadcast tapes held at the Vanderbilt Television News Archive. The index gives the names of sources quoted in news items, the amount of time devoted to each news item, the length of each newscast, and a brief description of the tape coverage.

A crisis period was identified for each of the two incidents. The crisis period begins on the day of the event, continues through the development of the story, and ends with reporting on the aftermath of the incident. For the Monument seige incident, a fourteen-day crisis period between December 8 and December 20, 1982, was used for the analysis. In the Pan Am hijacking incident, the crisis period was set between September 5 and September 30, 1986. All news items appearing in the six media outlets identified above were analyzed based on variables constructed to measure compliance with the following codes: 1) source reliance (terrorist, authority, other); 2) balance in the volume of news on the incidents versus other news; and 3) context, perspective, background, motivation, and causes reported.

Source reliance was measured by counting the number of sources identified or quoted in news items. The sources were placed into three categories—terrorist, authority, or other. The terrorist category includes, in addition to the perpetrators of the terrorist act, individuals who were identified as sources of terrorists' demands or claims for responsibility. The authority category includes police officials, elected government representatives, governmental spokespersons, leaders of foreign countries, or anyone acting or speaking in an official, law enforcement, or governmental capacity. The third category includes all sources who are neither terrorists nor authority sources.

The volume of coverage was measured by the number of paragraphs devoted to the incident in the magazines and the number of minutes in the network newscasts. The percentage of coverage devoted to the terrorist incidents was calculated on the basis of the number of paragraphs of coverage each incident received in relation to the total newshole (number of paragraphs) in the section of the magazine where the story appeared. The paragraph was chosen as the unit of measure because complete ideas are usually expressed in paragraphs, copy-fitting is done by paragraphs, and readers tend to read to the end of paragraphs.

The percentage of broadcast coverage granted to each incident was measured by the number of minutes each item received of the total news time for each broadcast. The news time was calculated by subtracting the number of minutes taken up by commercials from the total air time of each newscast. The number of paragraphs and details in those paragraphs that were devoted to explaining motivations, causes, and issues was used to measure the context provided in the print media coverage. The description of the broadcast coverage in the *Television News Index and Abstracts* was not adequate for identifying the context or background information in the networks' reports of the terrorist incidents. No attempt was made to measure the context of the broadcast coverage.

The total number of news stories on each incident was included in the analysis along with general reports and evaluation pieces on terrorism that appeared during the crisis period. These other items were included because TV newscasts often present them as a way to provide context and background to the dramatic crisis event and as an attempt to explore the issues and causes of the problem.

From the content analysis, the following evaluations and comparisons can be made: compliance of each media outlet with three of the common principles of responsible media coverage; compliance by print versus broadcast compliance; compliance by media with codes versus media without codes; and the change in media coverage and compliance between the two incidents.

FINDINGS

A total of fourteen magazine news stories and eleven days of network newscasts were analyzed. The two terrorist incidents combined had 181 sources in 172 paragraphs and 99 minutes of coverage. The media as a whole relied on terrorists as news sources only 6 percent of the time for coverage of both incidents (see Table 8.2 and Table 8.3 below.) The only pronounced difference in the source reliance variable is in the print media's use of terrorists as sources. There were no terrorists identified as sources in the broadcast coverage of either incident. The eleven times that terrorists were sources occurred in the magazine coverage. *Time* magazine had the greatest

Table 8.2. Source Reliance Terrorist Incident:
Monument Seige

MEDIA	SOURCES			
	TERRORIST	AUTHORITY	OTHER	TOTAL
Newsweek	1 (11%)	2 (22%)	6 (67%)	9
Time	1 (20%)	3 (60%)	1 (20%)	5
U.S. News	0 (0%)	0 (0%)	1 (100%)	1
ABC	0 (0%)	3 (60%)	2 (40%)	5
CBS	0 (0%)	2 (33%)	4 (67%)	6
NBC	0 (0%)	5 (56%)	4 (44%)	9
Totals	2	15	18	35
	(6%)	(43%)	(51%)	(100%)

reliance on terrorist sources with four of its twenty-five sources (16 percent)
in the two incidents being terrorists.

Authority figures made up 43 percent of the sources in the Washington
Monument seige story and 40 percent in the Pan Am hijacking incident. Of
the 181 sources identified in the coverage of both incidents, seventy-three
of them (40 percent) were authority sources (see Table 8.4 below.) The 40
percent authority source reliance indicates that the media have a high degree
of compliance with their responsibility criterion of not depending on officials
as the dominant source of information in terrorist incidents.

The assessment of a lower than normal reliance on authority sources
when covering terrorist incidents is also supported by other studies of

Table 8.3. Source Reliance Terrorist Incident: Pan
Am Hijacking

MEDIA	SOURCES			
	TERRORIST	AUTHORITY	OTHER	TOTAL
Newsweek	5 (10%)	25 (51%)	19 (39%)	49
Time	3 (15%)	5 (25%)	12 (60%)	20
U.S. News	1 (6%)	9 (56%)	6 (38%)	16
ABC	0 (0%)	6 (32%)	13 (68%)	19
CBS	0 (0%)	7 (37%)	12 (63%)	19
NBC	0 (0%)	6 (26%)	17 (74%)	23
Totals	9	58	79	146
	(6%)	(40%)	(54%)	(100%)

Table 8.4. Media Reliance on Authority
Sources, Both Terrorist Incidents

MEDIA	AUTHORITY	PERCENTAGE	TOTAL
Newsweek	27	47%	58
Time	8	32%	25
U.S. News	9	53%	17
ABC	9	38%	24
CBS	9	36%	25
NBC	11	34%	32
Total	73	40%	181

sources in news stories. In a recent study, Dan Berkowitz found that TV news uses more government officials as news sources than other kinds of news sources. He found that 48.6 percent of the sources on network news and 49.3 percent on local TV news are official government sources. "Television and newspapers do not differ meaningfully in their reliance on government sources for news information," according to the study.[2]

As shown in Table 8.4. only *U.S. News & World Report* had a reliance on authority sources (53 percent) that is higher than the percentages reported in the Berkowitz study. It might be argued, however, that media reliance on authority sources in their overall news coverage—and terrorism coverage—is too great.

The print media had the most reliance on authority sources with forty-four out of their one hundred total sources (44 percent) being authorities (see Table 8.5 below.) This compares with a 36 percent reliance by the broadcast media on authorities. Twenty-nine of the eighty-one broadcast sources were coded as authority sources. Although there is an 8 percent difference in reliance on authority sources between print and broadcast media, the findings of this analysis are not enough to conclude that the networks' codes for terrorism coverage are a significant contributing factor to the observed difference.

Table 8.5. Source Reliance of Print and Broadcast Media,
Both Terrorist Incidents

MEDIA	SOURCES			
	TERRORIST	AUTHORITY	OTHER	TOTAL
Print	11 (11%)	44 (44%)	45 (45%)	100
Broadcast	0 (0%)	29 (36%)	52 (64%)	81
Totals	11 (6%)	73 (40%)	97 (54%)	181 (100%)

Table 8.6. Volume of Print Media Coverage, Both Terrorist Incidents

MEDIA	INCIDENT COVERAGE	NEWSHOLE	TOTAL NEWSHOLE
Newsweek	91 paragraphs	35%	259 paragraphs
Time	37 paragraphs	19%	190 paragraphs
U.S. News	44 paragraphs	30%	147 paragraphs
Total	172	(29%)	596

The print media devoted 29 percent of their available news space to coverage of the two terrorist incidents during the identified crisis periods. And the broadcasters devoted 23 percent of their news time to the incidents (see Table 8.6 and Table 8.7.) The available news space or newshole was based on the number of paragraphs in the section of the magazine where the terrorism story appeared. The Monument seige story appeared in the national news section of *Newsweek* and *Time* and in the "Currents in the News" summary section of *U.S. News & World Report*. The hijacking incident also appeared once in the "Currents" section. All other coverage of the hijacking appeared in the foreign news sections of the three magazines.

Based on the available news space in each media, the print media gave slightly more (6 percent) coverage to the incidents than did the networks. The existence of broadcast media codes against crowding out other news with excessive terrorism coverage does not seem to differ much in absolute terms between print and broadcast media treatment of the incidents analyzed in the study.

Newsweek gave the highest percentage (35 percent) of its newshole to coverage of the two incidents. This was due to a special section in the September 15, 1986, issue that was devoted the hijacking incident. Coverage of the hijacking took 52 percent of *Newsweek*'s newshole and 41 percent of the available space in the print media (see Table 8.8.) The *Newsweek* special section adds to the appearance that the print media were a little heavy on their coverage of the hijacking incident and may have crowded out other

Table 8.7. Volume of Broadcast Media Coverage,
Both Terrorist Incidents

MEDIA	TERRORISM COVERAGE	TIME	TOTAL TIME
ABC	31 min. 20 sec.	21%	150 min.
CBS	31 min. 30 sec.	29%	110 min. 30 sec.
NBC	36 min.	21%	171 min. 20 sec.
Total	98 min. 50 sec.	(23%)	431 min. 50 sec.

Table 8.8. Volume of Print Media Coverage Terrorist Incident: Pan Am Hijacking

MEDIA	INCIDENT COVERAGE	NEWSHOLE	TOTAL NEWSHOLE
Newsweek	83 paragraphs*	52%	160 paragraphs
Time	29 paragraphs	30%	96 paragraphs
U.S. News	34 paragraphs	33%	102 paragraphs
Total	146	(41%)	358

* Includes special 45-paragraph section on terrorism in the 9/15/86 issue.

news of the day as the guidelines warn. It must be noted that none of the print media surveyed had adopted any written codes.

It must also be noted that the analysis of the broadcast coverage was confined only to those newscasts that appeared in the *Television News Index and Abstracts*. No special news broadcasts, such as the ABC News "Night-line" program, were included in the analysis. Also, not all three network newscasts were indexed for the weekend that fell during the crisis period of the hijacking incident. One day of the ABC and NBC coverage was not indexed and 2 days of the CBS weekend newscast were not indexed. Broadcast coverage of the hijacking is shown in Table 8.9.

Coverage of the two terrorist incidents in the six media outlets accounted for approximately 7 percent of the total available newshole or air time during the combined crisis periods. The percentage of space or time devoted to terrorism by each news organization was as follows: *Newsweek,* 15 percent; *Time,* 6 percent; *U.S. News & World Report,* 7 percent; ABC, 7 percent; CBS, 7 percent; NBC, 8 percent. Overall, the media did not focus on terrorism coverage to the exclusion of other news. But as already noted, the print media's coverage of the hijacking story accounted for a significant portion of the news volume for the period of the analysis.

It was considerably more difficult to measure coverage by the context-

Table 8.9. Volume of Broadcast Media Coverage Terrorist Incident: Pan Am Hijacking

MEDIA	INCIDENT COVERAGE	TIME	TOTAL TIME
ABC	25 min. 20 sec.	24%	107 min.
CBS	22 min. 10 sec.	33%	66 min. 30 sec.
NBC	27 min.	21%	127 min. 50 sec.
Total	74 min. 30 sec.	(25%)	301 min. 20 sec.

background-motivation-causes variable. Because the broadcast tapes were not viewed, measurement of the context variable would not be practical. Only a modest amount (10 percent) of context material was provided by the print media. Seventeen and a half of the 172 paragraphs of coverage were devoted to context and background material. The Monument seige story had a higher percentage of context information (21 percent) than the larger, more publicized hijacking incident (8 percent). Much of the seige background material emphasized the perpetrator, Norman Mayer, as a lonely, "troubled, but strangely sympathetic" fanatic incapable of making rational decisions. *Time* said this characterization of Mayer was "an appropriate epitaph for a flawed, ramshackled life that concluded with a bungled, irrational gesture."[3]

The context information in the hijacking incident was even more disappointing. Only twelve of the 146 paragraphs of coverage were coded as context-background material. And most of that information focused on the U.S. get-tough policy, revenge against Libya's Colonel Qadaffi, and Western frustrations over not knowing who to strike back at. One article concluded, "But with no solid line on the Karachi bloodbath's sponsors and therefore no target for reprisals, American officials could only fume and serve fresh warnings that attacks against American citizens would not go unpunished whether abetted by Qadhafi or anyone else."[4]

The print media did not score as high on the context-background measure of responsibility as they did on the other two criteria found in the codes. This is a very important measure of the quality of terrorism coverage since it indicates the depth of the reporting that was done. The media, no doubt, are concerned with giving the relevant background information without serving as mouthpieces for the various terrorist groups and individuals. This reasoning might have influenced the volume of background information in the items analyzed. But at best, the content of the coverage offered can be categorized as lacking in substance and capacity to inform the reader in any significant way about the causes of terrorism the possible motivation of terrorists.

EXAMPLES OF VIOLATIONS AND COMPLIANCE WITH CODES

Examples of violations of the voluntary codes and measures of responsible reporting abound. In an apparent attempt to castigate broadcasters for their coverage of the Monument seige, *U.S. News & World Report* committed the most flagrant violation of the letter and spirit of the responsibility measures. Coverage of the story in the magazine began with the following lead: "A 10-hour siege of the Washington Monument demonstrated that one determined person can tie up the nation's capital, disrupt the federal government and broadcast any kind of message through an ever available news media."[5]

The story continued to lend even more support to the media "contagion effect'' that many terrorism experts complain of. According to the account, ''For hours he [Norman Mayer] succeeded in getting his ideas publicized from coast to coast. . . . Hundreds of reporters—about as many as there were policemen—converged on the scene. Television networks interrupted soap operas and prime-time shows to broadcast on-the-spot developments.''[6]

U.S. News was not alone in its criticism of the broadcast media's coverage. The *Newsweek* report of the seige also stated that ''thanks to massive radio and television coverage—the whole nation, in a sense, became his captive.''[7] It could be said that the print media did one better for Mayer than did broadcast in that the print media also became his captives even after his death. The magazines may not have provided Mayer with a platform but there is a question as to whether their coverage may not have provided some other would-be terrorist with the additional motivation to stage an act that would bring similar uncensored exposure as Mayer reportedly got.

Although this study did not treat the common themes in the codes concerning proper, responsible behavior of journalists in getting a terrorism story, there are a few instances of apparent violations that surfaced even in the coverage that was analyzed. Journalists are involved in the most important aspect of terrorism, that of receiving and transmitting terrorists' demands. In the Monument seige incident, Associated Press reporter Steve Kamarow even served as a negotiator. One of the voluntary codes states that journalists should avoid participation in terrorist incidents and should *not* serve as negotiators.

Not only were the media responsible for publicizing Mayer's demands, one of their members helped to get him what he demanded. *Time* magazine reported details of how Mayer got his message to the park police that he intended to negotiate only with a member of the media. A section of the note was quoted. Mayer wanted to talk to ''a single person without dependents.'' According to *Time,* after the demand Steve Kamarow ''was selected as the emissary.''[8]

Another troubling finding of the study is the prevalent role of the media as the conduit of terrorists' demands and claims of responsibility. In this respect, the media seem not to be concerned about performing this function for even the most obscure groups seeking publicity, or at least name recognition. The hijacking stories were full of reports of conflicting claims of responsibility and denials by various anonymous callers and letter writers. The media also did not fail to give their speculations and impressions about the possible perpetrators.

The problem is perhaps best illustrated by quoting a portion of the coverage that was analyzed. An anonymous Arab reportedly called a

> Western news agency office in Nicosia, Cyprus, and claimed responsibility for the Libyan Revolutionary Cells, a previously unknown group. Denials came almost instantaneously from Radio Tripoli and from Gaddafi. . . . Next, an obscure Shi'ite organization calling itself Jundullah, or Soldiers of God, announced

it was responsible. Most Western intelligence agencies were skeptical. . . . As usual, even the identity and motivation of the terrorists involved were uncertain, though there was little doubt that they were Palestinian.[9]

When there is uncertainty, perhaps silence on the identification of the responsible group and directing callers and claimants to the authorities with demands and responsibility claims would be the most prudent and professional course of action for the media.

In addition to general compliance with the source and volume of coverage codes, there are a few other instances of compliance or responsible reporting that was done by the media. Although the context-background responsibility criterion received the least compliance of the three examined in the analysis, there is a good example of providing perspective, motivations, and causes of terrorism. *U.S. News* not only had the most flagrant violation of the codes, but it also had the most significant context-background information.

In its report on the hijacking, *U.S. News* concluded that

> most often, large-scale terrorism has at least vague policy objectives. Should current attacks continue, they could derail American efforts to promote Arab-Israeli peace and resolve the future of the Israeli-occupied West Bank of the Jordan River region. That is the real, if sometimes unstated, goal of several radical Arab groups and nations.[10]

This statement is the only one in the coverage that I would say exposed or identified the causes of international terrorism and the possible motivation of its perpetrators.

SUMMARY AND CONCLUSIONS

Based on the findings of the study, the media displayed no reliance on either terrorists or authorities as the sole news sources in covering the two terrorist incidents. The percentage of authority sources in the terrorism coverage is lower than the percentage found in overall news coverage by the media. The print media relied more on authority sources (44 percent) than the broadcast media (36 percent). This difference in source reliance and the heavier volume of coverage (29 percent) in print—broadcast (23 percent)—suggests that the print media ought not to lean so exclusively on their professional codes of ethics and on the First Amendment to ensure the highest standard of responsible terrorism coverage.

The lack of significant volume and substance in the context and background information in the coverage indicated that the media need to pay more attention to the larger issues and causes of terrorism. There is a lot of terrorism coverage and it tends to focus on the dramatic crisis event and reactions to it. But not enough perspective, explanation, and exploration of causes, motivations, and background information on perpetrators was presented. This missing element of coverage can be a significant media contribution to reducing and eliminating the terrorism problem. Norman Mayer wanted more coverage of a legitimate issue—the nuclear freeze—for which he was willing to stage the crisis event that the media agree brought an early end to his lonely, pitiful, and ramshackled life.[11]

This chapter should be viewed as a pilot study into the important area of media compliance with voluntary codes to ensure responsible reporting of terrorism. More analysis and research needs to be done. A survey-questionnaire of the journalists and editors involved in the coverage of these two incidents should be conducted to assess compliance with the "behavior codes" and the decision-making process that the media said they would follow.

The wire copy of the AP and UPI should be analyzed to assess the compliance of journalists under the gun of providing immediate information. The importance of the wire services in covering terrorism can be underscored by no greater claim than that made in the coverage of the Pan Am hijacking incident. According to the *Newsweek* account, "Pentagon officials learned about the hijacking from wire-service reports."[12]

Newspaper coverage needs to be included in any future analysis. The coverage of Cable News Network (CNN), "the AP of TV," should also be included in any complete analysis of media performance in covering terrorism. The inclusion of CNN would add more material—instant reporting—from which a more accurate reading on media compliance with the guidelines can be obtained. Not only could the content of the reports be analyzed, but the actions of reporters and editors are more easily documented when there is live reporting. Live reporting also holds out the possibility of the media influencing the outcome of a terrorist incident since the coverage often seems to be a dialogue between the media and the perpetrators.

Finally, the coverage provided by local TV and radio stations should be analyzed where archival tapes exist of their coverage of such incidents. Local broadcast media codes and compliance with those codes should be assessed since these outlets face the constant possibility of having to cover domestic hostage-takings, seiges, and bomb threats. Local stations, too, can have dramatic influence on the outcome of these incidents.

The scathing comments made in the *U.S. News* and *Newsweek* Monument seige stories are testimony to the need for studying this facet of the problem and for raising the question of local broadcasters' commitment to responsible presentation of terrorist events. Aside from network interruptions of soap operas and prime-time shows with live terrorism coverage, the assessment of local TV and radio performance might be a legitimate instance of broadcast bashing. Perhaps two different sets of responsibility standards and codes need to be developed by the media to adequately treat their coverage of domestic and international terrorism.

NOTES

1. Judy Henry, assistant to Ed Turner, executive vice president of CNN, telephone interview, February 10, 1988.

2. Dan Berkowitz, "TV News Sources and News Channels: A Study in Agenda-Building," *Journalism Quarterly* 64 (Summer-Autumn 1987): 510.

3. "One Man's Tragic Protest," *Time* (December 20, 1982):27.

4. "After the Lull: Terror, Death, Frustration," *U.S. News & World Report* (September 15, 1986):7.

5. "When Washington Was Hostage," *U.S. News & World Report* (December 20, 1982):13.

6. "When Washington Was Hostage," p. 13.

7. "The Man at the Monument," *Newsweek* (December 20, 1982): p. 37.

8. "One Man's Tragic Protest," p. 24.

9. "Carnage Once Again," *Time* (September 15, 1986):31.

10. "After the Lull," p. 7.

11. "One Man's Tragic Protest."

12. "A Rescue That Never Happened," *Newsweek* (September 15, 1986): p. 26.

PART IV

Covering Terrorism

CHAPTER 9

Broadcast Gatekeepers and Terrorism

by L. John Martin and Joseph Draznin

MUCH HAS BEEN SAID and written about the relationship between terrorist events and the media. This relationship is most commonly viewed as symbiotic. Terrorists conduct their "spectacular events" for the media, especially the broadcast media, and the media cannot resist covering them.[1] The ultimate objective of terrorists, mostly ideologically motivated individuals and groups, is to gain psychological effects through publicity. The media, especially television, are constantly being criticized for that coverage and for playing into the hands of terrorists.

Terrorism as news needs to be viewed from several viewpoints. From the viewpoint of the terrorist, he or she is "choreographing a news event," as Brian Jenkins terms it,[2] or as Gabriel Weimann puts it, is writing a script for a "theater of terror."[3] The terrorist's interest is in communicating something to the public.[4] To a lesser extent, of course, terrorists intend to do more than keep a cause in the public eye and at the same time add an important card—if not *the* most important card—to the negotiating deck of the group. The purposes include replenishing the coffers of the group; recruiting new members; reinforcing the commitment of existing members; freeing members who have been apprehended; providing a sense of importance to the group and especially to the leaders; fulfilling a need for adventure; and even satisfying a desire for revenge, an act not unlike sticking pins in dolls.[5]

From the viewpoint of the police or of public officials responsible for keeping the peace of the community, terrorism is a breach of the peace. In part they blame the "crazies" who violate the law—since all terrorist acts are a violation of some law or other; in part they blame the media for instigating the crime, since they assume that there would be little motivation for the terrorist act were it not for publicity. "Police negotiators should not have to compete with the news media for the time and attention of the terrorists," says Washington's assistant chief of police.[6] And "the news media must limit their coverage of a terrorist incident" to protect "a criminal's constitutional right to a fair trial."[7] Law enforcement authorities have criticized the media for jeopardizing police work by "disseminating information tactically useful to the terrorists . . . interference with effective law enforcement by exaggerating and making terrorists more extreme . . . reinforcing the terrorists' sense of power" and disturbing the efforts for crowd control.[8]

The public's interest in terrorism must be viewed under two, or possibly three, headings. The eyewitness sees terrorism as a scary, violent, and human event. His or her immediate reaction may be to flee or to assist the victims. The much larger mass media public that experiences terrorism vicariously through the eyes of news reporters, on the other hand, sees terrorism as drama—titillating, exciting, noteworthy, or possibly boring. Like any other news event, the reader, listener, or viewer can take it or leave it. A third type might be those few members of the public who are victims and therefore involuntary participants in a terrorist event.

By way of contrast, the reporter views a terrorist or any other event through a professional eye. The difference between the reporter's and the general public's reaction to a terrorist incident is clearly illustrated by an event that had nothing to do with terrorism but that was a violent act intended to transmit a message. W. Lance Bennett et al. described the media-grabbing effort of an unemployed laborer who set fire to himself after alerting the local television station and the police. The television cameras arrived before the police and the man began his self-immolation. The cameramen rolled their cameras while a fireman ran for a fire extinguisher. "You were two strapping men. You could have stopped him," the CBS correspondent covering the incident for national television said to the cameramen. But they did not. They saw their role as reporters of an event.[9]

The gatekeeper, who may of course be the reporter, but frequently is an editor or producer or even the anchor person on a television show, must decide whether to cover a terrorist incident at all, and if so, how to play the story. It is the gatekeeper who determines what aspects of a given news event are the most newsworthy. From a scholarly viewpoint, the gatekeeper has been a neglected member of the caste in the "theater of terror." The purpose of this chapter, therefore, is to examine that role, and, specifically, how television gatekeepers, who represent the principal medium of this phenomenon, view terrorism as a news event.

METHOD

This study is based on unstructured interviews with seven television network journalists—two editors, two producers, two correspondents, and one anchor man. An "interview guide," comprising twenty-five questions, was developed after a review of the literature from which many of the questions were derived. Based on analyses of general news coverage, other questions were added. Responses of our interviewees were classified under twelve headings and were compared for purposes of this analysis. Interviews were conducted separately by the two authors of this chapter. Four of the interviews were with the ABC network, two with CNN, and one with PBS.

DEFINITION OF TERRORISM

Like academics, broadcast gatekeepers could not agree on a general definition of terrorism. When asked to define terrorism some of them tried to characterize terrorism in one way or another. Some did so in terms of generalizations about terrorist acts, e.g., nongovernmental, political actions involving death or injury to noncombatants. Others looked at it in terms of the motives of the terrorists, e.g., acts that involve political-ideological motivation with international aspects to it. Others simply focused on a particular act, such as a hijacking, kidnapping, and car bombing or any other radical act against social norms. The gatekeepers' responses reflected the fact that they are less concerned about or familiar with general definitions of terrorism, but that they had a clear idea of what terrorism was when they saw it.

The news elements of media definitions of terrorism are: involvement of Americans; the number of hostages; the number of bodies; attacks on symbols; what other stories exist at the time; and the availability of video footage. The broadcasters could not agree on the relative importance of these criteria. One network producer said that hostages have a higher news value than the loss of lives, while a fellow editor, on the same network, said that dead bodies rank higher than live hostages.

The one criterion most broadcasters agreed on was the availability of footage. Availability of video can sometimes dictate the extensiveness of the coverage. As one broadcaster said, "It is important and sometimes crucial. The medium is video." The lack of continuous coverage of the hijacking of a yacht by the Abu Nidal organization may suggest that the media define terrorism in accordance with the above criteria. In this particular case, for example, there was no Americans involved, there were no bodies, and there was no available footage. This may still be a terrorist act, but it does not have the news value that the media are looking for and on the basis of which decisions are made.

AIMS OF THE BROADCAST MEDIA

All our interviewees agreed about what should be the primary aim of the broadcast media in covering a terrorist incident. The media job, as one broadcaster put it, "is first of all to get the information, get it fast, and do everything to get the story." Another broadcaster said "the basic instinct is to work, to make contacts, and to discover what is going on, as in any other journalistic work." For the gatekeeper, covering terrorism is like covering any other news event. It is another "story" they have an obligation to cover. Terrorism is viewed through professional eyes. If it has news value it will be covered. If it has high news value it will be covered extensively.

The responses of our gatekeepers to this question were similar to what broadcasters have said earlier. George Watson of ABC said: "Our basic responsibility is to report what is happening"; and Ford Rowan of PBS suggested that the media look at terrorism from the point of view of what is newsworthy.[10] Robin Walsh of the BBC describes media work when covering terrorism: "We try to do it by applying normal journalistic practices and principles and by applying that not too easily definable term news-value."[11]

As to the role of the broadcast media versus the print media, broadcasters agreed that although television needs to put terrorism in context, they will do so only if time permits and leave the explanation and background to the print media. "Pressure of time," said one newsman, "forces us to consciously leave the job of putting the event in context to newspapers. We have only twenty-one minutes a day."

COMPETITION

Competition has a lot to do with the way terrorism is covered. The interviewees could not agree specifically on how competition affects the coverage of terrorism; however, they all agree that the nature of the news business is based on competition and that this also affects the coverage of terrorism. "It does not affect whether we do or do not cover. It does affect our desire to be first," said one interviewee. It is unclear, therefore, how competition affects terrorism, in other words, the extent to which competition affects coverage and the part of the coverage that can be explained by the competitive nature of the media.

The interviews suggest that competition is a powerful constraint on the media and may explain not only how the media react when they are functioning together but also their behavior when they have an exclusive story. As one newsman said, reacting to the question, "Would a situation when you have no competition affect your coverage of terrorism?" "No," he said, "because then I would have an exclusive." Another newsman said that terrorism is going to stay with us in the future and the media are going to compete in the coverage of terrorism.

POOL REPORTERS

Most newsmen are opposed to pool reporting. As one broadcaster put it, "pooling exists when resources don't exist, like in wartime." However, not all of the newsmen rejected the idea of pool reporting, and there is room for further study of this question.

PARTICIPANT VERSUS NONPARTICIPANT OBSERVATION

The gatekeepers we interviewed generally agreed that the media are not supposed to be participants in the events they cover. However, they all rank the importance of getting the facts much higher than the value of not being participants. They say that the media are there to cover a story and if there is a need to participate in order to get the story they are going to do so. They say they would decide on a case-by-case basis, relying on their own judgment to be able to avoid interfering with the event as it happens. As one newsman said, "We should ask questions even about deadlines, but at the same time we must try not to make any suggestions. We should be accurate at all times and do nothing against the law."

CONTACTS BETWEEN THE MEDIA AND TERRORISTS

Related to this is the question of contacts between the media and terrorists. Law enforcement officials criticize the media for contacting terrorists. They are concerned not only about the publicity terrorists get but also about possible media interference with effective law enforcement. The media on their part say that they can't accept a general embargo and will not avoid contacting terrorists as a rule. All the broadcasters we interviewed said they were fully aware of terrorist attempts to take advantage of the media. However, their judgment on whether to make the contact depends on the circumstances. The driving force behind the attempt to contact terrorists, according to our interviewees, is the need to get as much information as necessary. It is part of the news-gathering process. None mentioned a desire to dramatize an event or competition among the media.

According to gatekeepers, the reporter in the field must do whatever he or she can to get the story, including interviews with terrorists. However, the decision on whether to broadcast the interview is made by the executives at the station after full consideration of the circumstances. These considerations will not hold in a case when other media decide to contact the terrorists. If one news organization contacts the terrorists or broadcasts an interview, the others will not stay behind.

RIGHT TO KNOW VERSUS SAFETY OF INDIVIDUALS

No story is worth a human life said one broadcaster. Potential loss of life cannot by itself justify regulations, said another. Most broadcasters agree that there is a need to prevent the loss of lives due to journalistic work. They give different reasons for it, however. Some said it is immoral intentionally to cause harm to innocent people. Another gatekeeper suggested that the media take very seriously the possible damage to them from hostile public opinion or even a lawsuit if they are found to be responsible for the loss of life. This is why, in general, they would not cross police lines. Nevertheless, broadcasters rejected any preregulation.

LIVE VERSUS EDITED COVERAGE

Network newsmen tend to avoid live coverage because of the lack of control such coverage involves. CNN newsmen, however, said they would cover terrorism live and take the risk of not getting the whole story. They are aware that live reports are dangerous because the situation is fluid. However, the nature of their network dictates live and immediate coverage. As to live coverage of law enforcement activities, a CNN newsman said they would not cover them live, because it is immoral to tip off either side.

POLICE RESTRICTIONS

As the tension between law enforcement officers and the media rises during a terrorist event, gatekeepers suggest that it might be wise for media coverage to be controlled or restricted to some extent. All our respondents except one did not totally reject the possibility of the authorities imposing some restrictions. However, they made it very clear that these restrictions should be applied only on rare and extremely explosive occasions. The possible loss of innocent lives is the only case when the media will accept the idea of being restricted by the authorities.

"We should listen to the authorities," said one broadcaster. "If the government asks us, we will comply," said another. The gatekeepers said that they are always on the lookout to see whether the authorities are attempting to restrict the media merely in order to prevent the press from embarrassing them. Instead of restricting the media, one broadcaster suggested, the authorities should work with the media as they do in the case of any type of story.

SELF-IMPOSED GUIDELINES

The 1977 Hanafi Muslim hostage-taking incident in Washington, D.C., led to an extensive discussion both among the media themselves and between the media and law enforcement authorities about the need for self-imposed guidelines for the media. The broadcasters that we spoke to said that, generally speaking, "guidelines are okay." But they should not be treated as unchangeable. Every incident is different, said the broadcasters, and therefore guidelines cannot cover each and every terrorist situation. The guidelines may be disregarded or changed in a matter of seconds. Among gatekeepers, those who do the legwork and get the story differed in their view on this topic from those who decide what to do with the story once it has been gathered. The correspondents among the interviewees generally rejected strict guidelines because they were afraid that such guidelines would constrain the reporter's freedom in the field and would limit his attempt to do the best he can to get the story.

The reporter or correspondent, the editor, the producer, and the anchor person, each is a gatekeeper at a certain stage of the news coverage effort. It is the job of each gatekeeper to make decisions at every step of the way about how to cover a story on terrorism. Each will make his or her decisions differently, depending on his or her responsibility in the news-gathering process. In the field, one must count on the judgment and experience of reporters to make wise decisions. As an alternative to fixed guidelines, one broadcaster suggested training for reporters on the subject of covering terrorism.

The reactions of many of our interviewees were similar to the opinion expressed by a *New York Times* executive editor more than ten years ago. He said: "The last thing in the world I want are guidelines—not from the government, not from professional organizations, or any one else."[12]

On February 22, 1989, Peter Jennings said on the ABC evening news that "the hostage holders clearly intend to use the media to put pressure on others; therefore, in this instance, we elected not to broadcast the tape." Jennings was referring to a seventy-second tape of Lieutenant Colonel William Higgins released by the kidnappers. However, one interviewee from ABC suggested the following:

> I think that the reason for not showing the video on the evening news is because there was no time and Sam Donaldson was not available. To do a voiceover by Jennings would have taken too much time and the video was already on "Good Morning America." I don't think there was a change in ABC news policy.

It would be interesting to find out whether Jennings knew ahead of time what he was going to say (was it on the prompter?) or whether he decided to ad lib it on the air. What made ABC not show the tape? Was it a self-imposed policy on how to handle terrorism or was it based on professional criteria of newsworthiness?

AWARENESS OF THE IMPACT OF THE MEDIA

The broadcasters' responses showed that they considered media coverage to have an effect on the public. Most of them said the main media effect is to form public opinion about terrorism. In their minds, the coverage of terrorism works against the objectives of the terrorists by forming public opinion that is hostile to terrorism and their goals. At the same time, coverage supports government efforts to fight terrorism. This is not an intentional support; it is merely the outcome of purely professional coverage.

The broadcasters could not agree, however, on the question of whether gatekeepers consider the possible impact of the coverage on the public in making their decisions about that coverage. Some thought their responsibility was to cover the story and let the chips fall where they may, while others said that when the gatekeeper is editing a story he or she must think about its possible impact.

The broadcasters could not agree either about the type of impact media coverage of terrorism might have on the public. They were willing to concede that the media might serve to alarm or frighten the public.

An example of media awareness of the impact of their coverage on the public and on terrorists is the abduction of Marine Lieutenant Colonel Higgins. The symbiotic relationship between the media and terrorism is seen in the treatment of the story. Immediately after Higgins's abduction, all major networks and newspapers knew about his being a senior staff member for then Secretary of Defense Caspar Weinberger. At the request of the office of the Assistant Secretary of Defense for Public Affairs, the American media did not publish that information. The reason for the request was the possible risk to Higgins's life if that information were to have become known to the terrorists. After the information was broadcast on Lebanese radio, the Pentagon released the information, too. Only then did the media broadcast and print the somewhat sensational story they had been holding for over forty-eight hours.

At the same time, the media were looking hard for pictures of Lieutenant Colonel Higgins's wife, who apparently works in the office of public affairs at the Pentagon. The Pentagon realized that it would not be possible to block the media from trying to get her picture. So it arranged for photo opportunity, letting the press know that she was going to be leaving her home at a specific time. Higgins's wife appeared at the exact time walking from her house to her garage. About ten camera crews were there to take her picture. They were satisfied, and nobody bothered her with questions.

STRAIGHT NEWS OR INTERPRETATION

All the broadcasters felt that the media's job is both to describe the news and to put it in context. They all agreed that the straight news story came first; then, and only if time permits and interest is still there, they can go on to explain it. As one newsman put it: "The basis is the coverage, but the main value of journalism is putting news in context. You can't just show, you have to explain."

CONCLUSION

In this exploration of gatekeeper opinions on the subject of terrorism, twelve topics were probed in some detail. While broadcast gatekeepers were found to disagree about many of them, there appeared to be some unanimity that they were serving society by covering the news of terrorism. They also agreed about the role of the news media, whether when covering terrorism or any other news event. In fact, our respondents could not see any difference between news of terrorism and any other news when it came to coverage. In every case, there seemed to be a consensus that the first responsibility of the news media is to cover the news—straight news. Interpretation comes later if time permits, according to all broadcasters.

Competition has a strong effect on gatekeepers, but it is not clear in precisely what way. While the decision to cover is not affected, they claim, they may decide to go in with whatever they have in the face of competition, even if it is not the whole story. Competition may also affect a newsman's views on pooling.

The importance of getting the story influences broadcasters' views on contacting terrorists directly. In the face of competition, they will do it even if asked not to by the authorities. However, they will consider a request to refrain from endangering the lives of innocent people. In every case, the gatekeepers' preference is to use an edited version rather than a live version of the story.

The question that remains to be answered is whether the economics of the media and the desire to beat the Olympian competition of being first and best at covering the news at any cost outweigh the desires of media owners and executives to play an important social role in the community. Since the media themselves suffer from this schizophrenic conflict, it is difficult for them to be responsive to the lofty role assigned to them by the community.

NOTES

1. See Grant Wardlaw, *Political Terrorism* (Cambridge: Cambridge University Press, 1982), p. 76; J.B. Bell, "Terrorist Scripts and Live-Action Spectaculars," *Columbia Journalism Review* (May 1978): 50; and M. Cherif Bassiouni, "Problems in Media Coverage of Nonstate-Sponsored Terror-Violence Incidents," in Lawrence Z. Freedman and Yonah Alexander (eds.), *Perspectives on Terrorism* (Wilmington, Del.: Scholarly Resources, 1983), p. 182.

2. Brian Jenkins, "International Terrorism: A New Mode of Conflict," in D. Carlton and C. Schaerf (eds.), *International Terrorism and World Security* (London: Croom Helm, 1975), p. 4.

3. Gabriel Weimann, "The Theater of Terror: Effects of Press Coverage," *Journal of Communication* 33, no. 1 (Winter 1985): 38–45.

4. See, in particular, chapter one of Alex P. Schmid and Janny de Graaf, *Violence as Communication* (Beverly Hills, Calif.: Sage, 1982); and L. John Martin, "The Media's Role in International Terrorism," *Terrorism* 8, no. 2 (1985): 127–46.

5. Martin, "The Media's Role," pp. 133–34.

6. Michael T. McEwen and Stephen Sloan, "Terrorism: Police and Press Problems," *Terrorism* 2, nos. 1 and 2 (1979): 72.

7. Ibid., p. 73.

8. M. Cherif Bassiouni, "Media Coverage of Terrorism: The Law and the Public," *Journal of Communication* 32, no. 2 (1982): 129–30; and Bassiouni, "Problems in Media Coverage," pp. 194–96.

9. W. Lance Bennett, Lynne A. Gressett, and William Haltom, "Repairing the News: A Case Study of the News Paradigm," *Journal of Communication* 35, no. 2 (1985): 50–68.

10. Sarah Midgeley and Virginia Rice, eds., *Terrorism and the Media in the 1980s* (Washington: The Media Institute, 1983), pp. 23–25.

11. J. Shaw et al., eds., *Ten Years of Terrorism* (London: Royal United Services Institute for Defense Studies, 1979), p. 89.

12. Yonah Alexander, David Carlton, and Paul Wilkinson, eds. *Terrorism: Theory and Practice* (Boulder, Colo.: Westview Press, 1979), p. 168.

REFERENCES

Alexander, Yonah, David Carlton and Paul Wilkinson, eds. *Terrorism: Theory and Practice*. Boulder, Colo.,: Westview Press, 1979.

Bassiouni, M. Cherif. "Problems in Media Coverage of Nonstate-Sponsored Terror-Violence Incidents," in Lawrence Z. Freedman and Yonah Alexander, eds. *Perspectives on Terrorism*. Wilmington, Del.: Scholarly Resources, 1983.

———. "Media Coverage of Terrorism: The Law and the Public," *Journal of Communication*. 32:2 (1982): 128–43.

Bell, J.B. "Terrorist Scripts and Live-Action Spectaculars." *Columbia Journalism Review* (May 1978):47–50.

Bennett, W. Lance, Lynne A. Gressett, and William Haltom. "Repairing the News: A Case Study of the News Paradigm." *Journal of Communication* 35:2 (1985):50–68.

Dowling, Ralph E. "Terrorism and the Media: A Rhetorical Genre." *Journal of Communication* 36:1 (1986):12–24.

Jenkins, M. Brian. "International Terrorism: A New Mode of Conflict," in D. Carlton and C. Schaerf, eds. *International Terrorism and World Security*. London: Croom Helm, 1975.

Martin, L. John. "The Media's Role in International Terrorism." *Terrorism* 8:2 (1985):127–46.

McEwen, Michael T., and Stephen Sloan. "Terrorism: Police and Press Problems." *Terrorism* 2:1,2 (1979).

Midgeley, Sarah, and Virginia Rice, eds. *Terrorism and the Media in the 1980's*. Washington: The Media Institute, 1983.

Schmid, Alex P., and Janny de Graaf. *Violence as Communication*. Beverly Hills, Calif.: Sage, 1982.

Shaw, J., et al., eds. *Ten Years of Terrorism*. London: Royal United Services Institute for Defense Studies, 1979.

Wardlaw, Grant, *Political Terrorism*. Cambridge: Cambridge University Press, 1982.

Weimann, Gabriel. "The Theater of Terror: Effects of Press Coverage." *Journal of Communication* 33:1 (Winter 1985):38–45.

CHAPTER 10

Of Christian Freedom Fighters and Marxist Terrorists: The Image of SWAPO and the Namibian Independence Movement in the Religious and Secular Press

*by Judith M. Buddenbaum**

For the most part we do not first see, and then define, we define first and then see.

Whatever we believe to be a true picture, we treat as if it were the environment itself.

The fiction is taken for truth because the fiction is badly needed.

Every newspaper when it reaches the reader is the result of a whole series of selections as to what items shall be printed, in what position they shall be printed, how much space each shall occupy, what emphasis each shall have. There are no objective standards here. There are conventions.[1]

IN THE MORE THAN HALF CENTURY since Lippmann wrote of Miss Sherwin of Gopher Prairie, the relationship between news and truth, and the power of the media to create the pictures in her head, social science research has generally supported his observations about the origin, uses, and influence of media-created labels—the stereotypes that create the pictures in our heads.

This stereotyping or labeling is a natural phenomenon. As Kelley points out, everyone is a naive social scientist routinely conducting analyses of variance in order to group external phenomena, including people and organi-

*The author thanks Thomas E. Caldwell, undergraduate student in technical journalism at Colorado State University, and Katherine E. Buddenbaum, graduate student in sociology at Indiana University, for help with data collection.

zations, into categories that help make sense of the world. Depending on the person's experience, categories will be employed to label some as "like" the individual and therefore "safe." Others will appear as "different" or even "deviant" and therefore "dangerous."

For the most part, labeling is unavoidable and benign. Labels and stereotypes are efficient ways of making sense of the world. However, they can also act as censors ruling out countervailing information. Therefore, in the hands of respected individuals or institutions, they become a powerful control mechanism.[2]

In the case of the media, labels are rarely neutral, objective facts. Nor are they independent observations. More often, reporters monitoring those agencies their society defines as legitimate news sources pick up and pass on the labels those sources use to define reality. Thus, the media reinforce the hegemony of other powerful institutions, especially that of the government, by setting "facts," including labels, in the context of simple "common sense" explanations reproduced out of the specialized knowledge of previously legitimated news sources.[3]

Although the body of agenda-setting research shows that the press may not be able to influence what people think, it also shows they are spectacularly able to influence what people think about;[4] recent work suggests much of that influence comes from the labels the media attach to people and events.

James Lemert's analysis, for example, indicates that by labeling some political candidates as "front runners" and "winners," others as "dark horses" and "also rans," the media prematurely narrow the field of candidates and can even destroy popular candidates by creating unattainable expectations of victory.[5] Similarly, David Weaver et al. document that the media teach their audiences labels to use in describing politicians. Even when candidacies are not destroyed, voters pick up on and use the media labels to describe both the politicians they support and those they oppose. Thus, during the 1980 presidential campaign, Ford opponents would often explain their choice by describing him as a "bumbler," while Ford supporters frequently prefaced explanations of their choice by saying, "He may be a bumbler, but. . . ."[6]

That "but" suggests that, in domestic politics at least, images contrary to the media stereotype are quite possible. Candidates rarely appear out of nowhere; they usually come with a long history of public service. Through their public work and appearances, as well as their public relations and advertising initiatives, candidates can create and present a countervailing image. Although it may take more effort than most people are willing to invest, voters can analyze candidates' histories. They can also see and hear the candidates themselves, or at least talk to trusted friends and colleagues who have, and compare their impressions to the candidates' own presentations and to those provided by the news media. Indeed, research on the effects of the media in election campaigns documents that voters often ignore the media image by electing candidates that the media oppose.[7]

However, the problem of media stereotypes may be more pervasive and more difficult to overcome in foreign news, and particularly in news from the Third World. While bias is often in the eye of the beholder, both media critics and media researchers agree that Third World news is limited both in subject matter and in nations covered.[8] As a result, the media-created image is often one of poor, benighted lands riddled by "coups and earthquakes."[9] And even those are open to question because they often become part of "justifying symbols."[10] Media may label the coup that succeeds as the justifiable act of freedom fighters, and the one that fails as the criminal work of terrorists, or the labels may be reversed, depending on the political system in the country involved and its relationship to the government of the country in which the media labelers live and work.[11]

Whatever the media image, the stereotypes in foreign news may be much more powerful than those in accounts of domestic politics. Because opportunities for first-hand observation and investigation are more limited, the mass media image may be the only one available. If that is true, the picture on which people act may be wrong, but there will probably be consensus about the wisdom and rightness of the act. However, on those occasions where multiple images exist, public opinion may divide according to whose image of reality people accept.

Because such a split in public opinion based on mediated images of reality can have serious repercussions for governments, the media, and, indeed, all of society, this chapter examines the images journalists working for the religious and the secular press have created for a situation beyond the realm of personal experience of their audience, and even sometimes beyond their own personal experience—the situation in Namibia and the activities of the South-West Africa People's Organization (SWAPO) in the campaign for Namibian independence from South Africa.

This chapter cannot, and is not intended to, determine the truth about SWAPO and Namibia. Rather, it examines the image created in two different presses and explores how journalists from the religious and secular press select sources, facts, labels, and justifying explanations to create those images.

BACKGROUND

Although there apparently have been no earthquakes or coups in the region, Namibia has been in the news more or less continuously for at least a quarter of a century because of efforts to create an independent nation. Those efforts have variously been led by outsiders and by Namibians themselves. Sometimes they have been conducted peacefully through diplomatic channels; at other times they have taken the form of violent confrontations.

However, Namibia is a remote region. Few average Americans have ever met anyone from Namibia. Even fewer have been there. The major Western media have apparently never stationed a correspondent there and rarely sent one to visit. Therefore, most journalists, political analysts and scholars, as well as average citizens, are at the mercy of their sources.

News coverage of Namibia, then, is ideal for this study because this combination of newsworthiness and remoteness means that images become reality. Indeed, ideologically motivated justifying explanations are so common that the facts themselves are often unrecognizable.[12] Writers cannot even agree on the region's name, referring to it variously as South-West Africa, SouthWest Africa, South West Africa, or more recently as Namibia for the Namib Desert, a prominent geographic feature of the region.

Originally Great Britain claimed the Walvis Bay area and coastal islands while Germany proclaimed a protectorate over the rest of the region. After World War I the region became a mandate of South Africa under terms of Article 22 of the Covenant of the League of Nations. However, the exact status of the region became an open question when the United Nations superseded the League of Nations.

Since then, the United Nations has considered the status of the trusteeship arrangement prescribed by the UN charter as a replacement for the original mandate, eventually concluding that the charter requires establishing a new nation independent from South African control. The United Nations recognizes the South-West Africa People's Organization (SWAPO) as the legitimate representative of the Namibian people.

METHODOLOGY

This study of image and image production is based on a qualitative and quantitative analysis of all stories about Namibia and the South-West Africa People's Organization published in the weekly news packets distributed by *Lutheran World Information (LWI),* the English language news service of the Lutheran World Federation (LWF), Geneva, Switzerland, during 1966, 1971, 1976, 1981, and 1986 and all stories about Namibia and SWAPO listed in the *New York Times* index during the same years.

These stories were read first to determine the dominant image of Namibia, the Namibian people, and SWAPO created by the entire body of published stories. Individual stories were then coded to determine both the general subject matter and the stylistic features that contribute to the production of a particular image of Namibia and SWAPO. Here the sources *LWI* and *Times* reporters rely on, and the use and arrangement of facts, labels, and descriptions, and explanations were of particular interest.

Lutheran World Information was selected as the religious press for this study because it is the English-language news agency of the Lutheran World Federation, which has been the major Christian proponent of Namibian independence since 1971 when the leaders of the two largest Namibian Lutheran member churches issued their "Open Letter" to South African Prime Minister B.J. Vorster.

The Lutheran World Federation is comprised of 104 autonomous member churches representing 93 percent of the world's 54.3 million Lutherans. LWF's English, German, and French news services are designed to facilitate communication among member churches and between Lutherans, other

Christian churches, and the secular press. Therefore, *LWI* is a major source of information about Namibia for the Christian press in the United States.

The English-language weekly news packets go to nearly two thousand subscribers in more than one hundred different countries. In the United States, several hundred Lutheran and non-Lutheran opinion leaders and about one hundred media outlets receive the packets. U.S. media receiving *LWI* include the three major television networks, the major weekly news magazines, and the religion editors at about forty-five daily mass circulation newspapers, most Lutheran publications, and about twenty non-Lutheran religious news services, newspapers, and magazines including *Christian Century, Christianity and Crisis,* and *Christianity Today.*[13]

The *New York Times* was selected as the representative of the secular press for this study because it is the premier elite newspaper in the United States with news-gathering resources that include a large staff of political specialists and foreign correspondents. Therefore, other newspapers throughout the United States look to the *Times* for leadership in covering foreign news. Although its religion writers receive *LWI,* they rarely use it for anything other than background information. They seldom, if ever, pass it on to other journalists because the religion writers are primarily responsible for covering U.S. religion news at the national level and because the *New York Times* prides itself on active news-gathering.[14]

FINDINGS

Coverage by *Lutheran World Information*

News from Namibia was extremely rare until mid 1971. However, after Dr. Leonard Auala, bishop and chairman of the Church Board of the Evangelical Lutheran Ovambokavango Church, and Pastor Paulus Gowaseb, moderator and chairman of the Church Board of the Evangelical Lutheran Church in South West Africa (Rhenish Mission), issued their "Open Letter" to Prime Minister B.J. Vorster of South Africa in June, stories sympathizing with and promoting independence became a regular feature in the weekly *LWI* news packets.

In its first coverage of the Namibian situation, *LWI* began the July 19, 1971, packet with a news release, apparently written by the *LWI* editor in Geneva, explaining the attached full texts of the "Open Letter" and an accompanying "Pastoral Letter" sent to congregations of the two churches. The "Open Letter" reminded the South African government of the World Court's decision and of United Nations resolutions and called for South Africa to "seek a peaceful solution to the problems of our land and . . . see to it that Human Rights be put into operation and that South West Africa . . . become a self-sufficient and independent state."

During the remainder of 1971, *LWI* provided the full text of a news release from the two churches reiterating the views expressed in the "Open Letter" as well as six other stories about the political situation. In 1976, twelve issues carried a total of sixteen stories. As a result of both a change in news policy and news editor that led to regular use of news releases from Third World churches and from the growing number of Third World Christian news services, coverage increased dramatically in the 1980s. By 1986, about three-fourths of the weekly news packets contained at least one story.

Of the sixty-three stories that year, three were "documentation"—the full text of important letters and statements on the Namibian situation. About one-fourth appear to have been written or heavily edited by the *LWI* editor in Geneva; another one-fourth were reprints of articles from Lutheran publications, or from Religious News Service. The rest, written in styles ranging from personal letters and first-person stories to true news releases, came from Lutheran churches in Namibia, the Namibian Council of Churches, African Christian news services, or individual Christians.

But in spite of the increase in number of stories and writers, the coverage remained consistent. Whether based in Geneva, Namibia, or elsewhere, the writers sometimes alluded to statements by political sources, but did not rely on them. In fact, few stories suggest government officials were contacted or that their opinions and concerns should be taken seriously. Instead, they relied on Christian sources for their facts, descriptions, and interpretations.

The first story about the political situation in Namibia, the news release[15] accompanying the texts of the "Open Letter" and the "Pastoral Letter," established the image and set the tone for subsequent coverage. Following a summary lead reporting that the two churches had released letters "sharply attacking South Africa's apartheid policies," the author explained that the "Pastoral Letter" was to be read from the pulpits in

> all congregations of the 178,000-member Ovambokavango Evangelical Lutheran Church (OELC) and the 108,000-member Evangelical Lutheran Church in South-West Africa (ELCSWA-Rhenish Mission Church). . . .

The story then concluded with additional information about the religious makeup of Namibia:

> Both of the churches issuing the letters are predominantly indigenous groupings, the Ovambokavango considered a "black" church and the ELCSWA working with a variety of linguistic and ethnic groups.
>
> In addition to these two churches, both of which belong to the Lutheran World Federation, there is a third LWF church in South-West Africa, the German Evangelical Lutheran Church. This 15,000-member body, which cooperates closely with the other two churches, is largely made up of German-speaking residents of the country.

Between these two passages which establish an image of Namibia as a Christian land, the author alludes to a political source while quoting directly from the bishops to present an interpretation which justifies their action partially by delegitimizing South African political authority in the land:

> Both documents refer to the World Court decision of June 21 which called South Africa's occupation of South-West Africa illegal and the letter to congregations states that because of the decision "we can no longer remain silent."

"We feel," the letter says, "that if we, as the church remain silent any longer, we will become liable for the life and future of our country and its people."

For Lutheran readers, who might be uncomfortable with overt political activity because of Martin Luther's teaching that all political authority is established by God and, therefore, should not be interfered with unless the government first attempts to influence church doctrine or interfere with worship,[16] the news release explains:

Both documents were received here by Lutheran World Federation General Secretary André Appel, who pointed out that their preparation was on the initiative of the two churches.

The release then adds Appel's assurance of the appropriateness of the bishops' action and the justness of their cause:

"At the same time," he [Appel] added, "the fact of their preparation and issuance is directly in line with the Resolution on Human Rights" adopted by the LWF Fifth Assembly last summer . . . which urges churches . . . to help their members correct human rights violations "at individual and corporate levels through available religious and secular instrumentalities and channels."

By 1976, references to Namibian Lutherans acting alone disappeared in the wake of news of support from Lutherans and other Christians around the world; most referred to the land as Namibia instead of as South-West Africa. But other features of the coverage followed the pattern established in the initial story.

At least one-fourth of the subsequent stories used church membership figures similar to those in the initial news release to further the image of Namibia as a Christian land, although by 1981 the descriptive paragraph often appeared later in the story and included references to non-Lutherans. For example, one 1986 story reported Lutheran church membership figures that account for at least half the population of Namibia:

The 360,000-member Evangelical Lutheran Church in SWA/Namibia (ELCIN) [formerly OELC], the 190,000-member Evangelical Church in SWA/Rhenish Mission and the 12,000-member German Evangelical Lutheran Church. . . .[17]

While another one about an international, ecumenical consultation on Namibia combined church membership data with suggestions of broad-based religious support for the Namibian cause:

The conference, with its theme "One in the Body of Christ—together a free people" was called by the three largest churches in Namibia. Lutherans, Roman Catholics and Anglicans make up more than 75 percent of the Namibian population. The Namibia conference was sponsored by the three world communions, who were also represented at the consultation.[18]

In 1976, 1981, and 1986, a similar proportion of stories mentioning or describing activities of average Namibians are reported from the Namibian perspective and use religious labels to further the image of a Christian Namibia whose people are engaged in a just struggle for human dignity and independence. The opening paragraphs of the first story from Namibia during 1976, for example, contrast images of illegitimate South African violence with ones of justifiable actions by Christian Namibians:

> Police wielding batons and using dogs broke up a singing demonstration by some 300 people as the trial of six black Namibians charged under the Terrorism Act opened here on February 16.
>
> All of the defendants—two Lutheran men, three Lutheran women and a Roman Catholic man from Ovamboland—are charged with offenses related to the assassination last August 16 of Ovamboland Chief Minister Filemon Elifas. . . .
>
> At the end of the morning session on the opening day of the trial, police moved into the crowd outside the small courtroom. The singing, placard-carrying demonstrators had remained peaceful and were asking to see the accused.
>
> Three persons were bitten by dogs and one reporter was assaulted by a policeman. . . .
>
> Lutheran, Anglican and Roman Catholic churches and a variety of other sources have provided funds for defense costs of the accused.[19]

Later that year, *Lutheran World Information* provided a page of photographs, including one of the attack dogs.[20]

Other stories told of black Lutheran students,[21] black Christian young people,[22] white Lutheran youths,[23] a Catholic journalist,[24] Lutheran nurses,[25] Christian lawyers,[26] and crowds of average people[27] supporting the independence movement or protesting South African rule. Although explicit mention of "freedom fighters" appeared only once[28] in the stories examined, that image was almost as strong in the stories about SWAPO as in those primarily about religious organizations, church leaders, and members.

Nearly one-fourth of all stories mentioned SWAPO; of those about half create the impression that SWAPO is a Christian organization by juxtaposing references to the political organization with church membership figures, as in a reprint from "Namibia 1975—Hope, Fear and Ambiguity":

> Inside the territory SWAPO aligns itself with four other parties in the Namibia National Convention (NNC). . . .
>
> With about 350,000 souls between them, the Evangelical Lutheran Ovambo-Kavango Church (ELOK) and the Evangelical Lutheran Church (ELK) [sic] are a force to be reckoned with as they preach the social gospel to the masses. . . .
>
> The language of politics is suffused with the language of religion in SWA. On public platforms, when SWAPO rallies its supporters, Pretoria is the "antichrist."[29]

Others use religious labels to identify SWAPO leaders and members. A 1976 story based on an interview with Sam Nujoma describes the SWAPO president:

> Sam Nujoma speaks in soft but firm tones. He is a stocky six-footer with a thick, graying beard—a 47-year-old exile from his own country, where his wife and three sons still live. In the chambers and corridors of the UN his neat business suit fits the scene; as commander of SWAPO guerilla forces he is equally at home in battle uniform. He is a Lutheran from north Namibia's Ovamboland, a slightly schooled but self-educated farmer's son.[30]

A 1981 story lists "the Rev. Bartholomew Karuaera, president of the African Methodist Episcopal Church in Namibia; the Rev. Sidney Witbooi, an AME pastor; the Rev. Joshua Hoebeb, vice president of the Evangelical Lutheran Church of South West Africa; the Rev. Philip Tjerije, Editor of Immanuel" as being among SWAPO delegates at a United Nations conference on Namibia.[31] One 1986 story mentions "the Rev. Hendrik Witbooi, vice president of SWAPO . . . who is an elder in the African Methodist Episcopal Church,"[32] while another tells the story of Ida Jimmy, a Lutheran and a SWAPO leader, who "continued her struggle against the South African occupation even while serving a seven-year sentence under the terrorism act" by conducting illegal Bible studies for other inmates:

> Her attempt to spread the gospel aroused the displeasure of the South African security forces. . . .
> "The prison matron stopped us. It was considered too dangerous. We just ignored her and went on in secret," Jimmy said.[33]

While that story's reference to the Terrorism Act alludes to the South African political interpretation of the Namibian situation, like all the stories provided by *LWI,* it accepts without question the Namibian-Christian-SWAPO version. Other stories more overtly discredit the South African viewpoint by using quotation marks in explanations of Namibian crimes under the Terrorism Act and by trivializing the offenses as in this passage from a 1976 story:

> All of the women had been accused of turning over 10 Rand (US$11.50) sums to "terrorists." Ms. Nambinga also allegedly visited people in Angola whose purpose was to overthrow the government of South-West Africa and supplied one of them with a dress, soap and sanitary napkins.[34]

About 10 percent of the stories acknowledge the South African image of Namibians as terrorists and SWAPO as a Marxist terrorist organization, but use religious sources to supply the appropriate Christian imagery. In a 1981 reprint of a Religious News Service story, Bishop James R. Crumley Jr., head of the Lutheran Church in America, explained the appropriateness of churches providing financial and moral support to SWAPO:

> "I don't see it as just a guerilla, Communist group," the LCA bishop said. "After all Namibia is predominantly Lutheran and an awful lot of our people, Christian people, are members of SWAPO and working in it."[35]

While a few stories state that Christians should first seek peaceful solutions,[36] strikes, rallies, and protests, and even guerrilla warfare are generally defended as justified responses to political repression and greater violence from South Africa:

> He [Mokganedi Thlabanello, Assistant General Secretary of the Council of Churches in Namibia] spoke of Namibia's heritage of colonial violence and emphasized, "It is essential to understand that it is against this background that Namibians, as a last resort, took to arms in 1966; Was it SWAPO," he asked,

"who in 1904 exterminated almost half the Herero-speaking people or was it General von Trotha? Was it SWAPO, who in 1917 killed Chief Mandume and his men, or was it Louis Botha? . . .

It was on Aug. 26, 1966, when "SWAPO decided to rise up with arms, and thereby said enough is enough." It was then "the Namibians decided to confront South Africa in the same language that she spoke."[37]

That story, like others reporting on acts by SWAPO and the Namibian independence movement, presents a sanitized version of Namibian and SWAPO violence, but lurid headlines such as "Namibians Plead Not Guilty; Police Send Dogs Into Crowd,"[38] "Terror in Namibia: The Bombing of the Church Press,"[39] "Eyewitness to Namibian Beatings,"[40] and "Namibian Teenager Roasted Over Fire by KOEVET"[41] are common introductions to the nearly one-fourth of all stories that include tales of atrocities committed by the South African government and its supporters inside Namibia.

Coverage by the *New York Times*

Stories about the Namibian situation appeared during each of the years between 1966 and 1986 that were examined for this study. However, the amount of coverage in each year varied dramatically depending on events on the international diplomatic scene. There were approximately 150 stories in both 1976 and 1981, but only ten during 1986.

But regardless of the number, at least three-fourths of the stories each year were written by political or foreign correspondents stationed at centers of political power outside Namibia: the International Court of Justice in The Hague; UN headquarters in New York and offices in Geneva; Washington, D.C.; and South Africa. Working from those vantage points, the reporters, most of whom apparently had visited Namibia only briefly if at all, relied on highly placed political sources, many of whom also probably had little first-hand knowledge of the land, for their facts, descriptions, and interpretations. About 10 percent of the stories during each year except 1986 were the full text or lengthy excerpts from UN documents or from speeches by political leaders; between 10 and 20 percent were editorials, commentaries, or letters to the editor, often written by American university professors, politicians, or diplomats with special expertise in foreign affairs but not currently holding a government position.

Because of heavy reliance on South African sources whose basic attitude toward the Namibian situation did not change over time, the mediated reality was largely the creation of South Africa. Although that reality was tempered by other perspectives, especially the United States' ever changing and somewhat ambivalent attitude toward the whole situation, the dominant feature of the coverage is that the image of Namibia, SWAPO, and the Namibian independence movement is largely the creation of outsiders.

The land itself is generally pictured as vast, empty, and inhospitable. A 1966 story, for example, reports:

South-West Africa covers 318,000 square miles—as much as France and West

Germany combined—compared with South Africa's 472,000. . . . With a population of only 384,000 and largely unexploited mineral deposits. . . .[42]

Similarly, one 1971 story describes the territory's Caprivi panhandle as "a geographical oddity that stretches from South-West Africa for 280 malarial miles,"[43] while another story describes the land as "a huge territory that is mostly desolate" before explaining:

In fact, the name Namibia, given to South-West Africa by the United Nations, is derived from the Namib Desert, a vast area of sand dunes and solitude flanking the South Atlantic Ocean.[44]

As the quote from that story suggests, the use of outsiders to define Namibia extended even to the name of the region. The *New York Times* indexed the coverage under South-West Africa and used that name consistently in stories even during 1981 and 1986 when headlines occasionally referred to the region as Namibia. Even in those later years, most continued the practice begun in 1976 of attributing that name to radical black African nationalists with Communist connections or to Third World representatives within the United Nations. Because none even raises the question of what name the region's indigenous people might use or prefer, the references and explanations contribute to an image of Namibians as uninterested in politics and submissive to outside authorities.

That impression of Namibians as relatively uninterested in their own fate is furthered by the stories that describe the people. Many create a psychological distance between Namibians and average *Times* readers by describing an unsophisticated people living in a tribal society wracked by ethnic and linguistic rivalries. Headlines promised features on "A Capital Where Go-Go Girls Are New"[45] and a "Tribe Still in Stone Age."[46]

Like that latter story, which was based on an interview with the white chief physician at a state hospital, most describe the people from the perspective of outsiders. In the process, a 1966 story based on information provided by South Africa about its policy of creating native homelands apparently confuses the "Bantustans," or black tribal homelands, with the Bantu tribe:

Two-thirds of South-West Africa has been reserved for development by Europeans, with natives, mostly Bantu tribesmen, restricted to segregated areas. . . .[47]

However, most report that Ovambos constitute a clear majority.[48]

Only about 10 percent of all stories even allude to religion, and most of those mention or suggest native tribal religion, as in a 1971 story that describes South-West Africa as comprised of "nine ethnic groups with neither language nor religion in common."[49] When Christianity is mentioned, it is usually in connection with white missionaries, in passages such as:

Only 500 whites, mostly missionaries, are said to live among the 350,000 Ovambos. White traders are forbidden to open shops in the area.[50]

The few that identify blacks as Christian often suggest they are not fully civilized. A 1971 story, for example, describes the Reverend Dr. Romanus

Kampungu as "a snuff-taking Roman Catholic priest who has a degree in canon law."[51]

Very few stories were based on interviews with Namibians, but those that featured or quoted them did little to dispel the impression of an unsophisticated people incapable of handling their own affairs. The only story during 1966 that featured a Namibian is typical of the descriptions based on reporters' investigations:

> Clement Kapuuo, the leader of the Herrero people, sat among sacks of corn meal and cans of evaporated milk in the back room of his small general store this morning and declared, "We have complete faith in international justice. . . ."
>
> The Herrero leader's store is in the middle of "the old native location" here, a shantytown made up of hovels known as pondoks. . . .[52]

While that story acknowledges the people's distaste for South Africa and their longing for independence, it, like all the other stories during 1966, emphasizes that Liberia and Ethiopia took the question of the status of the territory to the International Court of Justice and that those nations are the ones arguing the case in court.

On the few other occasions when reporters actually visited the land, they produced stories acknowledging that their access to people and places was arranged and controlled by South Africa, but pass on their limited experiences and their carefully selected sources' views as if they are representative:

> Officials of the South African Government and black notables sat side by side at the Finnish Lutheran Mission Hospital in this tribal capital today Ondangua.
>
> The scene would be impossible in Johannesburg, Pretoria, or Capetown, or indeed in any place in the South African Republic, where apartheid, or separation of the races, in day-to-day life bans any convivial contact between blacks and whites.
>
> At the end of the lunch, Roelof F. Botha, a member of Prime Minister John Vorster's Nationalist party, said in a toast, "Africa is like a zebra. It doesn't matter if you hit a black or white stripe—the animal dies." Blacks and whites applauded.
>
> Later, at a question-and-answer session, a black tribal leader told a group of 12 newsmen—the first foreign reporters to visit this remote area in many years— he approved of apartheid. . . .
>
> Father Kampungu, who is about 50 years old, explained that he was for apartheid on the grounds of morality. . . .
>
> Alex Kudomo, a 32-year-old tribal headman sitting next to the priest at the meeting broke in to say, "Our mother is South Africa. . . ."
>
> Both representatives of the Kavango tribe denied charges made in the United Nations that black people in the north of South-West Africa were oppressed and terrorized.[53]

Only those who read to the last paragraph of the twenty-inch story would learn "there are some signs of opposition to South African rule among the blacks." Fully half of the other stories that year passed on estimates from South African spokespersons that most blacks from all ethnic groups support South Africa.

Even during 1976, when reporters were more often on the scene because U.S. Secretary of State Henry Kissinger's "shuttle diplomacy" frequently took him to South Africa in an attempt to solve the problems created both by the presence of Cubans in Angola and by the status of Rhodesia/Zimbabwe and South-West Africa/Namibia, reporters usually accepted and passed on the South African interpretation of the situation. Stories continued to imply that most Namibians were not really oppressed by South African policies and had little real interest in independence.[54]

Both because of continued reliance on South African sources and the stronger U.S. interest in the issue evidenced by Kissinger's shuttle diplomacy, the first strong image of SWAPO as a Marxist, terrorist organization occurred during 1976 when at least half of the 147 stories mentioned the organization.

Although SWAPO was mentioned by outside sources in about 5 percent of the stories during 1966 and 1971, no one connected with the organization served as a major news source until March 1976. According to that story:

> A spokesman for nationalist guerillas fighting white minority rule of South-West Africa says that his group is prepared to invite Cuban forces to help it.
>
> This statement was made by Theo-Ben Gurirab, a member of the Central Committee of the South-West Africa People's Organization, who is accredited to the United Nations. . . .
>
> Mr. Gurirab declined to say when or how his organization would extend an invitation for Cuban troops. But he noted that Cubans began fighting in neighboring Angola last year after they were "asked to do so. . . .
>
> "We reserve the right to invite them, too," Mr. Gurirab said. . . .
>
> In the American intelligence estimate the South-West People's Organization remains relatively weak. It maintains headquarters and training camps in neighboring Zambia.
>
> Mr. Gurirab described himself as a 38-year-old from a "petit bourgeois family" in central South-West Africa and "some kind of socialist." He said that his organization had "over 1,000 but under 10,000" members. . . .
>
> "We had great logistical problems until recently," Mr. Gurirab said, "But . . . the situation is changed now. We have a 1,000 mile border with Angola and we are getting both infantry weapons and heavy stuff, too."[55]

That story established the common themes: SWAPO has little support within the country for its violent campaign against South Africa. It both supports and is supported by international Communism and thus poses a threat to stability in southern Africa and to U.S. interests abroad.

During that year about 10 percent of the stories included some comment from SWAPO sources, and one[56] identified a SWAPO leader, but not its president, as Christian. Two stories directly quoted SWAPO president Sam Nujoma and another provided a personality profile of him, but those pieces were developed within the context of the South African and U.S. interpretations of the Namibian campaign for independence as a dangerous one. The September 14 story[57] about a convention set up by South Africa to develop a constitution for the country begins:

This vast territory, twice the size of California but with a population of 900,000, is southern Africa's most serious problem after Rhodesia.

From the perspective of black Africa . . . South Africa's administration of the one-time German colony is a colonial anachronism. The South African system of separate development of the races is an indignity and an affront to black African nationalists. . . .

South Africa's point of view is different. The Government in Pretoria insists that its mandate over the territory was legally granted by the League of Nations after World War I. It insists that transition to independence is a question to be decided . . . by the people of South-West Africa. . . . It has categorically rejected any role for the militant black group SWAPO that the United Nations has endorsed as the people's legitimate representative.

Near the end, the story quotes Hannes Smith, editor of an English newspaper in Windhoek, to provide one of the few images of SWAPO from a non–South African perspective:

I know what they say—that SWAPO's claims to represent the people are fraudulent—but I travel around this country, and I can tell you that for the black man SWAPO represents the true nationalistic aspirations in the soul. Ach, I disagree with SWAPO in many areas. They get their arms from the East, but remember they get their ideas from the West, their clothes, their language. They are the only group in the country that can get 3,000 people at one of their meetings. You can't just wish them away because Mr. Vorster thinks that Sam Nujoma is a Communist.

However, the intervening paragraphs briefly quote Sam Nujoma in a way that suggests the SWAPO president is becoming less militant because of lack of support within Namibia, mention Kissinger's opinion that the Namibian issue "is less complicated than that of Rhodesia," and describe a "strong feeling in this clean, tidy, and dull town Windhoek that the forces shaping the territory's future are beyond its boundaries," provide additional details on South Africa's position, and present quotes from constitutional convention delegates, who were approved by South Africa.

Similarly, in the generally sympathetic personality profile, Nujoma is quoted rejecting the claim that he is a Marxist:

When Mr. Nujoma is at the United Nations or traveling on fund-raising activities which have taken him to many European cities as well as Moscow and Peking, he styles himself as "comrade"—not, he says, to establish any political identity but much in the way blacks use the word "brother."

"I am not a Communist," he said. "If in America you consider using that term to mean something, that is your interpretation."[58]

However, those paragraphs conclude a story which applies the "freedom fighter" label to him but which also includes passages reporting he has "led a liberation movement, sometimes with weapons," is on the South African "government list of terrorists," and that he is "commander of the guerrilla forces, and there are many photographs of him in battle dress."

Fully 90 percent of the 147 stories that appeared that year had no significant input from people living in Namibia. In sharp contrast, two-thirds quoted extensively from South African officials and from Kissinger and other U.S. diplomats and politicians to establish the dangers posed by Communist influence in SWAPO especially because of the presence of Cuban forces in neighboring Angola. Some note the impossibility of settling the independence issue as long as South Africa refuses to recognize SWAPO. However, at least one-fourth mention violent acts reported from the South African perspective and attributed to SWAPO.

The passages referring to that violence, often constructed as atrocity tales, tell of guerrillas engaged in a "hit and run war,"[59] ambushes,[60] and kidnappings.[61] No similar stories reporting violence by South African forces appeared that year. Even the mentions of repression are usually presented only as "reports" which can then be refuted by South African spokesmen or supporters.

Thus the coverage during 1976 left the firm impression that Namibians are relatively uninterested in independence and unsupportive of SWAPO, which is consistently described as a violent Marxist group recognized as the legitimate political representative of the Namibian people only by the United Nations.

By 1981 fully half of the 158 articles criticized or expressed some skepticism over U.S. policy in southern Africa. Therefore, the coverage was somewhat more supportive of independence for Namibia. While one story[62] and a letter to the editor[63] indicated support from the international Christian community, heavy reliance on U.S. and South African government sources tempered any enthusiasm for the cause.

In more than half the stories diplomatic sources from within the United States tied the question of independence to the problem of Communism in neighboring Angola and of Communist support for SWAPO. While South African sources also emphasized the problem of Communism, nearly half of all stories also told of SWAPO-led guerrilla warfare. But because South Africans were generally the only ones providing evidence or interpretation concerning the hostilities, these stories again sanitized South African behavior while fostering the impression of SWAPO as a terrorist organization. Because few stories used sources within Namibia and only one-fifth quoted a SWAPO leader, the coverage also maintained the image of SWAPO as an outside intruder with little support from within Namibia.

While news analyses, editorials, and letters during 1981 suggested some recognition of the justness of Namibian independence, that disappeared by 1986. Although there were only ten stories, the impression of SWAPO as a Marxist terrorist organization was particularly strong, at least partly because of increasing emphasis in U.S. diplomatic circles on the dangers of Communism abroad.

During 1986, six of the ten stories dealt with diplomatic activities between the United States and South Africa concerning the status of Namibia. These stories about negotiations between outsiders still clearly linked independence to the problem of Cuban troops in Angola; none suggested any urgency to the situation or any real concern on the part of U.S. negotiators. Three told of violence, linked directly or indirectly only to SWAPO; a fourth story acknowledged South African violence as a response to the situation. But all of these stories mentioning violence were again told from the South African perspective, without any SWAPO input, so they heighten the impression of a land overrun by dangerous Marxist terrorists:

> The South African military said today that its forces had attacked insurgents of the South-West Africa People's Organization at a camp in Angola.
>
> It said 39 people had been killed, all identified as insurgents. . . .
>
> The announcement by South Africa came after earlier assertions by Angola that Pretoria forces had struck deep into Angola, an avowedly Marxist nation.
>
> Angola provides bases for the South-West Africa People's Organization which has been fighting a low-key guerilla war for 20 years. . . .
>
> At this time of year, before the annual rains, the insurgents have reportedly been preparing for a wet-season offensive.[64]

CONCLUSION

This examination of news coverage of SWAPO and the Namibian independence movement suggests that *Lutheran World Information* and the *New York Times* rarely cover the same events or situations. They do not rely on the same or similar sources for their information. As a result, the images created by the two bodies of coverage are strikingly different.

Lutheran World Information has excellent access to information from the perspective of Namibian people who are church leaders, church members, Christian journalists, or Christian members of SWAPO. Because these sources are themselves Christians and are using a Christian news agency to tell their story to an audience assumed to be primarily Christian, the stories create a strong impression of a Christian land whose people are engaged in a just struggle for personal dignity and independence against an illegal, repressive, and violent South African regime.

However, *LWI* has limited access to political sources either in southern Africa or elsewhere, and its organizational mandate does not require including secular political positions in the stories it passes on to subscribers, so other perspectives on the Namibian situation rarely appear in the news releases. Because economic and political realities rarely intrude into the accounts, the solution to the problems in Namibia seems simple: Free Namibia and everything will be fine in southern Africa.

In sharp contrast, the *Times* stations its reporters in The Hague, Geneva, New York, Washington, Pretoria, Capetown, and other international centers of power where they have excellent access to official political and diplomatic sources. The story is told through the eyes of those important sources, but because they are not Namibian, the image is an outsider's impression of a large, strange land whose people are barely civilized. Both *LWI* and *Times* accounts confirm that outsiders, including Western reporters, have little access to the land and its people because visits to Namibia are controlled by South Africa.

At the *Times* the story has been defined as a political one. Therefore, there is no coverage from reporters assigned to monitor other influential institutions such as international businesses or religious organizations and little encouragement at a newspaper such as the *Times,* with its emphasis on active news-gathering by its reporters, to monitor news or other printed materials from such institutions. As a result, the emphasis is on what outside diplomatic and political sources think and are doing and how the situation there will affect Western interests. The facts, labels, and descriptions supplied by these sources appear to explain, but build little rapport between readers and the people of Namibia.

The striking differences between the two accounts of SWAPO and the Namibian independence movement suggest that both political leaders and average citizens who rely on the secular press, through the *New York Times,* and church leaders and members who rely on the Christian press, through *Lutheran World Information,* may be setting policy or attempting to influence it on the basis of factually accurate but wholly one-sided and incomplete images of reality. As with the situation in Iran, actions on the basis of partial images could lead to policy disasters. At the same time, those who happen to monitor both the secular and religious press undoubtedly experience cognitive dissonance that may lead them to lose faith in their government, their press, and/or their churches. That, too, could lead to disaster if citizen confusion and anger were to spill over into voting decisions.

One cannot fault religious sources for creating a religious interpretation of reality; nor can one fault political sources for defining reality according to their political ideology. One can only partially fault a religious press service for passing on without question images from its member-clients even if it might be wiser for that press's editors to insert a little more of others' impressions. Neither can one fault the *Times* for concentrating its news-gathering resources in centers of power; however, it is necessary to question why, in this situation, the *Times* so consistently failed to present countervailing images that were available to them through the presence of Christian church leaders at UN sessions and as lobbyists in Washington.

Preventing potentially serious problems would not seem to lie, as Lippmann suggested, in creating new and better collection agencies to provide information to the press. Rather, it would seem to lie within the journalists whose stories clearly indicate they know they are getting only a portion of reality yet are passing it on with little or no effort to find countervailing information.

NOTES

1. Walter Lippmann, *Public Opinion* (New York: Macmillan, 1922), pp. 81, 4, 19, 354.

2. Lippmann, *Public Opinion,* pp. 79–158; Walter Lippmann, "Stereotypes," in Bernard Berelson and Morris Janowitz, eds., *Reader in Public Opinion and Mass Communication* (New York: Free Press of Glencoe, 1953).

3. Richard V. Ericson, Patricia M. Baranek, and Janet B.L. Chan, *Visualizing Deviance* (Toronto: University of Toronto Press, 1987).

4. David H. Weaver, "Media Agenda-Setting and Public Opinion: Is There a Link?" in

Robert Bostrom and Bruce Wesley, eds., *Communication Yearbook,* vol. 8 (Beverly Hills, Calif.: Sage, 1984).

5. James B. Lemert, *Does Mass Communication Change Public Opinion After All?* (Chicago: Nelson-Hall, 1981).

6. David H. Weaver, Doris A. Graber, Maxwell McCombs, and Chaim Eyal, *Media Agenda-Setting in a Presidential Election* (New York, Praeger, 1981), pp. 162–93.

7. David H. Weaver and Judith M. Buddenbaum, "Newspapers and Television: A Review of Research on Uses and Effects," in G. Cleveland Wilhoit and Harold de Brock, eds., *Mass Communications Review Yearbook,* vol. 1 (Beverly Hills, Calif.: Sage, 1980).

8. Robert L. Stevenson and Donald Lewis Shaw, eds., *Foreign News and the New World Information Order* (Ames, Iowa: Iowa State University Press, 1984).

9. Mort Rosenblum, *Coups & Earthquakes* (New York: Harper and Row, 1981).

10. Harold D. Lasswell, "Nations and Classes: The Symbols of Identification," in Berelson and Janowitz, eds., *Reader in Public Opinion.*

11. Ericson, et al., *Visualizing Deviance,* pp. 47–48.

12. See, for example, Walter Darnell Jacobs, "A Special Study of South West Africa in Law and Politics," report prepared for the American-African Affairs Association, July 1966; Randolph Vigne, *A Dwelling Place of Our Own: The Story of the Namibian Nation* (London: International Defence and Aid Fund, 1973); J.H.P. Serfontein, *Namibia?* (Randburg, South Africa: Fukus Suid Publishers, 1976); Elizabeth S. Landis, "Namibian Liberation: Self-Determination, Law and Politics," report for Episcopal Churchmen for South Africa, New York, November 1982; and David Mermelstein, ed., *The Anti-Apartheid Reader* (New York: Grove Press, 1987), pp. 61–140.

13. Judith M. Buddenbaum, "Religion in the News: Factors Associated with the Selection of Stories from an International Religion News Service by Daily Newspapers" (Ph.D. dissertation, Indiana University, 1984), pp. 61–140.

14. Buddenbaum, "Religion in the News," pp. 194–96; and Judith M. Buddenbaum, "Analysis of Religion News in Three Daily Newspapers," *Journalism Quarterly* 63 (3) (Autumn 1986):600–606.

15. "Apartheid Protest Letters Issued by Two Lutheran Southwest Africa Churches," *Lutheran World Information,* July 19, 1971, pp. 1–2.

16. J.M. Porter, ed., *Luther: Selected Political Writings* (Philadelphia: Fortress Press, 1974); and Hugh Thomas Kerr, ed., *A Compend of Luther's Theology* (Philadelphia: The Westminster Press, 1943), pp. 213–32.

17. "News Analyis: Namibian Lutherans Will Attempt to Unite in 1992," *Lutheran World Information,* November 13, 1986, p. 6.

18. "First International Ecumenical Namibia Conference Demands Release of 22,000 Political Prisoners in Southern Africa; Supports Namibian Independence," *Lutheran World Information,* May 24, 1976, p. 8.

19. "Namibians Plead Not Guilty; Police Send Dogs Into Crowd," *Lutheran World Information* (February 20, 1976):1–2.

20. "Photo Page Namibia," *Lutheran World Information,* May 24, 1976, p. 8.

21. "Lutherans Plan to Bring Namibian Students to U.S.," *Lutheran World Information,* April 10, 1986, p. 18; and "Comment: Education in Southern Africa—a Namibian Student's View," *Lutheran World Information* no. 5 (May 1986):8.

22. "Namibian Youth Flee South Africa-Imposed Military Draft," *Lutheran World Information,* January 22, 1981, p. 3; "Young Namibian Refugees Flown to Zambia," *Lutheran World Information,* No. 7 (1981) p. 2; "Namibian Youth Leader Curbed by Court," *Lutheran World Information,* June 26, 1986, 18.

23. "Two White Namibians Refuse to Serve in South Africa's Army," *Lutheran World Information,* June 26, 1986, p. 20.

24. "Namibian Religious News Editor Detained," *Lutheran World Information,* May 22, 1986, p. 5.

25. "Namibians Plead Not Guilty"; and "Feature: Namibian Nurse Says, 'We Are in Hell,' " *Lutheran World Information,* December 18, 1986, pp. 15–16.

26. "Namibian Lawyers Use Rights Bill to Challenge South Africa," *Lutheran World Information*, November 6, 1986, p. 4.

27. "Namibians Plead Not Guilty"; John Evenson, "Namibian Independence Groups Defy Ban, Condemn US and South Africa," *Lutheran World Information*, May 7, 1986, p. 2; "4,000 Namibian Christians March for Freedom After Court Lifts Ban," *Lutheran World Information*, June 3, 1986, p. 2; "SWAPO's First Legal Rally in Years Draws 13,000," *Lutheran World Information*, August 7, 1986, pp. 4–5; and "8,000 Gather for Pre-Namibia Day Rally," *Lutheran World Information*, September 5, 1986, pp. 3–4.

28. " 'Freedom Fighters' Not Refugees Say Namibians," *Lutheran World Information*, May 6, 1976, p. 1.

29. Clive Cowley, "A White Assessment of Black Politics," *Lutheran World Information*, No. 10 (1976):9.

30. "Namibian Liberation Movement Leader Sees Role for Churchmen in Possible New Negotiations," *Lutheran World Information*, October 22, 1976, p. 11.

31. Edward C. May, "Feature: Namibia: Slaves of Hope," *Lutheran World Information*, February 23, 1981, p. 15.

32. "SWAPO's First Legal Rally," op. cit.

33. "Lutheran Namibian Woman Fights Prison Bible Study Ban, Endures Suffering," *Lutheran World Information*, May 14, 1986, p. 14.

34. " 'Bloodshed' Feared in Wake of Death Sentences Against Swakopmund Trial Defendants," *Lutheran World Information*, May 14, 1976, p. 16.

35. Richard Walker, "US Lutheran Leader Defends Grants Made to Namibia Guerilla Movement," *Lutheran World Information*, November 5, 1981, p. 16.

36. "Namibian Churchmen Appeal to Kissinger, Asking US Help for Independence," *Lutheran World Information*, July 10, 1976, pp. 1–2; and "Namibian Theologian Sees No Choice but Violence," *Lutheran World Information*, March 26, 1986, p. 18.

37. "8,000 Gather," op. cit.

38. "Namibians Plead Not Guilty," op. cit.

39. John A. Evenson, "Feature: Terror in Namibia: The Bombing of the Church Press," *Lutheran World Information*, March 5, 1981, pp. 5–6.

40. Gary Nelson, "Feature: Eyewitness to Namibia Beatings," *Lutheran World Information*, January 22, 1986, p. 15.

41. "Namibian Teenager Roasted Over Fire by KOEVET," *Lutheran World Information*, July 17, 1986, p. 5.

42. Max Frankel, "Crisis Seen Over South-West Africa," *New York Times*, July 17, 1966, p. 14.

43. Paul Hoffman, "Border Incidents Stall Vorster's Bid for Talks," *New York Times*, October 8, 1971, p. 18.

44. Paul Hoffman, "South Africans, Defying U.N., Say They Will Retain Disputed Area," *New York Times*, June 9, 1971, p. 10.

45. Paul Hoffman, "A Capital Where Go-Go Girls Are New," *New York Times*, June 26, 1971, p. 7.

46. Paul Hoffman, "South-West African Tribe Still in Stone Age," *New York Times*, June 15, 1971, p. 10.

47. Frankel, "Crisis Seen," op. cit.

48. See, for example, Paul Hoffman, "South-West Africa Being Split Into Reserves," *New York Times*, June 23, 1971, p. 18; and Alan Cowell, "Bomb Kills 4 in South African Enclave," *New York Times*, August 3, 1986, p. 14.

49. "Strong Words on South-West Africa," *New York Times*, October 2, 1966, Sec. 4, p. 3.

50. Hoffman, "South-West Africa Being Split," op. cit.

51. Paul Hoffman, "Black Officials in Tribal Capital Sit With South African and Laud Apartheid," *New York Times*, June 11, 1971, p. 6.

52. Joseph Lelyveld, "A Tribe Puts Faith in Far-Off Court," *New York Times*, April 25, 1966, p. 9.

53. Hoffman, "Black Officials," op. cit.

54. See, for example, Hoffman, "South-West Africa Being Split," op cit.

55. David Binder, "African Rebels Hint at Cuba Bid," *New York Times,* March 3, 1976, p. 4.

56. "Rebels Bar Plan for Africa Area," *New York Times,* August 20, 1976, p. 7; and John Darnton, "African Talks Close Without Ending Rift of Black Rhodesians," *New York Times,* September 8, 1976, p. 1.

57. "Rebels Bar Plan"; and Michael T. Kaufman, "Progress Is Seen in Constitutional Talks on Future of South-West Africa," *New York Times,* September 14, 1976, Sec. 2, p. 2.

58. Kathleen Teltsch, "South-West African Nationalists," *New York Times,* September 30, 1976, p. 3.

59. "South Africa Seeks Accord With Angola Leftists," *New York Times,* February 13, 1976, p. 3; and John F. Burns, "South-West African Talks Stall as Guerrilla War Continues," *New York Times,* December 11,1976, p. 6.

60. "4 South Africans Killed Near Angola," *New York Times,* April 24, 1976, p. 3.

61. "South-West Africa Rebels Kill Bodyguard, 4 Others," *New York Times,* July 11, 1976, p. 4.

62. "Namibian Rebels Given Grant," *New York Times,* September 22, 1981, p. 3.

63. Edward May, "On the Wrong Side in Namibia," *New York Times,* September 1981, p. 18.

64. Alan Cowell, "Pretoria Says It Killed 39 in Raid Against Namibia Rebels in Angola," *New York Times,* November 15, 1986, p. 3.

SELECTED BIBLIOGRAPHY

BOOKS

Adams, William C., ed. *Television Coverage of International Affairs.* Norwood, N.J.: Ablex, 1982.

Adams, William C., ed. *Television Coverage of the Middle East.* Norwood, N.J.: Ablex, 1981.

Alexander, Yonah; David Carlton; and Paul Wilkinson, eds. *Terrorism: Theory and Practice.* Boulder, Colo.: Westview Press, 1979.

Alexander, Yonah, and John M. Gleason, eds. *Behavioral and Quantitative Perspectives on Terrorism.* New York: Pergamon Press, 1981.

Alexander, Yonah, and S.M. Finger, eds. *Terrorism: Interdisciplinary Perspectives.* New York: John Jay Press, 1977.

Bassiouni, M. Cherif, ed. *International Terrorism and Political Crimes.* Springfield, Ill.: Charles C. Thomas, 1975.

Bell, J. Bowyer. *Transnational Terror.* Washington, D.C.: American Enterprise Institute, 1975.

Clutterbuck, Richard. *The Media and Political Violence,* 2d ed. London: Macmillan, 1983.

Committee to Protect Journalists. *Attacks on the Press 1987.* New York: Committee to Protect Journalists, 1988.

European Terrorism and the Media. London: International Press Institute, 1978.

Freedman, Lawrence Z., and Yonah Alexander, eds. *Perspectives on Terrorism.* Wilmington, Del.: Scholarly Resources, 1983.

Friedlander, R.A. *Terrorism and the Media: A Contemporary Assessment.* Gaithersburg, Md.: International Association of Chiefs of Police, 1981.

Gurr, Robert Ted. *Why Men Rebel.* Princeton, N.J.: Princeton University Press, 1971.

Hall, Stuart; C. Critcher; T. Jeggerson; J. Clarke, and B. Roberts. *Policing the Crisis: Mugging, the State and Law and Order.* London: Macmillan, 1978.

Herman, Edward S. *The Real Terror Network: Terrorism in Fact and Propaganda.* Boston: South End Press, 1982.

Livingstone, Neil C. *The War Against Terrorism.* Lexington, Mass.: Lexington Books, 1982.

Midgley, Sarah and Virginia Rice, eds. *Terrorism and the Media in the 1980s.* Washington, D.C.: The Media Institute, 1983.

Miller, Abraham, ed. *Terrorism, Media, and the Law.* Dobbs Ferry, N.Y.: Transnational, 1982.

National Advisory Committee on Criminal Justice Standards and Goals. *Disorders and Terrorism: Report of the Task Force on Disorders and Terrorism.* Washington, D.C.: Law Enforcement Assistance Administration, 1977.

O'Neill, Michael J. *Terrorist Spectaculars: Should TV Coverage Be Curbed?* New York: Priority Press Publications, 1986.

Picard, Robert G., and Rhonda S. Sheets. *Terrorism and the News Media Research*

Bibliography. Boston: Terrorism and the News Media Research Project, Emerson College, 1986.

Schlesinger, Philip; Graham Murdock; and Philip Elliott. *Televising "Terrorism": Political Violence in Popular Culture*. London: Comedia Publishing, 1983.

Schmid, Alex Peter. *Political Terrorism: A Research Guide to Concepts, Theories, Data Bases and Literature*. New Brunswick, N.J.: Transaction Books, 1984.

Schmid, Alex P. and Janny de Graff. *Insurgent Terrorism and the Western News Media: An Exploratory Analysis with a Dutch Case Study*. Leiden: Dutch State University, 1980.

———. *Violence as Communication: Insurgent Terrorism and the Western News Media*. Beverly Hills, Calif.: Sage Publications, 1982.

Snyder, Marie, ed. *Media and Terrorism: The Psychological Impact*. North Newton, Kan.: Mennonite Press, 1978.

Stohl, Michael, ed. *The Politics of Terrorism,* 3d ed. New York: Marcel Dekker, 1988.

Stohl, Michael and George A. Lopez, eds. *The State As Terrorist: The Dynamics of Governmental Violence and Repression*. Westport, Conn.: Greenwood Press, 1984.

Television and Conflict. London: Institute for the Study of Conflict, 1978.

Terrorism and the Media. Washington, D.C.: American Legal Foundation, 1986.

Terrorism and the Media. London: International Press Institute, 1980.

ARTICLES, BOOK CHAPTERS, MONOGRAPHS

Alexander, Yonah. "Communications Aspects of International Terrorism." *International Problems,* 16 (1977):55–60.

———. "Terrorism and the Media: Some Observations." *Terrorism* 3 (1980):179–80.

———. "Terrorism, the Media and the Police." *Journal of International Affairs* 32–(1978):101–113.

Altheide, David. "Impact of Format and Ideology on TV News Coverage of Iran." *Journalism Quarterly* 62 Summer 1985):346–51.

———. "Three-In-One News: Network Coverage of Iran." *Journalism Quarterly* 59–(Autumn 1982):482–86.

Anable, David. "Media, Reluctant Participant in Terrorism," in Marie Snyder, ed. *Media and Terrorism: The Psychological Impact*. North Newton, Kan.: Mennonite Press, 1978.

Atwater, Tony. "Network Evening News Coverage of the TWA Hostage Crisis." *Journalism Quarterly* 64 (Summer-Autumn 1987):520–25.

Baker, Brent. "The PAO and Terrorism." *Military Media Review* (July 1986), pp. 10–11.

Bassiouni, M. Cherif. "Media Coverage of Terrorism: The Law and the Public." *Journal of Communication* 33 (Spring 1982):128–43.

———. "Problems in Media Coverage of Nonstate-sponsored Terror-Violence Incidents," in Lawrence Z. Freedman and Yonah Alexander. *Perspectives on Terrorism*. Wilmington, Del.: Scholarly Resources, 1983.

———. "Terrorism, Law Enforcement and the Mass Media." *Journal of Criminal Law and Criminology* 72 (1981):801–851.

Bell, J.B. "Terrorist Scripts and Live-Action Spectaculars." *Columbia Journalism Review* (May 1978):47–50.

Bennett, James R. "Page One Sensationalism and the Libyan 'Hit Team'." *Newspaper Research Journal* 4 (Spring 1983):34–38.

Bryant, Jennings; Rodney Corveth, and Dan Brown. "Television Viewing and Anxiety." *Journal of Communication* 31 (1981):106–119.

Cairn, Ed. "The Television News as a Source for Knowledge About the Violence for Children in Ireland, North and South." *Current Psychological Research and Reviews* (1985).

Catton Jr., W.R. "Militants and the Media: Partners in Terrorism?" *Indiana Law Journal* 53 (1978):703–715.

Clawson, Patrick. "Why We Need More But Better Coverage of Terrorism." *Orbis* 30 (Winter 1987):701–710.

"Conference Report: Terrorism and the Media." *Political Communication and Persuasion* 3 (1985):185–90.

Consoli, John. "Covering Terrorism." *Editor and Publisher* (November 2, 1985):11.

Cox, Robert. "The Media as a Weapon." *Political Communication and Persuasion* 1 (1981):297–300.

Crelinsten, Ronald. "Power and Meaning: Terrorism as a Struggle Over Access to the Communication Structure," in Paul Wilkinson, ed. *Contemporary Research on Terrorism*. Aberdeen: University of Aberdeen Press, 1987.

Crenshaw, Martha. "The Causes of Terrorism." *Comparative Politics* 13 (July 1981):379–99.

Doob, Anthony, and Glenn Macdonald. "The News Media and Perceptions of Violence," in *Report of the Royal Commission on Violence in the Communications Industry*, vol. 5, *Learning from the Media*. Toronto: Royal Commission on Violence in the Communications Industry, 1977.

Dowling, Ralph E. "Terrorism and the Media: A Rhetorical Genre." *Journal of Communication* 35 (Winter 1986):12–24.

Elliott, Philip, Graham Murdock, and Philip Schlesinger. " 'Terrorism' and the State: A Case Study of the Discourse of Television." *Media, Culture and Society* 5 (April 1983):155–77.

Elliott, Deni. "Family Ties: A Case Study of Families and Friends During the Hijacking of TWA Flight 847." *Political Communication and Persuasion* 5 (1988):67–75.

Epstein, E.C. "The Uses of 'Terrorism': A Study in Media Bias." *Stanford Journal of International Studies* 12 (1977):67–68.

Friedland, Nehemia. "The Psychological Impact of Terrorism: A Double-Edged Sword." *Political Psychology* 6 (December 1985):591–604.

Graber, Doris. "Evaluating Crime-Fighting Policies: Media Images and Public Perspective," in Ralph Baker and Fred Meyer Jr., eds. *Evaluating Alternative Law-Enforcement Policies*. Lexington, Mass.: D.C. Heath, 1979.

Heyman, Edward, and Edward Mickolus. "Observations on 'Why Violence Spreads.' " *International Studies Quarterly,* June 1980, pp. 299–305.

Hickey, Neil. "Terrorism and Television." *TV Guide* (July 31, 1976):4.

Hill, Frederic B. "Media Diplomacy: Crisis Management With an Eye on the TV Screen." *Washington Journalism Review* (May 1981):23–27.

Jaehnig, Walter B. "Journalists and Terrorism: Captives of the Libertarian Tradition." *Indiana Law Journal* 53 (Summer 1978):717–44.

Jenkins, Brian M. "The Psychological Implications of Media-Covered Terrorism." *Rand Paper Series* (1981).

Johnpoll, B. "Terrorism and the Mass Media in the United States," in Yonah Alexander and S.M. Finger, eds. *Terrorism: Interdisciplinary Perspectives*. New York: John Jay Press, 1977.

Jones, Juanita, B., and Abraham H. Miller. "The Media and Terrorist Activity: Resolving the First Amendment Dilemma." *Ohio Northern University Law Review* 6 (1979):70–81.

Katz, Elihu. "Communications Research and the Image of Society: Convergence of Two Research Traditions." *American Journal of Sociology* 65 (1960).

———. "The Two-Step Flow of Communication: An Up-to-Date Report on an Hypothesis." *Public Opinion Quarterly* 21 (Spring 1957):61–78.

Kelly, Michael J. and Thomas H. Mitchell. "Transnational Terrorism and the Western Elite Press." *Political Communication and Persuasion* 1 (1981):269–96.

Larson, James F. "Television and U.S. Foreign Policy: The Case of the Iran Hostage Crisis." *Journal of Communication* 36:108–27 (1986):108–27.

Levin, Jerry. "Remarks to Committee to Protect Journalists." *Political Communication and Persuasion* 4 (1987):25–27.

Levy, Rudolf. "Terrorism and the Mass Media." *Military Intelligence* (October-December 1985):34–38.

Martin, L. John. "Mass Media Treatment of Terrorism." *Terrorism* 8 (1985):127–46.

———. "Violence, Terrorism, Non-Violence: Vehicles of Social Control," in Joseph Roucek, ed. *Social Control for the 1980s: A Handbook For Order in a Democratic Society*. Westport, Conn.: Greenwood Press, 1978.

McLeod, Jack, Lee Becker, and James Byrnes. "Another Look at the Agenda-Setting Function of the Press." *Communication Research* 1–(April 1974):131–66.

Meeske, Milan D., and Mohamad Hamid Javaheri. "Network Television Coverage of the Iranian Hostage Crisis." *Journalism Quarterly* 59–(Winter 1982):641–45.

Midlarsky, Manus I., Martha Crenshaw, and Fumihiko Yoshida. "Why Violence Spreads: The Contagion of International Terrorism." *International Studies Quarterly* 24–(June 1980):262–98.

Miller, Abraham H. "Terrorism and the Media: A Dilemma." *Terrorism* 3–(1979):79–89.

O'Donnell, Wendy M. "Prime Time Hostages: A Case Study of Coverage of the Hijacking and Hostage-Taking on TWA Flight 847." *Terrorism and the News Media Research Project Paper Series* no. 9 (1987).

Paletz, David L., John Z. Ayanian, and Peter A. Fozzard. "The I.R.A., the Red Brigades, and the F.A.L.N. in the *New York Times*." *Journal of Communication* 32, no. 2 (Spring 1982):162–272.

———. "Terrorism on TV News: The IRA, the FALN, and the Red Brigades," in William C. Adams, ed. *Television Coverage of International Affairs*. Norwood, N.J.: Ablex, 1982.

Palmerton, Patricia R. "The Rhetoric of Terrorism and the Media Response to the 'Crisis in Iran.' " *Western Journal of Speech Communication* 52–(Spring 1988):105–121.

Picard, Robert G. "The Conundrum of News Coverage of Terrorism." *University of Toledo Law Review* 18–(Fall 1986):141–50.

———. "News Coverage as the Contagion of Terrorism: Dangerous Charges Backed by Dubious Science." *Political Communication and Persuasion* 3–(1986):385–400.

———. "Stages in Coverage of Incidents of Political Violence." *Terrorism and the News Media Research Project Paper Series* no. 10 (1987).

Picard, Robert G., and Paul D. Adams. "Characterizations of Acts and Perpetrators of Terrorism in Three Elite U.S. Daily Newspapers." *Political Communication and Persuasion* 4:1–9 (1987):1–9.

Post, Jerrold M. "Hostile, Conformite, Fraternite: The Group Dynamics of Terrorist Behavior." *International Journal of Group Psychotherapy* 36–(April 1986):211–24.

Quester, George H. "Cruise Ship Terrorism and the Media." *Political Communication and Persuasion* 4–(1986):355–70.

Rada, S.E. "Transnational Terrorism as Public Relations?" *Public Relations Review* 11–(Fall 1985):26–33.

Rubin, Jeffrey, and Nehemia Friedland. "Theater of Terror." *Psychology Today* (March 1986):21–28.

Salomone, Franco. "Terrorism and the Mass Media," in M. Cherif Bassiouni, ed. *International Terrorism and Political Crimes*. Springfield, Ill.: Charles C. Thomas, 1975.

Stephens, Lowndes F. "Implications of Terrorism for Planning the Public Relations Function." *Terrorism and the News Media Research Project Paper Series* no. 2 (1987).

Stohl, Michael. "Outside of a Small Circle of Friends: States, Genocide, Mass Killings and the Role of Bystanders." *Journal of Peace Research* 24 (1987).

Terry, H.A. "Television and Terrorism: Professionalism Not Quite the Answer." *Indiana Law Journal* 53–(1978):745–77.

Weimann, Gabriel. "Conceptualizing the Effects of Mass-Mediated Terrorism." *Political Communication and Persuasion* 4–(1987):38–46.

————. "Terrorists or Freedom Fighters? Labeling Terrorism in the Israeli Press." *Political Communication and Persuasion* 2–(1985):433–45.

————. "The Theater of Terror: Effects of Press Coverage." *Journal of Communication* 33, no. (Winter 1985):38–46.

Wurth-Hough, Sandra, "Network News Coverage of Terrorism: The Early Years." *Terrorism* 6–(1983):403–422.

Zillman, Dolf, and Jacob Wakshlag. "Fear of Victimization and the Appeal of Crime Drama," in Dolf Zillman and Jennings Bryant, eds. *Selective Exposure to Communication*. Hillsdale, N.J.: Lawrence Erlbaum, 1985.

ABOUT THE EDITORS AND CONTRIBUTORS

YONAH ALEXANDER, Ph.D., is a professor and director of the Institute for Studies in International Terrorism at the State University of New York and research professor at the Elliot School of International Affairs of The George Washington University.

ROBERT G. PICARD, Ph.D., is professor of communications at California State University, Fullerton. He was the former project director of the Terrorism and the News Media Research Project of the Mass Communication Division for the Association for Education in Journalism.

JUDITH BUDDENBAUM, Ph.D., is an associate professor of journalism at Colorado State University.

THOMAS W. COOPER, Ph.D., is an associate professor of mass communication at Emerson College (Massachusetts).

JOSEPH DRAZNIN is a Ph.D. candidate at the College of Journalism at the University of Maryland.

TIMOTHY GALLIMORE is a doctoral candidate in the School of Journalism at Indiana University.

GEORGE GERBNER, Ph.D., is dean of the Annenberg School of Communication at the University of Pennsylvania.

JACK LULE, Ph.D., is an assistant professor of communications at the University of Tulsa (Oklahoma).

L. JOHN MARTIN, Ph.D., is a professor and director of graduate studies in the College of Journalism at the University of Maryland.

LOUISE F. MONTGOMERY, Ph.D., is an associate professor and chair of the department of journalism at the University of Arkansas.

RICHARD M. PEARLSTEIN, Ph.D., is an independent security consultant and author.

KRISTINA ROSS is a master's candidate in the school of journalism at Indiana University.

ROBERT TERRELL, Ph.D., is an associate professor of journalism at the University of Colorado.